Teaching Culture

Teaching Culture

the long revolution in cultural studies

Edited by
Nannette Aldred and Martin Ryle

NIACE
THE NATIONAL ORGANISATION
FOR ADULT LEARNING

Published by the National Institute of Adult Continuing Education
(England and Wales)
21 De Montfort Street, Leicester, LE1 7GE
Company registration no. 2603322
Charity registration no. 1002775

First published 1999
© NIACE

CATALOGUING IN PUBLICATION DATA
A CIP record for this title is available from the British Library
ISBN 1 86201 045 5

Typeset by The Midlands Book Typesetting Company, Loughborough
Cover design by Boldface, London EC1
Printed in Great Britain by Antony Rowe Ltd

Contents

Introduction

Some of the chapters in the present book began life as contributions to a conference held at the University of Sussex in 1996 on 'Teaching Culture and the Cultures of Teaching'. Those who attended that event turned out almost without exception to be either teachers of cultural studies in 'new' universities, or adult educators working in extra-mural departments in 'old' universities. The question 'Where does cultural studies in Britain come from?' has, it seems to us, always had two answers, institutionally speaking, both of them true: from the tradition of radical extra-mural education exemplified and advocated by Raymond Williams, which is having to redefine itself today with the 'mainstreaming' of continuing education departments (although these often remain the least conservative parts of their parent institutions); and from the 'intra-mural' practice of some humanities and social science lecturers in the former polytechnics, who have worked to adapt their teaching to the needs of a diverse – and increasingly 'adult' – student constituency. These may not have been the best-endowed or most prestigious places in British higher education over the past 50 years, but the encounter there between established academic disciplines and the worlds of diverse, marginal, 'other' students has stimulated some of the most interesting work (in teaching and writing) of the period.

The pace of change has not slowed in higher and adult education since 1996, and the essays now printed reflect those changes, and include subsequently commissioned work which has broadened the scope of the book. However, we have sought to sustain, in this collection as it now appears, the sense of dialogue, of drawing on common experiences and values as well as on particular settings and projects, which distinguished the conference.

The intellectual and institutional histories which make up this shared body of experience are reflected in several contributions. These consider cultural studies as a practical exercise in democratic education, and reflect on the theoretical strands and positions developed and used in that practice. Here, education's own role in the formation of 'culture', through postwar educational policy, is suggested – and in some chapters, actively addressed. Tom Steele offers an authoritative review of the 'project and formation' of the original extra-mural moment, and concludes with some thoughts on current radical possibilities. Richard Johnson and Jim McGuigan reflect on the changing settings in which cultural studies has been taught as a mainstream undergraduate subject. Johnson reviews his own experience, at Nottingham and (earlier) Birmingham, drawing on this to illustrate some of the 'constraints, contradictions and possibilities that run through the history of cultural studies in the academy'; McGuigan offers a wry overview of political and intellectual accounts of and rationales for work in the field, and concludes that students still have much to gain, and not just in narrowly vocational terms, from selecting it for their studies.

These chapters, like the other contributions which assess where the 'radical project' has now arrived at, are historically informed, rather than nostalgic. They all reflect continuing change in the wider political context, though most see current New Labour priorities as continuing rather than transforming the agenda of the earlier 1990s. Most of them emphasise that there remains 'scope for significant intervention', as Alan O'Shea puts it, today. Some point to elements of illusion, and to intellectual defaults or evasions, which may now be detected in the founding discourses and practices. Thus Angeliki Spiropoulou asks what has been lost and concealed (and to what ends) through the rather general exclusion of literary 'high culture' from the cultural studies curriculum, and Kate Soper questions whether a coherent critical project can be sustained outside the (admittedly problematic) utopian horizon of the earlier and explicitly Marxist critique of mass culture which 'cultural studies' in some ways displaced.

There is little sympathy here, however, with the journalistic claim that cultural studies has lost its way, or become a 'pick'n'mix' subject, where academic credit comes as part of 'infotainment'. The conviction that it remains a means for students to 'understand their world' is tied, for most contributors, to a belief that we can defend and retain the political impetus of earlier phases, while being prepared to question the content, methodology and sense of values which underpin our pedagogical work. All the chapters exemplify the belief that cultural studies, in its now various and increasingly international and postcolonial guises, must sustain such an active and self-questioning sense of its own formation if it is to retain critical purchase. This self-questioning edge, this awareness of itself as historically constituted and mutable, is perhaps what above all distinguishes cultural studies – in whichever of its variants – from other academic fields or disciplines, and provides the vantage-point from which it criticises them.

As editors, we have sought contributions exemplifying that kind of awareness, rather than expecting agreement about what is to be done. No consensus was sought, and none emerges. However, a number of themes recur. Most contributors take it as axiomatic that questions of pedagogy (by which we understand both classroom practice, and work on curriculum and on disciplinary boundaries) are central to any evaluation of the potential of higher education, whether for change or for containment; and many of them reflect explicitly on such questions. Most chapters engage with the transformation of higher education in Britain from an élite to a mass system: this has effectively mainstreamed the old extra-mural project of widening participation, and (as McGuigan notes) the 'new universities' generally, and not least their cultural studies departments, have played here the role of pioneers, or guinea pigs. Several authors comment on the recent intensification of vocationalist or neo-vocationalist policy discourses on the purposes of education: for some – McGuigan and O'Shea, for example – the development of 'skills' is in the end not incompatible with a critical education; for others (especially Martin Ryle, who argues that the 'usefulness' of cultural studies is a matter of the awkward incommensurability between 'culture' and 'work'), this is a tension we cannot and should not dispel.

Another common question, and one that underlies the division of the book into two parts, concerns the (in)compatibility between what Christina Lupton and Heiko Henkel term 'postmodern or culturally relative approaches to learning' and 'older models of socialist, progressive education'. A commitment to education's 'others', to the constituencies excluded or made invisible in dominant educational practices and discourses, underlay, of course, the original radical project of taking knowledge beyond the walls. From the start, the modes and content of 'knowledge' were themselves at stake in this, but (as Steele and others have argued, here and elsewhere) a negotiation of the curriculum and purposes of adult education was for many years possible which seemed both to respect the experiences of 'non-traditional' students and to advance a common, or at least widely shared, goal of democratic-socialist progress.

In education as elsewhere, such grand narratives have become harder to sustain. For some time now, work which addresses and draws upon the experiences and needs of particular marginal, excluded, or simply sub-cultural groups has flourished, even as a confident sense of some larger progressive project has ebbed away. Andy Medhurst describes and reflects on the experience of 'teaching queerly' in the innovative Sexual Dissidence MA at the University of Sussex, while also considering how queerness might be more widely diffused across the curriculum. The chapter by Jane Elliott on the diverse subjects and subjectivities which must be addressed in the teaching of women's studies, and Nannette Aldred's interview with Eddie Chambers (which explores how oppositional cultural practice can inform mainstream teaching about visual culture), indicate some of the difficulties and rewards of such work. However, 'cultural difference' is, of course, a problematic term, whether applied to social formations or to educational practice, as David Butler shows in his account of what 'teaching culture' can mean in Northern Ireland. The complexities involved are acknowledged, and carefully discussed, in the chapters by O'Shea, by Lupton and Henkel, and by Butler which foreground 'difference' as a theoretical and pedagogic problem, and in several other contributions too.

We shall not comment further on the book's chapters, since their titles sufficiently indicate the specific, but overlapping, concerns with which their authors engage, and their detailed arguments do not lend themselves to summary. While its focus is on 'teaching culture' in a range of particular settings, we believe that the book as a whole offers sharp and thoughtful discussion of some large questions about the relationship between culture, education and teaching: about the purposes, student constituencies and prospects of critical education in what one is tempted to call 'late social democracy'. In that context, we come neither to praise the great radical tradition, nor to bury it: rather, our concern has been to keep open lines of communication between the past of 'cultural studies' and a possible future in which it might continue to be more than just another academic specialism.

It remains to make some acknowledgements. We would like to thank colleagues in the Centre for Continuing Education at the University of Sussex for the practical and intellectual support they gave to the 1996 Teaching Culture conference. Dr Gerry Holloway and Mary Hoar undertook most of the administration. Dr Al Thomson worked with us on the planning of the event and was generous with ideas and time, as was Professor Roger Silverstone, in his (then) role of Director of the Culture and Communication Graduate Research Centre at Sussex. We are also indebted to the Director of CCE, Dr Fred Gray, for facilitating our work on this book. We recall with pleasure the positive, collegial atmosphere of the conference, for which all those who gave papers and attended must be thanked.

The contributors, those recruited then and those who have been brought on board since, have combined patience with promptness, and have made our editorial task pleasant. Finally, we would like to thank Virman Man at NIACE for listening to our ideas, asking difficult questions and agreeing to publish this book. We think it is appropriate that the National Institute of Adult Continuing Education (England and Wales) should continue its well established tradition of asking questions about culture, education and pedagogy, which this book aims to do.

Nannette Aldred
Martin Ryle
January 1999

Part I

Radical projects

Part I

1 Marginal occupations: adult education, cultural studies and social renewal

Tom Steele

In his essay *The Future of Cultural Studies* Raymond Williams insists that no intellectual or artistic project can be understood without also understanding its formation.[1] The relation between project and formation is particularly decisive in cultural studies because it engages with both rather than specialising in the one or the other. The artistic or intellectual project with which cultural studies engaged was not simply a reflection of the sociological formation to which it belonged. This was a key reformulation of the old 'art and society' paradigm because cultural studies no longer saw the object of study as the relationship between two separate entities 'art' and 'society' but as the critical and creative processes which take these different material forms. Thus a project may spring from a distinct social formation but changes in that formation will alter the nature of the project. The success or failure of the project alternatively, will have consequences for the formation.

So what formation gave rise to the project of cultural studies? Williams quite unequivocally locates it in the broader world of adult education in the immediate post World War II period, when he, E P Thompson, Richard Hoggart and many others found in adult education a radical political vocation. It was, for him, a renewal of that attempt at 'a majority democratic education' which had been present in the early days of English literary studies and then in Leavisism but which had got side-tracked into minority and élitist attitudes. Williams's own short lived journal, *Politics and Letters*, and a companion volume called *The Critic* were an attempt to engage politically with that world which Williams increasingly saw as the 'decisive' world for his political work.

> Virtually every WEA tutor was a Socialist of one colour or another. We were all doing adult education ourselves. So we saw the journals as linked to this very hopeful formation with a national network of connection to the working-class movement. If there was a group to which Politics and Letters referred, it was the adult education tutors and their students.[2]

It was significant that Williams saw the adult education universe as a 'formation', a term he later defined in his book *Culture* as having a specific sociological meaning. A 'formation' was capable of having a distinct political and ideological perspective. Williams later acknowledged, however, that the journals foundered because they were in effect too cultural and had failed to develop a properly economic critique. He was also unhappy that they had not made contact with

Communist Party intellectuals, whose understanding of Marxist economics could have been invaluable, in an organised way. The marriage of Leavisism and left politics had failed because it had not taken into account that, despite its oppositional standpoint, Leavisism was by definition hostile to socialism. Williams later said:

> The correct perspective was to try to help to build a very strong cultural mobilisation to take part in a battle inside the Labour movement. But we still shared one illusion with precisely the position we were attacking. We thought we could do so simply by literary argument, by cultural discourse. That was the influence of Leavis.[3]

Origins and influences

This chapter summarises arguments, presented at greater length elsewhere,[4] to suggest a pre-history of British cultural studies in the work of adult education between the 1930s and the 1960s and so locate the formation Williams refers to in a more precise social history. It suggests that the origins, nature and influence of the new approaches to working-class history, popular formations, the 'national' culture and socialist politics produced in the work of adult educators in the immediate postwar period were already prefigured in the controversies and pedagogy of the inter-war years and as Williams suggests can be traced even further back to the distant origins of English literary studies in nineteenth-century university extension. The subsequent work of E P Thompson, Richard Hoggart and Raymond Williams is of special interest because of their role in the 'founding' both of British cultural studies and the New Left, but they themselves should be contextualised within the broader creative milieu of experiment and re-alignment within adult education. The work of other figures in adult education such as Thomas Hodgkin, Sidney Raybould, A D Lindsay, Karl Mannheim, Karl Polanyi, G H Thompson and W E Williams and their interrelationships are also significant in constructing what Williams might have called a 'structure of feeling'.

There is an argument that adult education has, since the later nineteenth century, been a critical place of dialogue and negotiation between the forces attempting to modernise the British state and the emergent social movements, especially that of the labour or 'working-class' movement. While a revised conception of Englishness which could incorporate the newly enfranchised lower classes was being advocated by liberal intellectuals, the subaltern classes were developing their own forms of collectivist culture which relied on their own class nature. Hardly less important, although until recently relatively neglected, was the space provided by adult education for the education of women. Many women who came into adult education were the newly recruited teachers in the board schools created by the 1870 Education Act, who had a pivotal role in articulating the new cultures to the rising generations.

It needs to be asked how the practice of interdisciplinary work grew within adult education classes and how important were the identifying features of this work such as: dialogic democratic practice; mature and experienced students; political commitment and class-consciousness; links with the organised labour movement; the ethic of 'social purpose'; resistance to academic compartmentalising of knowledge; and other non-institutional aspects. It seems to be the case that interdisciplinary study in adult education was an important precursor of academic British cultural studies, the particular circumstances of which were focused by arguments over the role and status of the 'literary' and the 'sociological' in adult liberal studies. Further, the origins of the study of 'popular culture' in adult classes date from the early 1930s while the increasing importance of a totalising and theorised sociology dates from the work of Karl Mannheim, Karl Polanyi and other European émigrés who were involved in adult education in the late 1930s. Another important element in the reconstitution of adult liberal studies was the work of socialist and communist historians in the creation of a social history freed from mechanical determinisms and more open to 'cultural' effects, in which the Communist Party Historians Group and the work of R H Tawney and G D H Cole were of central importance.

From this innovative pedagogic climate there came a preoccupation with the term 'culture' which ultimately led to the foundation of the Birmingham Centre for Contemporary Cultural Studies by Richard Hoggart and subsequently the widespread flowering of cultural studies within polytechnics and the Open University. The strategic importance of the work of Thompson, Williams and their colleagues in adult education in Oxford, Leeds and elsewhere to the formation of the New Left is seen as organically related to their educational project. Finally, the development of the History Workshop movement from Ruskin College, and the subsequent origins of women's studies in adult education, with for example the work of Sheila Rowbotham and feminist critiques of the originating project, have further widened the reach of cultural studies.[5]

Thus the conventional assumption that British cultural studies emerged as an offshoot of a university school of English mistakes the nature of the formation from which it sprang and conveniently forgets the work of adult educationists who were shifting politics into the realm of symbolic values in the immediate postwar period. Ironically, cultural studies were enabled by the very decline of independent working class education, which many of the new adult educators held so dear, as a distinct formation; but they received much radical impulse from this formation. However the transition from a class-based to a 'national popular' (in Gramsci's terms) educational constituency was crucial in relocating the site of ideological contestation from the point of production to the realm of reproduction.

The term 'culture' is used in a variety of ways which are not always complementary, particularly when the contrast is made between culture as signifying on the one hand 'the high arts' and alternatively, 'a way of life' in the anthropological sense. These formulations can be mapped, consecutively, on to the ideals of the radical adult educators of the university extension movement, who believed in self-improvement through culture and on the other hand the actual development of working-class collectivist institutions which signified an emergent alternative and at times oppositional culture. Both class-based and national identities seem to have emerged at the same time in the late nineteenth century and in some of the work of adult education can be seen attempts to negotiate the contiguities of these identities. The rise of English studies as an academic discipline from their colonial roots in India to the Newbolt Report suggests that a colonial metaphor of missionary appropriation, first tested on the Indian subcontinent, was subsequently applied to the English working class and provincial regions. Thus, as Brian Doyle and others have argued, the development of English studies and the re-creation of English identity are interwoven.[6] However, it is not safe to assume that this was simply a top-down process of hegemonic imposition and identity erasure. Clearly the marginal space offered by adult education also allowed the contrasting voice to be heard and as a result a dialogic quality was inserted into the English settlement, which recognised some difference and diversity.

Much of this is well documented but what is less well known are the pedagogic wars of the 1930s over the teaching of the arts and culture fought out in adult education. On the one hand the metropolitan modernisers at the centre of the adult education movement, like W E Williams (the editor of the WEA's journal *The Highway*), wanted to construct a version of the national popular and on the other the provincial class-warriors, like G H Thompson (District Secretary of the WEA Yorkshire (North) District), were bent on maintaining an independent workers' education based on the needs and experience of the organised labour movement. In many respects this was an (eternally recurrent) argument between the 'literary' and the 'sociological' wings of the movement, the former wanting purity of textual study (and class harmony) and the latter wanting relevance to life (and class struggle). The fecundity and passion of the arguments no doubt contributed immensely to the emergence and quality of British cultural studies.

It was clear that by the end of the 1930s a different kind of voice was intervening in these debates, that of the European, mostly Jewish, intellectuals who had fled from Nazi persecution to Britain. What they brought was a much more sophisticated sociological reading of Marxism than had been developed in Britain. For many of these intellectuals adult education was the key pedagogical site of intervention. The most active members of this group were Karl Mannheim and Karl Polanyi whose book *The Great Transformation* (1944) was developed in the course of his lectures for the WEA and the Oxford Extramural Delegacy. Mannheim's views on the commitment and autonomy of the intellectual, the need for a totalising sociology or 'science of society' and the centrality of culture in creating social consciousness were of inestimable importance in shaping the debates to come. Similarly, Karl Polanyi's insistence on realigning the academic curriculum to reflect the needs of the political working class and supersede 'bourgeois' divisions of knowledge was extremely suggestive of new subjects of knowledge.

Edward Thompson's arrival in the West Riding of Yorkshire as a literature and history tutor in the late 1940s brought him into the heartland of the provincial class warriors and right from the onset of his career he was forced to mediate his passionate belief in Marxism with the expressed needs of working-class students. The fact that he was very nearly an early victim of the onset of the Cold War in academia makes the achievement of his *Making of the English Working Class* (1963) (his 'West Riding book') even more remarkable. As others have since remarked, this was not a book which could have been written in a mainstream university department of history at this time, and it must be seen as the outcome of his extra-mural engagement and political commitment. Thompson's distrust of American 'mass' culture, his sceptical approach to unhistoricised 'popular' culture, and his belief in the function of education for creating purposeful social consciousness put him at a distance from the direction cultural studies was subsequently to take.

Raymond Williams's attempts to unite cultural radicalism, left wing politics and adult education must be seen as the most ambitious and far-sighted project of the postwar period. This was in large part the core of the 'old' New Left project. Described by Edward Thompson as 'our best man', Williams, during his years in adult education, contributed some of the most politically incisive and creative commentary on cultural issues yet to be seen. Williams's principal task was to make the study of literature and writing a political activity and see it explicitly as an aspect of communications. He was one of the first to grasp the significance of film and television as objects of study, which he pioneered in adult classes. His reconstruction of the Romantic critique of capitalism in the nineteenth century for the first time suggested a way in which the goals and struggles of the working-class movement could be located within a broader struggle for a full, creative and just way of life – the 'Long Revolution'. His preoccupation with drama and especially tragedy provides an ironic counterpoint to this heroic project and the disillusion he felt on leaving adult education for an internal post in Cambridge may well have foreshadowed the end of 'utopian' socialist politics in Britain. In one of his last writings, Williams criticised the current academic practices of cultural studies as having strayed too far from their radical and grounded origins and wanted to return them to a more direct concern with political economy and social movements in order to renew the political project of a democratic cultural education. The point, Williams argued, was that cultural studies should understand its own formation.

Unlike Williams and Thompson, Hoggart was less interested in the grand political and historical narratives of the working class or in a 'common culture', a term of which he was always rather suspicious, and more interested in the detail of everyday life. How was it that a moral culture of resistance to the enfeebling hedonism and triviality of capitalist civilisation had enabled working people to survive with dignity, he asked. Could it now survive the onslaught of the mass media? His *Uses of Literacy* (1957) was the direct outcome of wrestling with his own journey of cultural development which cannot simply be dismissed as a nostalgic 'narrative of exile'. Necessarily partial, as autobiographical accounts must be, it nevertheless proved a galvanic text in altering Labour's educational and cultural policy. In its use of Leavisite methodology it was the first serious attempt at an academic study of popular culture and the model for the brilliant studies which mark the early years of the Birmingham Centre.

Class, culture and the national popular

In many respects the historical formation of 'adult education' had been a valuable marginal space which enabled creative experimentation and innovation in educational and pedagogic practices between the 1930s and the 1960s especially. This was a period of intense social and political change in which considerable modernisation of the British state apparatuses took place, not least in the function of education. One of the most important cultural shifts was the movement away from the class politics of the earlier part of the century to new concepts of the popular and the nation, which incorporated or at least mollified class divisions, a process that still continues. Although this is more a re-mapping of class identities than their obliteration in favour of other kinds of identity, the move to construct the national popular has been at the expense of the centrality of the working-class identity that was the core of the old Labour movement. The deliberate generation of mass unemployment and systematic destruction of working-class collectivist forms which was part of the political project of Thatcherism has of course grossly accelerated this. If this was the negative aspect of the process, the positive was that with the decentering of working-class identity other suppressed identities have emerged: most importantly, the distinct struggles for the liberation of women, minority ethnic identities and disability. The politics of anti-racism and anti-sexism must be regarded as two of the most important progressive outcomes of the decline of working-class politics. The contribution of cultural studies to these struggles has been invaluable in shifting the focus of enquiry from the workplace and production to the home and consumption.

Cultural study, always a significant part of liberal adult education, and the teaching of the arts, especially English literature, have had especial significance in constructing identity for the emergent democratic classes. One should not see this process as simply enforced hegemonic repression or surveillance, as has been the burden of older orthodox Marxist interpretations and newer uninflected Foucauldian ones, but as the outcome of mediated negotiations between necessarily unequal power blocs in which the liberal educator has been an important figure. It may have bought off revolution and allowed a revised bourgeois hegemony, but it also enabled substantial social reforms to be introduced and forced concessions from the hegemonic bloc which two decades of reactionary politics have still not wholly won back. If working-class identity has always been compromised by an infusion of bourgeois nationalism, it also true the nation has had to incorporate many 'working-class' values and institutions in order to be legitimated.

English studies may well have been invented by the liberal educators to incorporate the colonised masses into the new national settlement of Englishness but it had unintended consequences in suggesting other interpretations of labile texts. In adult education, one of the most significant factors in affirming these other interpretations and in casting suspicion on the intentions of the hegemonic institutions has historically been the fact of the working-class movement itself. Without the sceptical, though in many ways deeply conservative, approach to liberal education of this movement – as embodied in some districts of the WEA and in the Labour Colleges – the insistence on connectedness to everyday experience and social purpose would not have been possible. It was of course a limited connectedness and despite the presence of many women in these classes the question of their own exploitation was largely suppressed until the re-emergence of the feminist movement in the late 1960s. However, one of the most significant spaces in which this movement did appear was in WEA classes. Emblematic of this process were the courses taught by Sheila Rowbotham in Hackney and elsewhere, which began as courses in political ideas but underwent a paradigm shift to emerge as women's history and then women's studies in the early 1970s. Rowbotham is the first to acknowledge her debt to Edward Thompson in creating the conceptual space where those voices 'hidden from history' could at last be heard. Courses swiftly sprang up all over the country, in such subjects as single-parent families, women and technology, women and anthropology, women and literature and feminist approaches to film study, all of which were evidence of the interdisciplinary range of women's studies. Women's studies must not be allowed to suffer an analogous fate to cultural studies and be represented as emerging fully armed from the side of a university academic department; it too should be seen as linked intimately to a wider social movement which was testing its newly understood educational needs in the marginal spaces outside the academy.

Raymond Williams has suggested that in adult education, the 'truth' of English studies was always already cultural studies, in the sense that the study of English has continually strayed away from a singular concern with textual analysis to the implications of that text for life and identity. Although frequently forced back by the academicians to close textual analysis, the demands from outside the walls were for relevance – both from the adult student who wanted to connect it to lived experience and also from the liberal establishment which wanted to connect it to national identity. These tensions existed in university extension, were made explicit in the Newbolt Report and were fought out in the struggles over Leavisism in the 1930s.

There it might have ended had not the vitality of the adult educational movement attracted the attention of the European Marxisant émigrés, who, fleeing from Nazism, were also sceptical of the attenuated intellectual traditions of Stalinised Marxism. The new dimension they added to these debates suggested overhauling the élite intellectual traditions of the British establishment in favour of a democratised learning society from the cradle to the grave. Here hidebound academic specialisms, they argued, should be routinely transgressed in favour of new subjects of knowledge in a spirit of joyful interdisciplinary irreverence. Not surprisingly, specialist academic departments of universities looked askance at such iconoclasm and, consequently, the extramural space became for many the site of the educational avant-garde. The new totalising sociology suggested by Karl Mannheim, Karl Polanyi and others, which began from a radical conception of the worker's relation to society as a whole, was undoubtedly utopian but in the ways utopias have, it was remarkably suggestive.

The real effect of this interwar argumentation was not felt until the postwar generation of tutors took up their extramural positions and discovered ways of linking these insights to their work with adults. Freed from the imposition of the required 'neutrality' of the intramural university and committed to the general cause of workers' emancipation, this was the generation that made culture and social consciousness the centre of their investigations. If this was the 'moment of culture', it was also politics by other means, since the Cold War (from around 1947) informally outlawed communist politics in Britain and signalled the long-term attack on working-class industrial organisation (although many working-class social aims were maintained). Clearly the model of social revolution based on industrial mobilisation, the general strike and spontaneous mass upheaval was no longer a mobilising myth. The extraordinary proliferation of cultural forms, from those backed by the newly formed Arts Council to the importation of American comic magazines, meant that representation and expression offered themselves for analysis and critique as never before. Culture, which unequivocally served neither the dominant order nor the emergent one, was everywhere and unavoidable. Making sense of this with adult education classes became one of the most engaging common pursuits.

But with the decline of the working-class movement, the already fragile relationship between it and liberal intellectuals inevitably weakened further. Also, with other opportunities for further and higher education emerging from the Butler and Robbins educational reforms, a fragmentation of the public for adult education and a consequent dilution of aims began.

The growth of cultural studies as an academic subject of knowledge seems to be intimately bound up with the construction of the idea of postmodernism. Ironically, while the idea of the cultural struggle was a rejuvenating force for a tired Left, for which labourist politics no longer had any bite, it only accelerated the internal collapse of the categories of class upon which Left politics were historically built. Thompson's emphasis on the growth of class consciousness and Williams's construction of a tradition of a common radical culture oriented the New Left towards cultural symbols and the contest over ideas. However, while both Williams and Thompson were still wedded to a notion of political economy in which economics in some (very loose) sense determined the cultural sphere, a younger generation of intellectuals were not prepared to be so inhibited. Thus for many of the new students of cultural studies, political economy became identified with 'old-fashioned' Marxism and the enthusiasm of the 'old' New Left for grappling with the material aspects of culture and cultural policy was seen as rather quaint. The 'new' New Left had decided that British culture and British cultural theorists really had little to offer a revolutionary movement. Perry Anderson's famous 'Components of the National Culture' *tour de force* rather roughly ignored the work of the old New Left and diagnosed British culture as expiring from an 'absent centre' which only an injection of continental Theory could remedy. As Thompson so vividly put it, 'the lines were electrified for the speedy traffic from the marxistentialist Left bank'.[7] New Left Books' programme of rapid translation of hitherto unavailable continental Marxist texts and post-Marxist theory presented a younger generation of would-be cultural theorists with unimaginable riches. But the more the treasure houses of European theory were opened up, the more distant the theorising appeared to be from any sites of traditional political activity. Whereas Thompson and Williams still imagined their writings as a dialogue with a Labour 'movement', the arguments of the younger cultural theorists took place almost entirely within the boundaries of the academy. There were of course notable exceptions to this, in the flowering of journals such as *Radical Philosophy*, *Capital and Class*, *Race and Society* and, more problematically, *Marxism Today* (but that is another story). However, it was the flourishing of feminist theory that succeeded best in relating complex cultural argument to the needs of a rapidly emerging social movement.

By the mid-1960s adult education had lost many of those who had inspired the cultural studies movement. Williams left the Oxford Delegacy to take a lectureship in English at Cambridge University; Thompson left Leeds to spend a few unhappy years as Reader and then Professor of Social History at Warwick 'Business' University, and Hoggart left Hull for a lectureship in English at Leicester University and then Chair of English at Birmingham. Paradoxically, they benefited from the same expansion of higher education that, as a result of the Robbins Report, would now matriculate significant numbers of school-leavers from lower middle-class and working-class families who, previously, might have turned in their later lives to the WEA. The most radical innovation of the period was the foundation of the Open University which offered adults structured part-time degree programmes with a level of technical sophistication, student support and educational resourcing compared with which much traditional extra-mural provision looked like light entertainment.

The effect of this epochal change on adult and higher education was that the yoking together of the political struggle and the cultural struggle urged in the immediate postwar period was only fitfully possible. Cultural studies moved into the academic mainstream and, despite its interest in popular culture, became increasingly mandarin in its discourses. It was discussed in ways that even the intelligent lay members of adult education classes found hard to grasp, often leaving the field free for the return of a more conservative liberal studies or 'art appreciation' mode. Thus the mainstreaming of cultural studies left the initial project of a popular critical education in a New Left politics stranded in a time-warp which, except perhaps for the development of local studies and creative writing, eternally celebrated the moment of The Making but seemed not to be able to move on.

Cultural studies in and beyond the academy

The most concerted attempt to make cultural studies an academically credible subject was made by Richard Hoggart. Although his MA in Cultural Studies was dismissed by some of his élitist colleagues at Birmingham as 'Hoggart's line in cheap hats', his founding of the Birmingham Centre for Contemporary Cultural Studies on a grant from Allen Lane of Penguin marked the beginning of the long march through the institutions in which none of the humanities or social sciences remained untouched by its methods. The Centre itself has consistently contributed some of the most illuminating analyses of popular culture which have promoted the formation of similar departments throughout the 'new' university sector. Stuart Hall's subsequent move from the Centre to the Open University led to many innovative interdisciplinary undergraduate programmes and the ground-breaking 'Popular Culture' module of the early 1980s made a substantial impact on the rest of the Open University's arts and social science programmes. The impact of cultural studies has been most keenly felt in the 'new' universities of the former polytechnic sector, which, because of less well-entrenched subject specialisms, have embraced inter-disciplinary study. In the older universities a general move to devolve budgets has meant that Arts and Social Science departments have taken on board some of the theorising elements of cultural studies but resisted their institutional implications.

However, many commentators, like Jim McGuigan, now see cultural studies as in crisis. McGuigan was already arguing in 1992 that mainstream cultural studies had lost much of its political bite because of its dogmatic insistence in ignoring the political economy of popular culture, seeing an engagement with such questions as a form of economic reductionism.[8] Instead of seeing cultural studies as a dialogue with social movements, many of its practitioners prefer to see it as a purely academic discourse and have lost the will, or the ability, to engage with actual social life or political struggle (notable exceptions include Stuart Hall, Angela McRobbie and Paul Willis). The idea of a material reality beyond discourse is itself seen by many as quaintly old-fashioned and has led to an increasingly distanced and ironic commentary on social life, with critics unwilling to grapple with the material implications of their analyses. Williams's insistence that 'culture is ordinary' has in many cases been turned into a cruel parody which celebrates each manifestation of popular culture – even shopping – as politically progressive. McGuigan insists that such a stance 'produces inadequate explanation of the material life situations and power relations that shape the mediated experiences of ordinary people'.[9] It's also not much help, he believes, for falsely modest intellectuals merely to record how well people are doing in the face of overwhelming odds.

Despite this, there is still a version of cultural studies which is more sociological in style and more indebted to the traditions of enlightened rationality that Williams and Thompson respected. The work of Habermas, Bourdieu, Frederic Jameson and David Harvey, for example, has shown a more determined attempt to take on board the valuable critiques offered by the new cultural theory while retaining a stance of principled opposition to actual capitalist relations. Much of this work has identified postmodernism as a cultural and ideological configuration of late capitalism which has produced both an authoritarian populism and antagonistic social movements. So is it possible to imagine a popular adult education which can benefit from the genuine insights made by cultural studies over the past two and a half decades and recover the tradition of social purpose education that inspired its founders? If so it could be invested in what William Morris called 'the education of desire'.

From its origins in the late eighteenth century popular education has been energised by the desire for change and a different way of life. Initially the desire for scientific, or 'really useful', knowledge was not merely to facilitate training needs of individual artisans but to understand the liberatory possibilities of science itself. Scientific knowledge promised the working class its evolutionary place in a world rid of priests and monarchs. As such, this knowledge was not just functional but utopian. Utopian thinking, as Ruth Levitas has shown, is as much about tutoring desire to imagine alternative futures to what is prescribed by quotidian reality, as constructing elaborate, and usually unworkable, 'ideal' social systems.[10] Without such utopian thinking, the Labourist Commonwealth of the mid-twentieth century, which came to fruition in Attlee's 1945 Labour government, would not have been possible. Whatever its faults as a system, the desire it encapsulated for collectivist solutions to social problems such as education, health, housing and old age has, despite nearly two decades of market economics, never been supplanted. Even against the grain of hegemonic policy making, adult education has shown in recent years that it can be effective in stimulating new social thought in, for example, widening access to higher education, third-age education and women's education.

The drive to incorporate adult education under the guise of 'continuing' education into the mainstream of higher education should not be allowed to threaten this marginal and highly creative space, for it is here that, as so often in the past, the new fields of knowledge, such as cultural studies itself, have been created and direct engagement with social movements has taken place. This should be a space in which communities and social movements can secure the services of intellectuals and universities for their own projects and utilise the insights of academic cultural studies in context. On a broader scale, cultural studies can enable the project of 'citizenship' to be reconsidered within much more flexible narratives of subjectivity, identity and cultural needs and with less aesthetic impoverishment than were entailed by the Puritanism of the old Labourist cause. In this way the education of desire could stimulate genuine social renewal.

That positive engagement with the outside world is essential. For example, after two decades of 'Black Studies', 'multiculturalism' and 'work with ethnic minorities', we seem in some respects to be little further forward and have retreated from the militancy of the 1970s and 1980s. Short-term funding for research and outreach projects, and the ending of local authority community education policies, have led to an incessant reinvention of the wheel. Instead of being embedded in educational practice, the achievements made are frequently lost among the filing cabinets of institutions forced into a perpetual pursuit of government-inspired targets and never owned by the communities themselves.

Communities remain impoverished. In a recent keynote speech at a Black Studies conference in Leeds, Amrit Wilson, unfashionably, bemoaned the disjunction of 'identity politics' from class politics. In the name of 'ethnic cultural studies', she argued, there now existed many courses in colleges which denied the link between racism and colonialism and taught the 'saris and samosas' syndrome, a notion of culture that was static. Since dynamic conceptions of culture which included struggles against racism were entirely absent from these courses, the inference that could reasonably be drawn by students was that history had ended and that their everyday experience of racism was somehow nothing to do with their 'culture'.

Notable exceptions to this are participative literacy schemes such as those in Sheffield which have altered the agenda by genuinely empowering local communities rather than institutions.[11] Such schemes only occur where local authorities are prepared to entrust serious long-term funding to local communities and allow members of those communities to influence the outcomes. This suggests that a modest shift of funding from institutions to communities may produce more beneficial effects than institutionally dictated curricula. An educational policy that recognised cultural difference and funded communities to negotiate their own educational needs could begin to construct supracommunal identities which no longer relied on the suppression of the Other or the fossilisation of 'Culture' described above. This shift would recognise the power of marginalised cultures to contribute to the positive transformation of a 'common culture' since, as we have seen, such cultures are not dens of ignorance which only middle-class enlightenment can illuminate, but sites of resistance and communal value. As orthodox notions of 'Englishness' or 'Britishness' lose legitimacy, a new settlement needs urgently to be agreed. Education can aid and benefit this process only if it becomes a medium of dialogue for those with circumscribed power to discover their own needs and learn how they may satisfy them. In this their own cultures can be reservoirs of wisdom and hope and the tradition of informed and committed dialogue in adult education the means of enlightenment.

Reflecting on the enduring value of Williams's *Drama in Performance* nearly 40 years since its first publication, Graham Holderness[12] has written:

> This book actually emerged from one of the most supportive educational environments in which it is possible for a teacher to work. It is probably easier to grasp and sustain the notion of culture as a collective social activity, and as a material process of production, in the context of a continual engagement with thinking and learning adult students, than in any other space in the educational system. At a time when, amid extreme political contradictions, those values that used to be sharply differentiated as 'extra-mural' and 'adult education' are becoming major priorities within the central system of higher education, it is appropriate to reinsert into active circulation a book which testifies so eloquently to the possibility of democratic educational culture.

If, educationally, the centre has begun to engulf the margins, then the project now must be to ensure those values of a 'democratic educational culture' so dear to the old extra-mural formation also shape the new 'mass' higher education.[13] It may be that, as Williams suggests, cultural studies can best rejuvenate its project within the formation of industrial training, which New Labour's Green Paper 'The Learning Age' appears, rhetorically if not financially, to support. If so, it may begin to deinstitutionalise itself once more. It should also seek out those constituencies increasingly marginalised by the changed conditions of production which will otherwise be condemned to receive little more than an attenuated skills training which takes no account of their human and social needs. However, it will need to recreate some independent and autonomous organisational form as did the WEA at the turn of the century.

The phenomenon of globalisation may have made the older project of a nationally located cultural studies, and hence 'Englishness', archaic. The reach of metropolitan capitalisms, especially American capital, has arguably reduced all forms of previously 'national' difference to that between the global and the local. McLuhan's 'global village' has been made possible by electronic communications systems barely imaginable when Williams held his first classes in communications. Yet the local still persists as a site of difference and a potential source of resistance, even if it is perhaps to be located in cities and regions rather than nation states. Hence the renewal of interest in the city – pioneered in Britain at the turn of the century by Patrick Geddes. There is also a sense of the local as a 'virtual' locality made possible by almost instantaneous communication through the internet; virtual communities regularly form around multiple campaigns and debates and dissolve just as quickly, an Athenian democracy of PC users (but one which also excludes its helots). The locality in this sense is one that dissolves space and incorporates difference on a global basis.

Cultural strategies cannot therefore ignore globalisation however it is formulated – and a useful typology is given by Lawrence Grossberg.[14] It has to centre on different constructions of identity which owe less and less to national determinants and more and more to issues of sexuality, age, ethnicity and disability. With the precipitous decline of the culture of organised labour and the international socialist movements on which the original project depended so heavily, social class seems to have faded as an agent of identity. However I still believe it would be presumptive to write it off: although it has been discursively enfeebled, 'class' still cuts swathes, economically and socially, through other forms of identity.

Paradoxically, Grossberg argues that cultural studies has now to escape culture, itself, and centre on questions of power. Culture has to be increasingly seen as the codification of powerful operations. For Grossberg, the task of cultural studies is

> to understand the operations of power in the lived reality of human beings, and to help all of us imagine new alternatives for the becoming of that reality. Culture is both its site and its weapon, but it is not the limits of cultural studies' world. In the end, I am trying to disarticulate cultural studies from the modern 'discovery' of the social construction of reality, to find a way, not to get rid of discourse and culture, but to de-imperialise them by bringing back notions of space and material reality.[15]

Ah, back to reality at last! Yes, but this reality is different. We now all agree on how provisional it is and how, dare we use the word, 'dialectical' it is. But what Grossberg seems to suggest conforms with what has been argued here, namely a twofold strategy: first, that cultural studies re-engages with political economy and sociological analysis and second, that it develops an intellectual and affective curriculum that encourages people to imagine and put into practice desirable ways of living. The wings of desire on the feet of reason. The concern for a rationally grounded cultural studies should not therefore mean any retreat from the aesthetic dimension. On the contrary, it should encourage engage-ment with it just because its concern with the other two dimensions of modernity, the scientific and the moral, may be said to have inhibited its affec-tive power. Similarly, the contemporary fascination with the aesthetic, fol-lowing Nietzsche, which has rejected the moral and scientific as, merely, discourses of power, seems also to have led to a theoretical and practical impasse. The point is that the aesthetic also has its reasons and the leap from reason to taste always leaves one foot anchored: aesthetic judgement requires reason and taste not merely to be a matter of passing whim. Habermas has argued against Nietzsche that he did not recognise that 'the critical capacity for assessing value that was sharpened through dealing with modern art' was also a moment of reason.[16] If this is true, then the education of desire is a realisable project and cultural studies, which has already mapped out much of the terrain, should work on the implications for the curriculum.

Notes

1   Williams R, 'The future of cultural studies', in Williams, *The Politics of Modernism*, Verso, London, 1989.
2   Williams R, *Politics and Letters: Interviews with New Left Review*, NLB, London, 1975, p. 69.
3   Williams, 1989, p. 75.
4   See Steele T, *The emergence of cultural studies: adult education, cultural politics and the English question*, Lawrence and Wishart, London, 1997.
5   Swindells J and Jardine L, *What's left: women in culture and the Labour Movement*, London, 1990; Rowbotham S, *The past is before us: feminism in action since the 1960s*, Pandora, London, 1990.
6   Doyle B, 'The invention of Englishness', in Colls R and Dodd P (eds), *Englishness: politics and culture 1880–1920*, Croom Helm, Beckenham, 1986, pp. 89–115; Baldick C, *The social mission of English criticism 1848–1932*, Clarendon Press, Oxford, 1987; Eagleton T, *Literary theory: an introduction*, Blackwell, Oxford, 1983.
7   Thompson E P, 'The peculiarities of the English', in Thompson E P, *The poverty of theory and other essays*, Merlin, London, 1978, p. 35.
8   McGuigan J, *Cultural Populism*, Routledge, London, 1992.
9   McGuigan, 1992, p. 244.
10 Levitas R, *The concept of utopia*, Philip Allen, Hemel Hempstead, 1990, p. 181.
11 See Gurnah A (ed.), 'Literacy for a change' (a special issue on the Sheffield Black Literacy campaign), *Adults Learning*, Vol 3 No 8, April 1992.
12 Holderness G, 'Introduction to this edition', in Williams R, *Drama in performance*, Open University Press, Milton Keynes, 1991.
13 Scott P, *The meanings of mass higher education*, SRHE and Open University Press, Milton Keynes, 1995.
14 Grossberg L, 'Cultural studies, modern logics, and theories of globalisation', in McRobbie A (ed.), *Back to reality? Social experience and cultural studies*, Manchester University Press, Manchester, 1997, pp. 7–35.
15 Grossberg, 'Cultural studies, modern logics, and theories of globalisation', in McRobbie, *Back to Reality*, p. 31.
16 Quoted in Rasmussen D M, *Reading Habermas*, Blackwell, Oxford, 1990, p. 13.

2 'Politics by other means'? Or, teaching cultural studies in the academy is a political practice

Richard Johnson

There are two key settings for this chapter. The first is the neglect, in public writings and debates, of questions of educational purpose and pedagogy in the teaching of cultural studies in the universities. It was strikingly novel to be asked, in the same year (1996), both to contribute to a book on teaching cultural studies[1] and to give a paper at the conference on 'Teaching Culture and Cultures of Teaching' from which this volume sprang.[2]

The second setting is the revival of often polemical criticism of cultural studies as a project, a marked feature of the late 1980s and the 1990s. A main burden of criticism has been the alleged disengagement of cultural studies, as an 'established' academic subject, from three Ps: 'Politics', 'Policy' and 'Practice'.[3]

There are several versions of this argument, with their own points of departure. In recreating 'the emergence of cultural studies' from new-left adult education in the period from 1945 to 1965, Tom Steele also argues, at the end of a persuasive and fascinating volume, that (by the 1970s?) cultural studies 'moved into the academic mainstream', became 'increasingly mandarin in its discourses', only entering (by the later 1980s) into a creative crisis of its own.[4] Steele's stance in adult education, the generative point of cultural studies as a formation, is unusual and refreshing. Other authors write from adjacent academic disciplines: usually sociology, or the study of media or of 'mass communication' or political economy. A common 'sociological' criticism, shared by a cultural studies 'materialism', has been that we have lost our way in an overly 'textual' version of culture than neglects social relations, institutions and lived cultural forms.[5] Some of the most trenchant (and long-standing) criticisms come from political economy in its intersections with media studies. From this point of view, cultural studies has become over-preoccupied with questions of popular culture and consumption. In celebrating popular creativity it has vacated the domain of hard political choices and judgements of value. Founded in a critical tradition, it has become complicit with the ideologies of 'consumer sovereignty' characteristic of the New Right. It has also vacated the study of cultural production and the fuller analysis of the effects of commodification and of capital's global power.[6] These critics are joined by others who argue that cultural studies has neglected questions of 'policy'.[7] What is meant by 'policy' or 'policy-makers' here is not always clear, but it certainly includes 'those who control and run the major institutions of public culture and those who decide on their regulation and funding'.[8]

To respond to wider criticisms would divert us from issues of educational practice – an unintended consequence of the critics' non-educational terms of debate. Three brief general points will have to do to re-orient discussion.

First, critical accounts of cultural studies often work with reduced portrayals of what cultural studies is, has been and is becoming. To typify cultural studies research as 'populist' for instance – in the sense of always celebrating popular resistance – is to ignore the prolonged attention given to hegemonic forms, their power, their contradictions and limits, and their common enclosure of popular forms.[9] If, however, 'populism' is taking the popular or subordinated sides in social struggles and working out what Gramsci called 'the good sense in common sense', well, I plead guilty to that.[10]

Second, it is surprising to find familiar intellectual refusals riding on the back of telling criticisms. I agree, for instance, that to neglect or pre-empt matters of political-economic tendency and organisation will not do; but neither will the refusal to rethink 'the economic' or 'production' or variants on the base/superstructure metaphor in relation to cultural critique.[11] The reiteration of limited state-centred views of politics and of policy is another case in point. These closures around politics and policy and the cultural aspects of struggles make it hard to recognise education as a politics at all.

Finally, I do wonder if the debate tells us more about the general academic scene – and our dilemmas within it – than about cultural studies specifically. As some critics admit, cultural studies is itself very diverse nowadays, especially internationally. It has many local variants, which combine in different ways with adjacent disciplines (cultural history, literary studies, literary theory and sociology especially) or with other interdisciplinary clusters (media studies, communication studies, women's, gender or sexuality studies); sometimes it even addresses practitioners and policy-makers, within a 'professional training' paradigm for instance. But what we all have in common, possibly, is our sense of a crisis in our approaches and a pressure to subordinate the elements of critical thinking in our work, especially those that cannot easily be accommodated within a dominant (eg Blairite) version of the future. I wonder if there is not a general loss of nerve in intellectual practice in the academy, partly to do with the intense ideological commercialisation of academic institutions and the slipping away of criteria other than 'what pays'. This seems to me to fuel desire to seek recognition from policy-makers, media and political professionals. Again, I am not arguing against 'policy-making' ambitions and cross-professional connections; I think all our work should address policies or strategies (but of which agents?) as a matter of course. But I do feel there is some self-disgust in this writing: in phrases like 'spouting seminar-room politics' or 'the curiously hermetic world of cultural studies in general' for example.[12] In seeking to make ourselves useful to others we surely need more confidence in what we have to say. Maybe we also have some practices of our own to defend, upon which our future usefulness depends.

These two settings form a pattern. The fear that cultural studies has lost validity and direction is fed by silence about a central practice – teaching students how to study culture (and learning with them how to do it better). The critics are as silent about this activity as its promoters have been. In the Ferguson and Golding collection, for instance, only one contributor out of 13 gets to mention teaching and he only to attack cultural studies for abandoning the possibility of 'truth'.[13] Tom Steele is unusual in centring on education, especially adult education, as the critical nexus of politics and a popular connection. His hopes for the future of cultural studies are phrased in the last words of the book:

> If the centre [the academic 'mainstream'] has begun to engulf the margins [popular adult education], then the project must now be to ensure that those values of a 'democratic educational culture', so dear to the old extra-mural formation, also shape the new 'mass' higher education.[14]

For participants in the 'new, "mass" higher education' this may seem a rather belated recognition, but our own silences play a part in this, including silence on the continuities between Steele's story and our own. Many of the preoccupations of extra-mural university education have been carried, latterly, in the parts of Further and Higher education where questions of access and expansion have been prioritised. As a particularly expansive area, cultural studies, in connection with media and communication, but also as a salt in traditional disciplines, has played a large part. It has, however, taken adult educators (among others) to put educational practice on to the public cultural studies agenda again.

This is why I want to concentrate on our central practices, especially those of teaching and learning. I want to argue against some aspects of Tom Steele's argument while recognising the ache of loss which seems to me to pervade it. I do not think that the move from (university) adult education to other parts of the academy necessarily involved a depoliticisation. It generated quite enough 'politics and practice' to outlast anyone's life time – and continues to do so. It was not a removal from political movements or cultural currents, not a disengagement; rather, these met up on a different site, in a different way.

Of course, politics by other means within the academy is shaped by the structures of these institutions, with their class-exclusive histories. It is a politics with definite horizons, what Marx would have called a limited material practice. It is not enough of a politics in itself. Moreover, after a period of expansion and a limited democratisation of intake, on the cheap, the horizons may be closing down again. It is a critical question who gets to participate in 'higher education' and who is in on the conversations. But 'limited horizons' also fits all other social sites, including the politics of media institutions and the politics of Politics. The academy is not unique in having limits and contradictions which have to be recognised even as we try to go beyond them.

So first I want to explore some parameters of everyday practice in the academy, trying to address today's realities. In this I also describe my standpoints as a teacher. In the second part of this chapter I offer a case study in learning how to teach. My example is the practice of theoretical review, or review of theories, a common practice across a range of 'cultural' disciplines – and one full of contradictions.

My main method is autobiographical reflection, based on memory, teaching archives and written retrospects of students.[15] Of course, my own experience has been specific. I taught and studied with MA, PhD and first degree students for nearly 20 years at the Birmingham Centre for Contemporary Cultural Studies (CCCS). It is not the case (as is sometimes said to me) that this was a postgraduate experience only. I taught on a steadily expanding BA programme through the 1980s, usually on three courses each year. In the 1970s and 1990s postgraduate work did take priority. Pedagogies must be contextually specific: what works in one place and time does not work in another. It is a question for other practitioners whether CCCS experiences have relevance today. I have also drawn on more recent experiences, especially three and a half years in a lively interdisciplinary Humanities Faculty, much influenced by 'the cultural turn', at Nottingham Trent University.

Inaugural troubles

Perhaps Nottingham is the best place to start. The contradictions of cultural studies in the academy were highlighted, once again, when I was preparing a professorial inaugural lecture.[16] I approached this occasion with feelings of extraordinary ambivalence. It was a confusing occasion: I was the second Professor of Cultural Studies to be inaugurated in the single institution in a single year. Compared with the struggle to establish cultural studies at Birmingham, our inauguration at Nottingham Trent was disorienting. Cultural studies had arrived at last – but wasn't it supposed to be marginal?

A conventional inaugural lecture should involve, I took it, some celebration of a discipline, to the credit of a professor himself, of a faculty, a university, and (in the old Polytechnic context) of a City. At Nottingham Trent the model event (which you get unless you ask otherwise) involves invitations to city and university worthies, a prestigious hall (on a city site not on the suburban Humanities teaching site) and minimum festivity (sherry before, no meal after). Publication is in a form evidently not meant to be read, since all the inaugurals of each year in all disciplines are bound in a single volume. Inaugurals are rather part of the corporate display that now preoccupies university administrations. In the course of panicky preparation, an image came recurrently to mind – the cap and the gown (would I *have* to wear them?) not as insignia of an honourable if pedantic profession, but as a masquerade, a turncoat. A switch of the gown displays . . . nothing but a bag of gold!

There were other difficulties too. The inaugural lecture is an individual didactic performance. Discussion is not encouraged. Yet much of my work has been cooperative. In cultural studies this has often been a strategy to try to break down the individualism and competitiveness of academic work. I knew that 'on the day' there would be several people in the hall who had contributed to my lecture, whose words and ideas it was as much as mine. My script also grew from ongoing dialogues with postgraduate students and colleagues at Nottingham Trent about political values and intellectual uses and abuses. The contradictions were sharp: Can you have a *collective inaugural*? Can you have a *dialogic inaugural*? Can you have a *marginal inaugural*? Can you have an inaugural which does not confer individual privilege or celebrate disciplinary identities? It doesn't sound very plausible, does it?

I wondered whether to refuse the occasion, which amounts to asking whether it would be better to do cultural studies outside the academy. In the end, I tried to negotiate a space to 'inaugurate' differently. I asked two postgraduate students (friends, coworkers not people I supervise) to introduce me. I asked a younger colleague, independently engaged on some of the same questions, to sum up. I wrote a script on issues of marginality in the academy, and about how academic work could, none the less, have a wider usefulness. I argued this through my main example – the contemporary politics of sexuality. While my professorial colleague spoke eloquently on how cultural studies must grasp the problem of violence,[17] I was embroiled (professionally of course) in the contemporary crisis of sexual ways of living. At least we were taking on 'current issues'! I asked the university to finance a meal afterwards for everyone and allow more time. As well as friends and coworkers from elsewhere and members of my complicated family, I invited all my Nottingham colleagues and all the students I teach or have a responsibility to. I tried but failed to shift the venue to the main humanities teaching campus, from corporate territory to intellectual home ground. I managed, however, to change the hall to one technically equipped for teaching. This process was interesting. Was it possible to use the privileges of a new professor to make things happen differently?

Similar processes – constraints, contradictions and possibilities – run through the history of cultural studies in the academy. Minor events, everyday events, even privileged events, can carry a political charge, a significance, an excitement. These are signs – to say it again – not of a depoliticised practice, but of a practice political in very particular ways.

Marginal histories

From adult education beginnings, cultural studies in Britain has been associated with marginal positions. This marginality did not go away because Richard Hoggart was a Professor of English. Cultural studies remained marginal in the academy for quite similar reasons to its marginality in the early adult education years. It was an intellectual approach which took its agenda not from the state of academic debates but from the priorities of social movements, from contemporary cultural currents and from the lives of individuals whose key questions were not addressed in the established academic disciplines. This was a recurrent pattern – which continues – and it was always in tension with the pressure to found a discipline in a more conventional sense.

In these respects – though not in many others – a teacher of cultural studies in the 'mainstream' (not extra-mural) academy shares much with the adult education tutor. A central dynamic is the encounter between an agenda that comes from everyday experience on the one side and the more institutionalised literatures and knowledges on the other. This includes appropriations from established academic disciplines and elements which previous challenges have sedimented in curricula, core texts and methods. The cultural studies teacher must listen for the new questions: this is a way to engage with what Raymond Williams called 'the emergent'.[18] But it is also our responsibility to make available what is present in our 'selective tradition' and add to it in terms of criticism. What do our critical resources offer for the new inquiry? How are older truths repositioned in the new agenda?

So the emergent has often appeared on my landscape as students and what they want to study. Making space for choice (in essay titles, projects, dissertations, theses, group work, working papers, collective books, and so on) and engaging, sometimes critically, with the choices and accompanying ambivalences are important practices here. This goes for all 'levels' including postgraduate work. Teaching postgraduates is a privilege and is rewarding. It is also a form of adult education. It is a dialogue with subjects who are, transparently, both inside and outside the institution and often feel ambivalent about it. They have invested in an intellectual identity and are poised for acceptance. They are trying the academy for size at close quarters. They are the marginal academic subjects *par excellence*, because marginality is not simply exclusion, but a borderline or 'liminal' state. It includes the desire to belong or take the place (skills, knowledges, rewards) of a more powerful Other. Recognition of the marginality of studentdom in the academy and its creativity has stayed with me since Student Movement days. Teaching in regular lecture rooms and in an occupation on the same days gave me a sense of the power that lies on the engaged edges of things. Similarly, constructions around academic centres and margins have been formative in my own self-identity as a teacher. This has included the need for recognition from students and the pleasure and the energy, when this seems fairly won.

The marginality of studentdom is intertwined with larger social marginalities.[19] Students are also positioned as working-class or women or black or lesbian or gay or as men critical of their own power or sexuality, or as foreigners in a xenophobic or culturally secretive country – or as combinations of all these positions. Who gets to be a student, or not, is pressured by these and other positionalities. Some 'marginalities' are 'chosen' and reversible. Like my inaugural experience, they carry the possibility of reclaiming centrality and privilege. Most marginalities, however, are direct, personal and imposed. The academic hierarchies are articulated to the larger social divisions.

Teaching cultural studies means making alliances with students and colleagues to struggle against such marginalities. With recognition and support, marginalities can be turned into resources. Much fine, strong, original, intellectual work, critical of orthodoxies and faithful to social allegiances, has been produced by young (and older) people, writing from a margin, barely started on an 'academic career'. Where local spaces are less transformed, individuals can pass – with difficulty – as *academic* as well as straight or as middle class. The underlying marginalities, however, will always mean that there are costs. At each stage of an academic progression it is extra hard to succeed and flourish if you are a woman and/or working class and/or 'black' and/or gay, and/or disabled, and/or a 'foreigner' – all terms that must be understood as reductive shorthands for complex structural-cum-biographical patterns. These patterns themselves interact with the small-scale politics of particular units and universities.

Because of this association with marginal positions, teaching cultural studies involves recurrent personal transformations and shifts in points of view.[20] It also involves a critical relation to the dominant social relations and ways of handling knowledge within the academy. At best, we have produced partially transformed spaces – always highly contradictory – where marginalities are recognised and room is made for work that is impossible or too costly elsewhere. This involves a particular teaching stance. We have to be clear about our own expectations and 'standards' and try to ground them in our politics. But we may also have to incite students to make a difference between the academic norms and critical intellectual work. We cannot 'ally otherwise' or produce good work unless we free up academic practices and take some distance from anxious pettiness, 'realistic' closures, and the cunning, brain-dead, instrumental cynicism of the day. We have to make a distinction between the academy as an apparatus, and critical, popularly allied intellectual practice; between the usual competition, and work which is cooperative in spirit and possibility. From this point of view, the academy looks strange. It ought to feel uncomfortable.

It looks stranger and stranger as I write. The reason lies in the scandalous history of academic institutions – in the transformations of ethos in the Thatcherite years, the deepening of a managerialist practice into the 1990s and probably, the coming centralised neo-vocationalist 'reform' of teaching and curricula. The more that academic institutions are articulated to markets, to the divisions of capitalist labour, to the culture of the corporate boast, to inter-institutional competition and to the social forms of unequal power in our world, the more academic activity becomes intellectual commodity production aimed to enhance the marketability or the cultural and economic capital of the individual or institution. The distance between critical intellectual work for broader public benefits and a conventional academic practice widens still further.

If this was the whole story, the solution would be relatively simple; the tensions of marginality could be relaxed by simply going or staying away. Perhaps cultural studies is not proper to the academy. Perhaps it belongs to informal, political, self- or mutual education, outside the academy. Tom Steele's and other histories reveal the different modalities of adult education in the past from the 'extra mural' (itself a privileged half-way house) to 'voluntary' or movement forms. There are possible, tempting spaces, minimally institutionalised, domestic, dispersed, networked, more cooperative, in which research and study can ally with living differently and with campaigns. Yet the academy remains a significant political site with resources worth struggling over. It is hard to imagine a political–intellectual project which does not have a foothold there. It is one place where new ideas and practices emerge or where alternatives emerging elsewhere get some public recognition, reinforcement and refreshment. The academy is not just theory as opposed to practice; it is a site of practice itself.

This is still a scandalous assertion for older theories of knowledge. It is a scandal for some 'critical' positions too: 'Oh it's all very well taking about theory! What about political practice in the real world?'[21] This rightly rebukes academic self-importance. It won't do to identify academic writing, research and even teaching as politics *per se*. But it won't do, either, to strip everyday practices in the academy (or anywhere else) of their significance and possibility and imagine that somewhere else – in street, factory, political party or the House of Commons – *anywhere* but *here* – there is *real politics* pure, unproblematic and with no conditions of its own.

Judith Butler puts the opposite case well writing about the 'performativity' of sex–gender categories and relations. Sexual and gender identities are perform-ances of more or less transgressive kinds. For sexual transgression we might read more transgressive performances in the academy, inaugural or otherwise (with which it should ally):

> Performativity describes this relation of being implicated in that which one opposes, this turning of power against itself to produce alternative modalities of power, to establish a kind of political contestation that is not a *pure* opposition, a transcendence of contemporary relations of power, but a difficult labour of forging a future from resources inevitably impure.[22]

It follows that the contradictions never go away. In any intellectual activity in the academic space it is hard to sort out what is oppressive and what transforms. We could explore these contradictions across the whole range of academic practices, from 'admissions' (viewed as a question of access) to curriculum and pedagogy (viewed as a negotiation with socially urgent questionings). Progressive politics in the academy has to address the cycles of return from critical intellectual work to social movements and to other contested sites. Though it is intrinsically difficult to audit past performance, and especially to trace the offshoots of new ideas,[23] cultural studies in the academy has probably benefited more from progressive social movements than they have gained in return. A thorough self-assessment would attend to the destinations, skills and political sensitivities of students, to the relevance and political pointedness of research, and to the accessibility and pertinence of writing and other representations. Important too are the politics of daily routines, aside from teaching: how to make policy and administer it in actively anti-democratic conditions, how to unravel teacher/taught relations and colleague hierarchies as productions of social difference, how to cooperate in research and teaching. Small-scale cooperation (which need no longer be 'local' only) is a key condition for challenging managerially imposed norms of competition. In cooperative work (sometimes called, unfortunately, 'collaboration') alternative values can be articulated. Of course, without larger engagements, the bigger structures stay in place, but it is surprising how in criticisms that hinge on 'policy' and 'practice', immediate and intermediate scales of action are so often missing. Missing too is that focus, over a considerable time, on doing some thing better, often the source of improvement.

'Mapping the field': didactic practice unrevised or abandoned

The practice and the metaphor of 'mapping' was in common use when I arrived in CCCS in 1974.[24] 'Mapping the field' was laying out and critically reviewing possible approaches in a particular domain. CCCS mappings were about theories of culture – 'problematics' in the Althusserian sense. Mapping was central to different versions of the MA programme at Birmingham, from Stuart Hall's formative Cultural Theory course of the 1970s to the core unit 'Frameworks of culture and power' of the 1990s. The aims of the 1970s course were described in these terms: 'This course is intended as a – necessarily condensed and selective – résumé of the field and its problems and definitions. Naturally it traces over again, in a summary form, the historical path which the Centre itself has followed to its present position.'[25]

This course, and the collective readings which preceded it, helped create the field of cultural studies in its second (that is, Gramscian) formation. Mappings were always interventions of course and this was a very influential one. Including some theories, excluding others, maps become a kind of canon, a guide to what is deemed indispensable in a new, fluid, interdisciplinary field. By the 1990s, 'Frameworks of culture and power' was constructing a sequence of positions from theories of ideology to issues of 'hybridity' and syncretic cultural production, from Marxisms to various Postmodernisms.

Pedagogically, mapping was problematic. It took the form of exemplary individual performances by strongly 'leading' teachers in a context of a research centre where, in general, democratic or 'collective' modes were preferred. Some of the difficulties were anticipated when the programme was set up in the mid-1970s: would not a 'taught course' sit ill with the practice of 'collective work'? Tensions were especially marked at moments of some new insurgency – of feminism for instance – when the 'story so far' was being sharply challenged and needed revision.[26] But there was also a difference between 'the story so far' as a complex contemporary struggle, and the story as heard by new generations. It could sound authoritative, accomplished and closed.[27] Whenever the sense of new production was lost, mapping the field accentuated the academic side of cultural studies not the side turned toward the larger social world and the movements (from New Left to Queer politics) from which theories often derived.

What is involved in this practice? I am interested, first, in the experience of the teacher. I can imagine myself as a balloonist with a superior vision – an over/view, a super/vision. I can see the twists and the turns of routes, and the choices that are involved, in ways that cannot, I imagine, be anticipated on the ground. Down there, in the high-banked lanes or muddy, misty fields, students and colleagues need some direction. 'Up' in that imaginary space arguments can be abstracted from their concrete contexts, for only the bold shapes are visible. It is easy to get into the way of making judgements-in-general. It is possible to imagine yourself as outside or above the social geographies and subjectivities of people 'on the ground'.

Of course these are not sustainable imaginings. Their complicity with power and self-aggrandisement are familiar from all the critical debates about 'objectivity' and standpoint, particularly within feminism.[28] The more 'masterly' the mapping the more it tended to silence students and to set up discussion in unhelpfully competitive ways. To provide a map for others is to seem to know your way around all the difficult and dangerous bits. The more comprehensive the map seems, the less space there is for new work – except by redrawing the map completely or adding a supplement which repositions the rest. Mapping, at least as solo performance, is certainly related to what Peter Redman and Máirtín Mac An Ghaill, on the basis of autobiographical work, have termed 'muscular intellectualness'.[29] It reproduces forms of 'mental' masculinity very familiar in the academy. There is a danger that 'overview' becomes the model for intellectual practice as such, or stands at a hierarchical apex of 'skills'. A persistent pedagogic delusion of the CCCS MA was that staff 'presentations' (lectures really) could be followed by animated discussion in which anyone could participate 'if they had done the reading'. This sometimes worked for a confident minority, already in possession of 'the basics'. As so often in the would-be radical academy, critical content and participatory gestures were stymied by fundamentally conservative pedagogy, by failing to see that participation has to be produced.

Further very particular dynamics may be involved, stemming from academic hierarchy, student expectations, the particular (eg rationalist) epistemologies of the day and a desire to emulate. Some such tight, confusing intellectual–emotional knot meant that when I became Director of CCCS, 'mapping' (something a director must do?) filled me with panic. Would I be able to carry it off? I made myself sick and sleepless (over-) preparing sessions. When I finally 'flew' I was never really off the ground, and not a bit above the battle. Any super/vision was dependent on wobbly mental technology, not God-like at all. The balloon floated intoxicatingly high and free, but was also very conspicuous. I could be shot at, boarded, high-jacked or exposed as a producer of hot air. Of course, if you take up a powerful stance, you should expect to be a target. Too much, however, can seem to hang on a performance to risk care, modesty and thought for others. Anyway, though frightening, the practice could be, can be, exhilarating.

Mapping was also a source of vulnerability for those positioned as students. Cultural theories are never really abstracted intellectual positions. This is obvious when questions of identity are explicitly discussed. Every position discussed in the 'Frameworks' course of the 1990s touched on someone's lived identities. Every exclusion was personally significant. Even deferral of discussion to later in the programme could cause strong feelings. Critical discourses, if they hit the mark, incite identification, exclusion and antagonism. They threaten personal change, so may prompt fierce defences. I am thinking of a session in the late 1980s about 'taking psychoanalysis seriously' (of course!). The teaching plan had soon to be laid aside and the argument had out for two and half hours. Always, however, the various positions were not 'out there', but 'in here', in the classroom, round the table, today.

Didactic practices reframed

So mapping seems both oppressive and necessary, one instance of the familiar, 'stuck' binary between didactic and 'progressive' approaches. My own responses to this paradox changed. In a long middle period – much of the 1980s – I gave up or held back from mapping in its more didactic moment. More energies went into surrounding activities, on the CCCS participatory model, including collective research projects with groups of MA students. We also instigated reading groups which became the central motor of the course, constructing maps through readings instead. Even here, however, there was tension between questions coming from members' concerns and what had so far been deemed important in the texts. I learned, however, that 'mapping the field' and masterly performance were not necessarily connected. Yet I often felt I was cheating students. A common, well-aimed student criticism from this period was that the MA programme lacked 'coherence'.

The didactics of mapping became available again, as I became more thoughtful about the vulnerabilities involved. Perhaps this was also a sign of confidence which came from having made most of the mistakes. Vulnerabilities were often revelations too. Why should the uncomfortable sides not be made to lead? This meant sharing puzzles and uncertainties, even bits I could not understand. But there was another paradox here: reviewing worked best when frameworks were laid out and compared with some coherence, trenchancy and purpose, when the lines were nice and firm. This seemed a condition for the most exciting moments, when the map went into crisis, challenged by some half-glimpsed contradiction or some new emergence 'on the ground'. A certain didactic clarity conveyed that the project mattered. A laying out of 'the basics' was best done by lecture or talk. This needed to be combined, however, with more open and discursive methods and strong permissions for difficulties and exclusions to be expressed.

There had always been plenty of challenges from students, whether about pedagogy or about 'content'.[30] Responding to crises was my most important learning experience as a teacher. But successful teaching should not really depend on such (partly) accidental happenings. It is better to *set up* mapping as dialogue or as a struggle, especially one where outcomes are deferred.

Such strategies do not depend on pedagogic gestures or performance merely. They require a rethinking of 'content'. A different method of teaching followed the recognition that theories of culture, power and political identity were aspects of a many-sided struggle, a struggle within radical social movements, between them, and also with liberal and conservative forces and positions. There were also dynamics, in which the course was always caught, between more 'academic' and more 'activist' versions. So why not follow this process in course content and method? Many past difficulties, many current tensions were then doubly present, in texts and positions round the room. Their presence was more fully recognised in advance; they were easier to deal with productively. 'Theory' could be taught as a series of moves and counter-moves, referring to a historical context all the time, negotiating contemporary differences. Part of the argument also came to be about what was meant by 'Theory'. Evidently frameworks are found everywhere, not only in high-intellectual texts. As the 1990s course outline put it:

> 'Framework' is preferred to 'theory' because it is more inclusive. Frameworks are elaborated explicitly in theoretical writings of course, but there are theories in the practical strategies of movements and in detailed empirical studies too. Nor are frameworks only intellectual constructs – there are 'structures of feeling' too.[31]

The stress was not on a canon or set of texts (though important writers and texts remained) but on ways of reading positions which occurred in many different forms. In this way theory moved closer to substantive cultural analysis.

'Reading for framework' is a way of making implicit assumptions speak themselves, absences present themselves, political horizons become explicit, emotional investments utter gasps and sighs.

In the earlier 1980s, like everyone else, we tended to teach the different fields of force – 'class', 'race', 'gender' and so on – in separated ways; and therefore implicitly to prioritise. It was hard to get back to some more unified view of the theoretical movement. By the 1990s, it became plainer that there were common features and debates within each field. It became possible, for example, to treat not only kinds of socialism and labourism, but also some kinds of feminist, gay and anti-colonial theory, under the general heading of 'Ruling ideas', usually seen as a distinctively Marxist framework. It was clearer too that there were political as well as academic dynamics to the take-ups of structuralist and poststructuralist theories – strategies to handle complexity, coexistence, intersection and competing claims, and more generally break the essentialist log-jams.

Learning to teach is also related to epistemological issues. One key break, associated for me with feminist influences, was to stress the personal, conventional, contingent, situated nature of 'maps'. The exclusion of lived points of view is solidified when the mapper objectifies his or her own point of view. A sequence of positions can also be rendered as a teleology leading to the mapper's preferred position, his word. Reversing this, but still unhelpfully, the story can be of original political engagement succumbing to theoretical over-complication and the entrapments of the academy. Even more mystifying is the usual academic disguise where positions are laid out adjacently, with no argu-ment contrived between them. In all these modes, the obtuseness of academic practice doubles the oppressions and non-recognitions of other sites, so that some positionalities are plentifully recognised (and inappropriately rewarded) and others are remarginalised and pressured towards silence. For every text invites powerfully differential readings and responses, though there are also texts with a particular capacity to trouble and to polarise. One key incident in the struggle over whiteness at Birmingham was a group discussion in 1991 of the chapter in Frantz Fanon's *Black Skin, White Masks* which starts with his experience of being pointed out as a 'nigger' by a white child.[32] After much confusion and silence, it became clear how sharply this text had polarised the group. It signifies very differently if you identify as black or (however 'anti-racist' in sentiment) are averagely unconscious of your whiteness. Such differ-ences are more painfully and much less productively produced when the teacher's discourse assumes that everyone is similarly placed in relation to the task, and that we are all to operate under rules of polite, white, English, middle-class behaviour.[33]

So perhaps the most important transformation is to disrupt the academic objectifications (or lordly relativisations) that often accompany the art of overview. It is important to 'subjectivify' the account without implying that, from your point of view, all positions are equally valid, useful or politically just. This involves teachers putting their own positions, perhaps their own identities on the line. It is also possible to be clear about the contingent and positional character of frameworks, yet argue for preferences in particular situations. Similarly it is possible to avoid simple teleologies. Key movements in theory – from Marxisms to postmodernisms, from humanism to anti-humanism, or from essentialism to constructivism and deconstruction – can be presented as a layered history, with complex gains and losses, tensions between the academy and broader politics: as an accumulation of repertoires, with all elements repositioned, certainly, but all still relevant sometimes.

Related to epistemology is the open recognition of the limits of theoretical clarification as an intellectual practice. According to this view, which runs against the current privileging of theoretical review in both 'critical theory' and in sociology, theoretical work is enabling not decisive. It is not the exemplary, master activity. A better candidate might be theoretically informed research into specific issues of practical importance – a practice which we did in CCCS, but which was more often done elsewhere.

Finally, there are more strictly pedagogic resources. Though the didactic moment – interruptible talks with plenty of concrete instances – remains important, these are best surrounded by other activities, including group work inserted into the same teaching occasion: discussion of shared readings or viewing, 'brainstorms', collective assemblings of critiques, close working on policy-rich examples. Surrounding occasions may also include, as they did at CCCS, group research projects and other forms of cooperative work. Essential everywhere are some one-to-one sessions where tutors can recognise and support individual projects and appear to the student in a different personal guise. If this combination works, your own map is subjected to students' readings and genuinely tested and revised each year. At the same time, conditions are created – challenge but also recognition and support – for the marginalised voices and the emergent agenda to be heard.

Collectivised, 'subjectified', and pluralised in these ways, mapping at least institutes some accessible *version* of the cultural studies field, and informs dialogues of many different kinds. It can enable conversation across positions. It can set up richly educative relations in which follow-ups are crucial. The advantages of the convention are plainest to me in encounters with traditions where the function of argumentative overview is absent or where a crazy-paving modularity has abolished any conception of a 'core'.

In conclusion, then, like all academic practices, mapping must be qualified by a sense of the academy as a place of power, where power can exclude, regulate and confine, but can also open doors.

Notes

1 Published as Canaan J E and Epstein D (eds), *A question of discipline: pedagogy, power and the teaching of cultural studies*, Westview Press, Boulder, CO, 1997. The refusal of Westview Press to publish this volume in more than a limited hardback edition suggests that publishers in the United States do not see a market for books on teaching cultural studies.

2 I am grateful to the editors of this volume and to the participants at the conference itself for discussion of the original paper and for editorial patience and support. Thanks also to Jean Pierre Boulé, Joyce Canaan, Mariette Clare, Dave Clayton, Debbie Epstein, Umut Erel, David Jackson, Pat Noxolo, Deborah Steinberg and Joanne Whitehouse for particularly generative and memorable discussions on these themes.

3 There are other important strands of criticism including the questioning of foundational concepts and of conceptual 'banality': eg Frow J, *Cultural studies and cultural value*, Clarendon Press, Oxford, 1995; Morris M, 'Banality in cultural studies', *Block*, No 14; and the earlier Hunter I, *Culture and government: the emergence of literary education*, Macmillan, London, 1988. See also Mulhern F, 'The politics of cultural studies', *Monthly Review* Vol 47, No 3, July–August 1995, pp. 31–40; and two book-length assessments, the first preoccupied with the loss of political edge, the second with over-politicisation: Harris D, *From class struggle to the politics of pleasure: the effects of Gramscianism on cultural studies*, Routledge, London and New York, 1992 and Inglis F, *Cultural studies*, Blackwell, Oxford and Cambridge, MA, 1992. One problem with many criticisms is that cultural studies is still identified with its earliest or classic texts, especially the work of Raymond Williams and the Birmingham work on sub-culture. These texts have been criticised particularly from positions influenced by poststructuralist theory (though others criticise the turn to 'French theory'). Practitioners of cultural studies have often in the meantime adopted positions very like those of their critics.

4 Steele T, *The emergence of cultural studies 1945–65: cultural politics, adult education and the English question*, Lawrence and Wishart, London, 1997.

5 This is a key theme in several contributions to the useful collection, mainly from US writers, Long E (ed.), *From sociology to cultural studies: new perspectives*, Blackwell, Malden MA and Oxford, 1994 and the somewhat more polemical Ferguson M and Golding P (eds), *Cultural studies in question*, London, Thousand Oaks, CA, and Delhi, 1997.

6 See especially McGuigan J, *Cultural populism*, Routledge, London and New York, 1992 and the chapters by James Carey, Nicholas Garnham, Todd Gitlin, Douglas Kellner, Jim McGuigan, Graham Murdock, and the editors' introduction in Ferguson and Golding (eds), 1997.

7 For example, Bennett T, 'Putting policy into cultural studies', in Grossberg L, Nelson C and Treichler P (eds), *Cultural studies*, Routledge, New York and London, 1992, pp. 23–37; Bennett T, 'Towards a pragmatics for cultural studies', in McGuigan J (ed.), *Cultural methodologies*, Sage, London, Thousand Oaks, CA, Delhi 1997 pp. 42–61; McGuigan J, *Culture and the public sphere*, Routledge, London and New York, 1996; McQuail D, 'Policy help wanted: willing and able media culturalists please apply', in Ferguson and Golding (eds), 1997, pp. 39–55.

8 Graham Murdoch referring to the arguments of McQuail and Bennett in 'Base notes: the conditions of cultural practice', in Ferguson and Golding (eds), 1997, p. 94. One of the difficulties here is that those who discuss cultural policy restrict

their view of appropriate agencies to governments or established institutions and also often the definition of culture to traditional and restricted definitions.

9   Examples would be the work on Thatcherism and on education policy at Birmingham: eg Hall S, Critcher C, Jefferson T, Clarke J and Roberts B, *Policing the crisis: mugging, the state and law and order*, Macmillan, London, 1979 and Centre for Contemporary Cultural Studies, *Unpopular education: schooling and social democracy in England since 1944*, Hutchinson, London, 1981 and Education Group II, *Education unlimited: schooling, training and the New Right since 1979*, Hutchinson, London, 1990.

10 Hoare Q and Nowell Smith G (eds), *Selections from the prison notebooks of Antonio Gramsci*, Lawrence and Wishart, London, 1997, p. 328.

11 This theoretical conservatism (in political economy) is most marked in the work of Nicholas Garnham among the critics. See, for example, his 'Political economy and the practice of cultural studies', in Ferguson and Golding (eds), 1997, pp. 56–73.

12 McGuigan in Ferguson and Golding (eds), 1997, p. 153.

13 Garnham in Ferguson and Golding (eds), 1997, p. 67.

14 Steele, 1997, p. 210.

15 For a fuller account of the methods and sources used in the cluster of studies to which this belongs see Johnson R, 'Teaching without guarantees: cultural studies, pedagogy and identity' in Canaan and Epstein (eds), *A Question of Discipline*, pp. 43–45.

16 See 'Scandalous oppositions: cultural criticism and sexual regulation in contemporary Britain', unpublished inaugural professorial lecture, Nottingham Trent University, June 1997. (Copies available from the author.)

17 Bromley R, 'What shall we do without the Barbarians? Violence, inequality and contemporary culture', unpublished professorial inaugural lecture, April 1997, Nottingham Trent University. (Copies available from the author.)

18 For a fuller application of this idea of Williams to academic practice and to 'theory' see Johnson R, 'Sexual Emergenc(i)es: cultural theories and contemporary sexual politics', *Keywords: A Journal of Cultural Materialism*, No 1 (1998), pp. 74–94. For the original formulations see Williams R, *Marxism and literature*, Oxford University Press, Oxford, 1997, pp. 121–27.

19 My discussion of marginality throughout is influenced by the discussions in Bhabha H, *The location of culture*, Routledge, London and New York, 1994; Dollimore J, *Sexual dissidence: Augustine to Wilde, Freud to Foucault*, Clarendon Press, Oxford, 1991; Stallybrass P and White A, *The politics and poetics of transgression*, Methuen, London, 1986; Fanon F, *Black skin, white masks*, Grove Press, London, 1986; and bell hooks' various discussions of these issues, eg 'The politics of radical Black subjectivity' in *Yearning: race, gender and cultural politics*, Turnaround, London, 1991.

20 I deal with this aspect in more detail in 'Teaching without guarantees: cultural studies, pedagogy and identity', in Canaan and Epstein, 1997, especially pp. 65–69.

21 For a recent polemical example of this kind of argument, a policing of the boundaries of the political, see Gitlin T in Ferguson and Golding, 1997, especially pp. 32–37.

22 Butler J, *Bodies that matter*, Routledge, London and New York, 1993, p. 241.

23 For such an attempt, briefly, at a political audit for cultural studies, see Johnson R, 'Reinventing cultural studies: remembering for the best versions' in Long, 1997, especially pp. 473–480.

24 See, for example, one of the issues of the early self-produced CCCS journal, *Working papers in cultural studies*, No. 4 (1973).

25 MA in Cultural Studies, Course I, 1975–76.

26 For accounts of early struggles see Brunsdon C, 'A thief in the night: stories of feminism in the 1970s at CCCS', in Morley D and Chen K-H (eds), *Stuart Hall: critical dialogues*, Routledge, London and New York, 1997; and Hall S, 'Cultural studies and its theoretical legacies', in Grossberg, Nelson and Treichler, 1982, p. 282.

27 This became a problem especially by the early 1980s when CCCS texts began to be published and our reputation grew.

28 For example, Mackinnon C, 'Feminism, Marxism, method and the state: an agenda for theory', *Signs*, Vol 7, No 3 (1982), pp. 515–44; Harding S, *The science question in feminism*, Open University Press, Milton Keynes, 1986; Stanley L and Wise S, *Breaking out: feminist ontology and epistemology*, Routledge, London and New York, 1993.

29 Redman P and Mac An Ghaill M, 'Educating Peter', in Steinberg D L, Epstein D and Johnson R (eds), *Border patrols: policing the boundaries of heterosexuality*, Cassell, London, 1996.

30 The role of student 'rebellions' in the MA course is discussed more fully in Johnson in Canaan and Epstein, 1997.

31 M Soc Sci in Cultural Studies, CSGHI: 'Frameworks of cultural study', 1992–93.

32 Fanon, 1986, pp. 109–40.

33 I am especially grateful to Rozena Maart, Claudette Purville and Shruti Tanna for discussion around these themes.

3 'Relevant provision': the usefulness of cultural studies

Martin Ryle

The 'political project of a democratic cultural education' began, as Tom Steele has convincingly argued in *The emergence of cultural studies*, in a particular marginal space; and while cultural studies is now in the academic mainstream, its origins (or some of its points of origin) lie in those margins.[1] Steele's detailed history, recapitulated in his contribution to the present volume, reminds us how the landscape looked before subsequent, and continuing, large shifts in academic and political formations. A left social–democratic government in postwar Britain provided a relatively hospitable climate in which the long established project of workers' education was taken forward. In the encounter between the institutions of what was still an overwhelmingly élitist academy and the largely excluded constituency of working-class adult students, dominant conceptions of 'culture' were significantly reworked, and the leading figures of the moment (Raymond Williams, Richard Hoggart, E P Thompson) drew on their experience and practice as extra-mural tutors in research and writing which took that reworking back into the academic and scholarly mainstream. In Williams's well-known claim, 'that shift of perspective about the teaching of arts and literature and their relation to history and contemporary society began in Adult Education'.[2]

However, if cultural studies today is to 'understand itself as a formation' (as Steele urges that it should),[3] it is not clear that we can any longer ground that self-understanding in the original project. Everyone teaching and writing in the field may share a commitment to reading cultural practices and texts in their implication with forms of social power; and radical critics within the academy may relate their work to what Terry Eagleton calls the 'counter-public sphere' of dissenting or oppositional social formations and movements outside its walls.[4] But changes since the 1950s have displaced the broad alliance between social democracy, adult education, and organised trades unionism from the position which it might be seen to enjoy, post-1945, as the bearer or agent of a more general historical progress. Cold War politics and economic neo-liberalism have undone those hopes of social advance, while the particularity of the 'universal' subject on which that political–educational formation was centred – actually, or rather ideally, the male worker – has been made increasingly clear. Adult classes, in the WEA but also in the GLC of the radical 1980s, have been one important site for feminist education, whose impact has in my view been systematically understated in histories of cultural studies. In the last two decades, academic criticism has been most productive when it has sought to represent and form alliances with people whose cultural–political identity has been centred on questions of gender, 'race'/ethnicity or sexuality never addressed in that earlier emancipatory project. Meanwhile, in a discourse increasingly inaccessible to non-specialist audiences, theoretical challenges have undermined the confident notions of subjective autonomy and cultural value which were the implicit presuppositions of critical–humanist pedagogy from Arnold through Leavis and up to Williams's *Culture and society.*

Teachers in higher education who see their work as part of a radical and democratic project have also had to negotiate changes in immediate institutional contexts. Those in the post-binary 'new' universities, where mainstream cultural studies has most strongly developed and where most of the interesting work is being done, have had to contend with growing material pressures and, often, with increasingly dirigiste ideologies and practices of institutional management (some of the consequences are noted in the chapters in this volume by Richard Johnson and Jim McGuigan). Those of us who hold positions in surviving Continuing Education departments in the pre-1992 universities may in some cases have been sheltered from the worst of these pressures, but sustaining the extra-mural project – even defining it – is a more complex matter than it was in the 1950s and 1960s. Then, 'extension work' would involve students ready and eager to acquire existing academic knowledges: the reworking of disciplinary boundaries and curricular fields took place within a horizon shared by this extra-mural 'other', whose 'difference' was never seen as radically disruptive, but rather as a specifically class-based difference to be integrated into a revised but recognisably continuous national culture. Raymond Williams could write, in 1959, that the 'whole spirit' of adult education 'is of growth towards a genuinely common culture, and educated and participating democracy', as if the first objective were the condition of the second.[5] Williams's *Long revolution* was criticised at the time, by Thompson, for understating the tensions between nineteenth-century bourgeois culture and the project of socialism; but the aspiration for a 'common culture' which underwrote both his own work and the broader educational–cultural politics which it aimed to serve would have been shared by many on the Left. Thirty years later, Alan Sinfield, while acknowledging his indebtedness to Williams, would offer an important critique of that kind of 'left culturism', and insist that 'a divided society should have a divided culture'.[6] Today the 'culture' represented in academic knowledges is a great deal more internally fractured and contested, while those who have begun to find their way into a less monolithic HE classroom are seen as bringing with them, even as representing or embodying, a series of valued and properly intransigent 'differences'.

The project of widening provision is no longer marginal, something which committed academics do on the edges of the institution; on the contrary, for many years it has been central to the rhetoric, and policy, of government's intentions for HE – even if (as I shall argue below) there is limited space for 'culture', however interpreted, in what has been an increasingly vocationalist discourse. However, today's non-participants in higher education, in contrast to many of those shut out by an earlier and more selective system, may often lack the cultural literacy necessary before negotiation or reworking of institutionally accredited knowledges can begin. 'Outreach work' in a continuing education department nowadays might mean the provision of English language classes for recently arrived refugees, or of courses on sexuality for women with learning difficulties.[7] The value of these and similar projects is unquestionable, but they cannot (it seems to me) necessarily expect to engage their students in the kinds of discussion that take place – in the setting of the same department – when part-time undergraduates in our Cultural Studies degree discuss Edward Said on the colonial context of *Mansfield Park* or consider the impact of feminist scholarship on the writing of art history. The professional self-understanding of marginal radicals in HE and also many of the roles they are called on to play tend to be defined in terms of 'outreach', but the lines of communication between that work and the increasingly specialised discourses of academic cultural studies are not easy to keep open.

In short, the coherent project that we may like to think of as the origin of our own practice depended on a set of mutually reinforcing conjunctions: between a broadly supportive, left social-democratic national educational policy and a specifically socialist notion of agency and progress; between particular critical readings and a collective sense of the developing critical consciousness to which they might contribute; between a still largely homogeneous working definition of 'culture' and a student body apt to engage (albeit 'critically') with its texts and disciplines; between a project of extending education 'outside the walls' and an extra-mural constituency already possessed of many requisite skills and knowledges.

Those conjunctions, that conjuncture, are not going to recur. If 'cultural studies' can still own any collective self-understanding, as a 'formation', it has to be articulated in new terms. Other contributors to this volume offer a variety of perspectives and arguments towards such an articulation: while not all of them would subscribe to the view that a collective project called 'cultural studies' remains viable, they all witness to a continuing belief that although the space in which we work has changed, it is still possible, within it, to pursue radical or emancipatory projects.

My own argument, in what follows, while it is among those that attempt to sustain a quite general claim about the potential (and historical) importance of teaching culture in higher education, opens and in some ways remains with a negative kind of self-definition. If at an earlier time 'cultural studies' emerged in a space of uneasy negotiation between educational radicals and social democratic policy makers, its current stance *vis-à-vis* New Labour's (rhetorical?) project for HE needs to be in some important respects oppositional.

That opposition, I argue here, begins in the rejection, or at any rate the qualification, of the reductive vocationalism of current educational-policy discourse. In sorting out its proper terms, one finds oneself pushed towards a difficult reconsideration of relations between the radicalism of 'cultural studies' and the liberalism of the academy. Liberal notions of the (relative) autonomy of the university and the value-freedom of its disciplines were criticised or deconstructed in books such as *Ideology in social science* (1972), *Criticism and ideology* (1976), *Old mistresses* (1981), or *Re-reading English* (1982),[8] which mark out the stages by which socialist and socialist–feminist work, on the margins, contested the claim that the academy offered a space for neutral or disinterested knowledge. In the aftermath of that intellectual work, cultural studies is now established as a more self-reflexive alternative to established disciplines (especially English) which declined to acknowledge their own history or to avow their implication in ideological and social processes. Yet self-reflection also impels us to recognise that any kind of cultural study, insofar as that term can and must imply a critical relation to 'the world of work' rather than just a formation of professional skills, must rely on the notion of a 'disinterested' space: a notion indeed impossible of full achievement in conditions of highly unequal wealth and divided labour, but which can still be a regulative ideal. It seems to me that it is presently more important to argue for the social useful-ness and value of such an ideal than to expose it as an illusion that cannot be realised. In so arguing, one acknowledges relations of continuity as well as antagonism between the forms of cultural study and critique which have developed since the 1960s, and the older modes of literary and critical educa-tion against which they initially defined themselves.

The notion of 'disinterestedness' which grounds liberal conceptions of the purposes of education has turned, importantly, on the idea of an antagonism between 'work' and 'culture'. This is an ambiguous ideology, but one which has (I argue in my final section) an emancipatory aspect: its larger implications call into question both the forms of the social division of labour, and the productivist orientation of overdeveloped societies. I conclude that the horizon within which a fully coherent democratic defence of 'teaching culture' can be made is also the horizon of the general utopia of a diminution in socially necessary labour and an expansion and redistribution of free time.

Perhaps I should say that I am not sanguine about the likelihood that any such utopia will be realised. It seems much more probable that productivism and the new work ethic will maintain their ideological hegemony, and that their 'values' will come to determine what is taught in the academy: especially, perhaps, in those more open but more exposed spaces, the accessible institu-tions and institutional margins where radical education has been possible. (What Leavis called 'humane culture' will no doubt go on being taught much the same as ever at Oxbridge.)

Relevant provision

Today's New Labour project, in HE policy as in many other areas, carries forward an already powerful momentum. For well over a decade, the policy advisers, commentators and researchers who have promoted wider access have also criticised the institutional élitism of the 'old' universities, in terms with which radical educators must have sympathy. But this has been within a discourse of outcomes and competences that leaves no obvious space for 'teaching culture'.

The stress on capability, competence and skills is nothing new: Jane Thompson recalls that when James Callaghan gave a speech in memory of Steve Biko at Ruskin College in 1976, he chose that occasion to lament education's alleged failure to 'meet the needs of industry'.[9] But of late, in an ideologically crucial mutation, what is called the 'producer-led' culture of higher education, in which academic disciplines, discourses and expertise have predominated in shaping curricula and defining knowledge, has been presented not just as a hindrance to the vocationalism which many politicians advocate, but as a major obstacle to the widening of participation. The facts that higher education in the past has catered only for 'a tiny, élite minority', and that 'many of the subjects . . . regarded as "academic" . . . are frequently centred on scholastic disciplines with only an indirect relevance to the world of work', are seen as necessarily, rather than historically, coincident. And they are presented as equally regrettable, and ripe for change.[10]

Thus John A Andrews, writing as Chief Executive of the Further and Higher Education Funding Councils for Wales, recently criticised the 'monastic and élitist' tradition of the European University (Oxford, Bologna). Andrews contrasts this unfavourably with the more locally responsive, open and variegated mission adopted by some civic universities, by the former Polytechnics, and now also by 'the enormous range of further education provision . . . much of it . . . developed to meet the needs of students for user friendly delivery'.[11] He is clear what is needed for the future:

> The higher education students of tomorrow will require flexibility in provision and increasingly are likely to look for provision which is relevant to their world of work. Part-time courses, distance learning, outreach provision, collaboration between institutions, targeting the needs of special groups, women returners, unemployed men, students with disabilities, employees needing up-skilling, and so on, will become major features.[12]

This dominant policy discourse, while identifying many reasonable priorities in terms of whom and how we might want to teach, tends to reduce to a simple binary the complex relationships between institutions, students, curricula and the actual and potential uses which education may have for individuals and in society. On the one hand the institution is presented as reactionary, self-serving, both slow and reluctant to change; and on the other, there are the students – who already know what they need, and who when they require 'what is relevant to their world of work' are seen as pursuing not only their own primary interests but also the general, collective interest. So academic institutions and those who teach there had better abandon their 'monastic and élitist' conceptions and get on with the job of providing 'provision'. And this simplification itself depends on larger, and still more problematic, assumptions about social and economic futures, to which I shall refer later in my argument.

Vocational education for students who want and need it is of course part of what higher education should offer: to question the simplifications of a vocationalist discourse is not to deny this, still less to defend the disparities of esteem which were for so long embodied in the divide between polytechnics and universities, and which have meant (for example) that nursing is only now becoming a graduate profession. And within radical adult education, there will be space to do valuable work in these now dominant terms of 'relevant provision'. The collection in which Andrews's paper appears (*Communities and their universities*, 1996) also has an account by Kevin Ward of a partnership between the Continuing Education Department at Leeds University and the local Training and Enterprise Council, whose focus was on social exclusion and community regeneration;[13] and in the same volume Rob Humphreys and Hywel Francis describe the setting up of the Community University of the Valleys, in which adult educationists at the University of Wales at Swansea have worked with communities hard-hit by the closure of the South Wales coalmines following the defeat of the 1984–85 miners' strike. This builds on a long radical tradition of popular education in the region, and also exemplifies the new push for 'flexibility' and institutional collaboration.[14] However, Humphreys and Francis remark on the 'differing nuances and emphases within this coalition', especially as regards 'outcomes measured in terms of employment for students, and those measured – more intangibly – in terms of individual and social well-being'.[15] Ward similarly identifies a tension, in community development projects, between a free-market, individualist stress on the acquisition of skills by individual students, and a collectivist 'focus on active citizenship, decentralisation and democratisation'.[16]

These tensions and differences of emphasis are at play in that same space, between the academic mainstream and those excluded from it, in which the earlier radical project originated, and I think it is as true today as it was then that those teaching in the margins (less prestigious universities, and their less prestigious corners) are likely to be both more sensitive and more exposed to shifts in policy and their implications. We may also feel that it is part of our responsibility to be 'public intellectuals', rather than to rely solely on the kinds of validation by academic peers which provide the basis of the Research Assessment Exercise; and that this in turn requires one to engage with (rather than evading) discussions of educational policy and principle. Institutional managers will in general avoid pushing at points of tension, and will prefer to find ways of adapting pragmatically to new discourses: for example, by stressing how HE inculcates 'transferable skills'. One hardly blames them for this; but there is also a need for that engaged, intransigent response, not only in defence of institutional spaces and values, but also because redefinitions of the purpose of education are contestable statements about desirable social futures. (We should respond, I believe, not only by arguing about educational policy in publications or in university committees; but also by considering how far what we teach encourages our students to engage with debates about the nature of work, about socially necessary labour time, about the relations between culture and labour, and about cultural representations of work, including its place in utopian, revolutionary and progressive political visions.)

For teachers in higher education, the most significant difference between the postwar moment and the present seems to me to lie in the different relations now proposed between education, culture, democracy and the economy. Some of this agenda remains contestable, to be fought out in whatever margins of autonomy or dissent remain in the new relationships between institutional management and government, as mediated by HEFCE, and by the bureaucratised surveillance of teaching and research; but it is clear enough that (in Richard Johnson's words, in his contribution to this volume) a 'centralised neo-vocationalist "reform" of teaching and curricula' is envisaged.

The postwar expansion of educational opportunity may have been figured, on a somewhat quasi-colonial model, as the induction of new subjects into a largely continuous national culture,[17] but its democratic potential was the more effectively realised thanks to the dialogic challenge to which it was then subjected: if the goal of cultural inclusiveness was paternalistic, its democratic/collectivist aspiration was made more tangible, rather than negated, by the subsequent acknowledgement that 'culture' must include cultural difference. That emphasis on 'culture', which grounded what was paternalistic in the original project but which has also allowed that ground to be so effectively re-mapped, belongs to a moment when there was, to put it simply, a commonsense view among social democrats that the economy was for the people, rather than the other way round. Today, the primary goal of education is said to be to equip individuals with skills which will allow them to participate in a modern economy which will itself be competitive and successful providing that the skills base is there. It is the Prime Minister's insistent aspiration that Britain may have 'the best educated *workforce* in the world'.[18] This certainly accords no special importance to 'culture': in which we must include not simply the specific cultural forms and texts which some academics work on and transmit, but the cultural values of education itself insofar as this is conceived as relatively autonomous of immediate economic imperatives.

Cultural education and the division of labour

The new policy discourse is peculiarly challenging to those working in radical adult education and critical cultural studies, and to the whole 'left-culturist' project and its more diverse and fragmented latter-day successors. Much of our own orientation and sense of purpose has been based in the critique of an élitist institution, whose boundaries we have wished to extend or breach while seeking to modify what goes on inside it.

From that perspective, new right radical populism spoke some salutary truths to universities which were, and are, conservative in many ways. Some, perhaps many, who work in their margins will be broadly in sympathy with the claim that academic institutions have been 'producer-led' domains, places where students are expected (in the words of one advocate of the accreditation of prior experiential learning) to 'absorb pre-packaged knowledge and élite culture'.[19] Even adult educationists have no doubt (and inevitably) been prescriptive in defining 'socially acceptable forms' of knowledge; noting that some radical adult educators have had problems in seeing the value of dress-making classes, two recent commentators observe sharply that 'even liberatory discourses, such as feminism, have [ignored] "other" feminine knowledge'.[20] In their recent *Cultural politics* (1995), which pushes to its limit the tendency within cultural studies to see all established forms of culture and knowledge as inherently oppressive, Glenn Jordan and Chris Weedon often present the academy as no more than an agency of the monolithic Liberal Humanism which they are concerned to attack.[21]

To me, these manoeuvres seem to be inversions, reversals of the signs, poor ways of handling inescapable contradictions. In a divided society, whose divisions are reproduced through education (though education is also a site of progressive challenges to them), there is no non-contradictory place for critical intellectuals to be. By meditating on this we may arrive only at what may seem, in Bruce Robbins's phrase, a 'strenuous complacency': but I think Robbins is right when he goes on to urge (in *Secular vocations*, 1993) that 'there is no complacency . . . in admitting that the privileges of the university are real and sometimes useful, or that they depend on a relation to the outside that is both precarious and politically polyvalent'.[22] Institutions of higher education are indeed a collective resource, which should be accessible to all those who can benefit from what they offer. But what they offer, in a society marked by an extreme division of labour, essentially includes the special knowledges and expertise of the intellectuals who work there; and to demonise this in a populist rhetoric about the 'producer-led' academy, about 'socially acceptable' knowledge and 'Liberal Humanism', is to serve no one's real interests.

This is all the truer given the recent opening-up of academic knowledges to dialogue with much wider constituencies than they ever engaged with in the past. If, after 20 years of dialectical teaching/learning, the 'liberatory discourse' of feminism is now part of the curriculum offered by many British universities, this may not be the time to devalue such an achievement by suggesting that the pastoral wisdom of the dress-making 'other' might hold the key to some more authentically radical knowledge. Jordan and Weedon may be right to suppose that most students will not have encountered the work of Fanon in the course of their academic studies, but they are most unlikely to have been led to engage with his ideas anywhere *but* in the academy.[23] In other words, while the results of the dialogic encounter should be made open to the widest constituency and must remain available to further redefinition and change, they are registered, and stored, as resources within the institution. Fifteen years ago, Terry Eagleton wrote that 'like others of us, but more poignantly and dramatically, [Raymond Williams] was driven to occupy an indeterminate space mid-way between an actual but reactionary academy and a desirable but absent counterpublic sphere'.[24] But what is 'actual but reactionary' may also be more 'desirable' than some possible alternatives; and the 'indeterminate space' has been, determinately, an institutional margin, dependent on the institution and on the parameters within which public policy defines its mission.

No doubt cultural intellectuals are too much the successors of Dostoevsky's 'liberal idealist' Stepan Verkhovensky, who likes to feel that he stands 'a living monument of reproach' before his country, but whose bills are paid by the landowner with whom he has an interminably ambiguous relationship. Verkhovensky's defence of culture takes the form of an insistence that 'Shakespeare and Raphael are higher' not only than 'chemistry' but also than 'the emancipation of the serfs'.[25] Dostoevsky reminds us that while the realm of culture, in the idealism of the cultural interpreter, may be figured as representing a 'higher' and in that sense universal value, it is part of this lower world of social and economic inequality, caught in a 'precarious and politically polyvalent' dependency on those who hold power. Moreover, when the intellectual – whether 'liberal idealist' or socialist–feminist cultural historian – secures a living by becoming at once the critic and the transmitter of culture, she or he adopts a highly specific place within the social division of labour even while seeking to represent the case that 'culture' is of general import. My argument here is that cultural intellectuals in the academy may be more useful when they accept this contradictory role, and work with a sense of its contradictions, than when they imagine they are able to escape from it.

This question of how we see our own work in relation to general social labour is not mainly a matter of the good karma of teachers, of course, or even of the entitlements of students. Dostoevsky's map has no space for the role of the state; but we can welcome our dependence on public funds (even if the Vice-Chancellor of the University of Cambridge for his part regards this as a regrettable 'encumbrance'),[26] because it obliges us to give some account of what we do in terms of the general social good. We can undoubtedly argue that the cultural foundations of a more pluralist and internationalist civil society have been strengthened by the acknowledgement, within cultural studies, of diverse oppressions, subjects and emancipatory projects; by the displacement of 'Shakespeare and Raphael' by a more heterogeneous body of texts and cultural practices – although these in my own view certainly should still include plenty of examples of 'high culture' (such, perhaps, as Dostoevsky's novels). We can argue, too, as Jim McGuigan argues in his chapter here, that cultural studies will equip students with a range of skills for both life and work.

I believe that we should also argue that it is in society's collective interest to foster, alongside specific skills useful for work, a certain scepticism about 'work' as such: its often unsatisfying quality, the tension between its demands and those of conviviality and child care, its reproduction of and dependence on undemocratic forms of hierarchy, its implication in productivist and economic–nationalist discourses which are problematic in terms of sustainability, human flourishing, global justice.

Existence beyond constraint

To acknowledge an unease with the aspiration that Britain may have 'the best educated *workforce* in the world', to dissent from the view that one's socially useful educational task is properly defined in such terms, is to concede that there are continuities as well as breaks between radical cultural studies and liberal–Arnoldian–Leavisite ideals of culture and education. Cultural studies in Britain can of course be seen, historically, as developing (most obviously, through the link between Leavis and Williams) out of earlier modes of literary criticism. More generally, our faith in the usefulness of teaching/learning 'cultural studies' depends on a conviction that cultural texts and representations are important because their distance from less mediated forms of social being may endow them with the power to embody and to occasion a certain critical, dissenting, subversive or utopian moment of reflection. This conviction is surely related by similarity as well as by difference to the Arnoldian project of valuing, and studying, literature as 'the best that has been known and thought'. Indeed, without some notion of 'the best' (complex, provisional and subject to debate as this must be) I do not know how we are to further a critical engagement: what project of emancipation are we involved in if we present our students with undifferentiated 'cultural production' or 'textuality', scanned for its symptomatic value as evidence but never subjected to aesthetic, political or ethical scrutiny? (In this connection one may well be concerned at the dominant tendency to regard judgements of aesthetic value, in particular, as entirely ideological; and by the consequence this may have in removing from the curriculum those works of 'high culture' which – here I am an unreconstructed modernist – pose searching cultural–political questions in modes that depend on their formal difficulty and originality. But I digress.)[27]

We should acknowledge continuities between liberalism, social democracy, and the critical project which led from the New Left to cultural studies today. However, we need to press the old notion of an antagonism between 'work' on the one hand and 'culture' and 'education' on the other out of and beyond its original liberal terms. The labour/culture antithesis used often to register only the disdain of the educated gentleman for the artisan or labourer. But it is also true that most kinds of work offer a very circumscribed space for the play of imagination and critical intelligence. As Adorno puts it:

> The anti-philistinism of Athens was both the most arrogant contempt of the man who need not soil his hands for the man from whose work he lives, and the preservation of an image of existence beyond the constraint which underlies all work.[28]

That 'image', of a space where self-development is unconstrained, is the '"good" in its own right' which John Andrews of the Funding Councils for Wales tells us that society cannot be expected to pay for, because it is not useful: 'society no longer funds higher education simply because it is regarded as a "good" in its own right'.[29]

The liberal defence of that 'good' was always fatally limited, from any democratic perspective, by precisely what made the 'good' easily affordable: what was defended was a privilege available exclusively to the few. Exclusivity, in the actual, liberal practice of HE institutions, made them vulnerable to radical–populist modernising rhetoric; just as abstract Leavisite formulations of liberal humanism were vulnerable to left-wing critiques of their élitism. Leavis's ideal English school was to produce the '"educated man", the man of humane culture who is equipped to be intelligent and responsible about the problems of contemporary civilisation'.[30] Rather too clearly a Senator or philosopher-king, this 'educated man' was to be produced in sufficiently small numbers: no supernumary square pegs were to be turned out for round holes, and in fact the 'humane culture' was in that sense just a peculiar type of professional (non-) training.

Those who work in the less prestigious corners of HE have done what can be done, on those margins, to break down exclusivity. What we have to argue against is any presumption that the spaces for reflection once available to the select few are becoming an unnecessary luxury now that they might be occupied by the (relatively) many. That kind of rationing has suited the division of labour which consigns most people for life to jobs for which 'humane culture' is unnecessary. But such an education remains, and will remain, unnecessary for most jobs: very general de-skilling is the reality (rhetoric aside) of 'flexible specialisation'. To make the critical study of culture available as an entitlement for anyone able to engage with it is thus not especially functional, so far as the reproduction of social labour goes.

So: might cultural studies be better conceived as 'educating for leisure'? A cultural education can indeed both awaken and satisfy a need for critical reflection and intellectual self-development. However, the space for such 'leisured' education, currently threatened by powerful discourses of neo-vocationalism and instrumentalism, may only survive in the framework of a general reconsideration of the nature and extent of leisure's counterpart, socially necessary labour. In André Gorz's terms,[31] the psychic and cultural dominance of heteronomous labour will need to be reduced by a reduction in the time it takes, if the sphere of autonomy – which is the proper setting for the old extra-mural project of 'a democratic cultural education' – is to grow.

Despite (or because of) their utopian aspect, such arguments have an immediate purchase on the collective choices that European polities, and all overdeveloped economies, confront. The dominant discourses of economic modernisation present capitalist globalisation as compelling a retreat from social democratic interventionism and from legislation in defence of general social interests, including workers' employment and social security rights; and the argument that we cannot afford (in a society that has never been richer) the 'good in itself' of liberal education is of a piece with this bleak pseudo-realism, and especially with the general subordination of 'culture' to 'work' which it aims to enforce. But there are also countervailing forces and tendencies. Greens, and some social democrats and trades unionists, are arguing for the shortening of the working week, which envisages a greater space for 'autonomous' life. This is part of a more variegated and nuanced conception of social and ecological–economic development which might replace the secular pursuit of undifferentiated economic growth, which is increasingly recognised as bringing, along with material abundance, growing social, cultural and environmental damage and distress.

In the discourses of continuing and higher education, these competing conceptions of the future find expression in the tension between learning as work-related 'upskilling', and learning as the democratic entitlement to that space beyond immediate constraint where access to knowledge serves the development of 'culture' in its broadest sense, as a resource for individual and collective pleasure, self-reflection, and autonomy.

Notes

1 Steele T, *The emergence of cultural studies 1945–1965: cultural politics, adult education and the English question*, Lawrence and Wishart, London, 1997, p. 7 and *passim*.

2 Williams, 'The future of cultural studies', quoted in Steele, 1997, p. 15.

3 Steele, 1997, p. 208.

4 Eagleton T, *The function of criticism*, Verso, London, 1984, pp. 110–123.

5 Williams R, 'Going on learning' (from *The New Statesman*, May 1959), in McIlroy J and Westwood S (eds), *Border country: Raymond Williams in adult education*, National Institute of Adult Continuing Education, Leicester, 1993.

6 See my review of Sinfield's *Literature, politics and culture in post-war Britain* (Oxford, 1989), in *New Left Review*, 188 (July/August 1991), p. 159.

7   These examples are among projects described in Stuart M and Thomson A (eds), *Engaging with difference: the 'other' in adult education*, National Institute of Adult Continuing Education, Leicester, 1995.

8   Blackburn R (ed.), *Ideology in social science*, Fontana, London, 1972; Eagleton T, *Criticism and ideology: a study in Marxist literary theory*, NLB, London, 1976; Parker R and Pollock G, *Old mistresses: women, art and ideology*, Routledge, London, 1981; Widdowson P (ed), *Re-reading English*, Methuen, London, 1982.

9   Thompson J, 'Preface', in Mayo M and Thompson J (eds), *Adult learning, critical intelligence and social change*, National Institute of Adult Continuing Education, Leicester, 1995, p. 1.

10   My quotations are from Andrews John A, 'The wider educational scene', in Elliott J, Francis H, Humphreys R and Istance D (eds), *Communities and their universities: the challenge of lifelong learning*, Lawrence and Wishart, London, 1996: see pp. 110, 109. On the 'producer-led' character of HE, see Tight M, 'The ideology of higher education', in Fulton O (ed.), *Access and institutional change*, SRHE and Open University Press, Milton Keynes, 1989; and Ball Sir C, *More means different: widening access to higher education*, RSA, London, 1990, especially Ch. 6. See also the glossy document entitled *Higher education developments: the skills link*, produced in 1990 by the Training, Enterprise and Education Directorate of the Employment Department Group, with a Foreword by Robert Jackson MP (then Parliamentary Under Secretary of State): Employment Department, London, November 1990.

11   Andrews, pp. 107ff, 112.

12   Andrews, p. 114.

13   Ward K, 'Community regeneration and social exclusion: some current policy issues for higher education', in Elliott *et al.* (eds), pp. 204–15.

14   Humphreys R and Francis H, 'Communities, valleys and universities', in Elliott *et al.*, *Communities and their universities*, pp. 230ff.

15   Humphreys and Francis, p. 243.

16   Ward, p. 205.

17   Tom Steele's argument in *The emergence of cultural studies*.

18   So Mr Blair has just been reported (again) as saying, on 'The world at one' (BBC Radio 4, 12 February 1998): the emphasis is added.

19   See Tight, 'Ideology of HE'; Ball, 'More Means Different'. My quotation is from Usher R, 'Qualifications, paradigms and experiential learning in HE', in Fulton, *Access and institutional change*, pp. 64–79; p. 79.

20   Stuart M and Thomson A, in their 'Introduction' to Stuart and Thomson, *Engaging with difference*, pp. 9ff.

21   Jordan G and Weedon C, *Cultural politics: class, gender, race and the postmodern world*, Blackwell, Oxford, 1995.

22   Robbins B, *Secular vocations: intellectuals, professionalism, culture*, Verso, London and New York, Verso, 1993, p. 223.

23   Jordan and Weedon, p. 34.

24   Eagleton, *Function of criticism*, p. 112.

25   Dostoevsky, *The devils*, trans. David Magarshack, Penguin, Harmondsworth, 1979, pp. 27, 483.

26   'Our dependence upon the state [is] an encumbrance not shared by our leading American competitors': Alec Broers, V-C of Cambridge University, quoted in the *Times Higher Education Supplement*, 30 January 1998, p. 7.

27   See, for some further discussion of this and related questions, Ryle M, 'Long live literature', *Radical Philosophy*, Vol 67 (1994).

28 Adorno T W, 'Cultural criticism and society', in Adorno (ed. J M Bernstein), *The culture industry*, Routledge, London, 1991, pp. 26ff.

29 Andrews, p. 110.

30 Leavis F R, *Education and the idea of a university: a sketch for an 'English school'*, Cambridge University Press, Cambridge, new edition of 1948, repr. 1979, pp. 29ff.

31 See Gorz A, *Farewell to the working class*, Pluto, London, 1982, and *Paths to paradise*, Pluto, London, 1985. See also my *Ecology and socialism*, to which I refer readers who want a more adequate presentation of arguments which can only be gestured at here: Ryle M, *Ecology and socialism*, Radius, London, 1988.

4 The marginalisation of literature in the teaching of culture

Angeliki Spiropoulou

What is the place of literature in cultural studies? It seems that having enjoyed an exemplary status within the study of culture, literature has increasingly assumed a marginal position *vis-à-vis* popular and media culture studies in the recently institutionalised discipline of cultural studies in Britain. The near absence of literary texts both in the taught bibliography of most cultural-studies related courses offered by a number of British universities and in cultural studies publication catalogues of major houses such as Routledge and Sage raises the question of what underlies a process of marginalisation of literature evinced in a field which, nominally at least, is supposed to encompass the study of all forms of culture.

The shift of focus from the study of literary to other cultural forms can be related to the objective cultural studies set itself at its emergence, which was, in Stuart Hall's words, 'a critique of humanities', 'the unmasking of the unstated presuppositions of the humanist tradition itself';[1] a tradition of which the national literary heritage has formed a basic part. This turning away from the traditional educational project of the humanities was originally meant as a distancing of cultural studies from the élitist Arnoldian project of 'teaching through literature and history the histories and touchstones of the national culture to a select number of people'.[2]

Within the British context, the vicissitudes of the process of establishing 'English' as an academic subject point to the nationalist, sexist and bourgeois ideology which it was made to serve. Eagleton sketches the 'Rise of English' according to these three basic ideological tasks. In his account, English literature, as opposed to the 'classics', was first institutionalised outside the traditional universities with a view to educating the (working class) masses into humanist identification with the higher classes and to forming a consciousness of national identity. Next, the admission of English into universities coincided with the gradual admission of women into the doors of these 'great' institutions, as the 'softening' and 'humanising' effects of English were thought to be suitable to the feminine 'nature'. Besides, the rise of English, as Eagleton continues, was concomitant with the high imperialist spirit England was experiencing at the time and which found in the literature of the national language an appropriate vehicle of justification and dissemination.[3] In addition, the canonisation of English literature, effected by its introduction to universities, was further implicated in the ideological project of defining and transmitting the 'national' culture and, most importantly, of identifying it with so-called 'high culture'.

The recorded struggle over the canonisation of literature along the lines of language, genre or author indicates that literature was until recently seen as a privileged form of culture, almost a paradigm of it.

The object of cultural studies

The move away from this tradition in the name of the cultural studies project was a significant moment in the history of the humanities, and, undoubtedly, a necessary one too. The genesis of cultural studies is associated with the rejection of an exclusive equation of culture with 'high culture' and with the articulation of the need to study all forms of cultural production in relation to socio-historical structures and other cultural practices. But in order to achieve its radical objective, cultural studies was defined not only in relation to a new method, an interdisciplinary one, but also in relation to a new object, that of 'popular culture', of which the media have lately come to be seen as the main instance. As a result, communication, media and cultural studies programmes, which have gained a significant place in British universities since the 1970s, mostly concentrate on cultural texts other than literature with an emphasis on popular culture and the mass media. The titles of undergraduate degrees offered by British universities are telling in that Cultural Studies tends to appear alongside either Media or Communication Studies while in the content of such courses the stress is on the social sciences and those forms of popular culture more closely associated with the new technologies and the media, with literature as an object of study represented minimally if at all.[4] Hence, not all cultural forms seem to qualify equally as analytic and teaching objects of cultural studies, despite the all-encompassing title of the new project.

The object boundaries of cultural studies can also be traced through the corpus of publications in the field born out of the research and educational project of the Birmingham Centre. The focus of most such publications has initially been on working class culture and youth lifestyles. Since then, the increasing popularity of cultural studies among students and researchers has widened the field significantly to include, for example, questions of race and sex determinations at the same time as it has effected the establishment of cultural studies as a discipline; a development which has gone hand in hand with a demand for a delineation of the field, a boundary-marking of what constitutes cultural studies.

As both a conscious response to and an inevitable consequence of that demand, there have appeared numerous histories as well as (critical) reviews of the development of cultural studies.[5] Most significantly for the constitution of cultural studies as a separate field of teaching and study, there has been the publication of Readers and 'key-text' editions providing textbooks for the growing number of cultural studies students. Two such cultural studies Readers, published by Routledge in 1992 and 1993 respectively, are a good example of how analysis and teaching in the field are generally conceived.[6] The contents of both readers are organised around representative areas of work in cultural studies and despite their many differences, they share similar perspectives; for example, both use categories such as nation and ethnicity, gender and sexuality, and the theory of culture to mark established areas of writing in cultural studies and reflect more contemporary concerns within the field. What is most interesting, however, is that in both Readers there is a separate section on 'popular culture', whereas those (few) articles concerned with literature come under the headings 'Theory and Method' or 'Discourse and Textuality'.

In the politics of selection underlying these publications, what is at stake is not so much an omission of the category 'literature' or 'literary studies', but rather the inclusion of the heading 'popular culture' which automatically invokes its absent 'other', high culture. Moreover, denied a constitutional place in the field, literature is subsumed under the category of 'textuality' in general while textual theory and analysis, which initially developed within literary studies, features as a dominant method in cultural studies.

One could argue that this trend of treating culture as text might be the common ground on which literature and cultural studies stand, thus obviating any value-laden distinctions between 'high' and 'popular'. This is indeed what Antony Easthope asserts in his book *Literary into cultural studies*, where he sets out to prove that a merging of the two disciplines has been effected after the legitimacy of a literary canon collapsed under the pressure of theory.[7] He even proclaims enthusiastically that 'the established distinction between high and popular culture has been broken down this time on the side of cultural studies', because by 'co-opting frames of analysis from work in semiology as well as in the analysis of ideology and of gender, cultural studies has advanced into the supposedly subjective realm of literary studies and reclaimed analysis of the text for itself'.[8] The appropriation of textual theory on the part of cultural studies is then seen as the basis on which literary and cultural studies can happily co-exist.

Wishing to offer some pragmatic evidence in support of his view, it is ironic that Easthope refers to the well-known Open University course U203, claiming that students on this course 'testified that they had been more analytically aware of the specific problems of textuality than they would have been on a conventional literary course' (!).[9] Textual theory, developed within literature departments, has indeed problematised accepted notions of literary value which underlie the identification of literature with 'high culture' and has even caused what has been described as a 'crisis' in English.[10] However, it is difficult to concur with Easthope's claim that cultural studies has broken 'the established distinction between high and popular culture' which had tended to prevent it from encompassing literature. Nor is the invocation of U203 very convincing. To begin with, the fact that this course, emblematic as it has been of the field of cultural studies, is entitled 'Popular culture' already involves a reproduction if not a reinforcement of this 'established' distinction between high and popular culture, literary and cultural studies. Furthermore, the syllabus itself makes no mention of literature as a topic, while the only unit in the syllabus which would implicitly involve literature is unit 15, entitled 'Reading and realism'. This would lead one to argue instead that the concern with textuality displayed in more recent developments in cultural studies neither automatically concedes a place to literature as an object of study nor necessarily breaks down the distinction between high and popular culture.

My own experience as a tutor in a communication studies course offered by Coventry University,[11] which, like many other cultural studies-related courses, was heavily influenced by the work of the Birmingham Centre, has been that textual analysis features independently of literary studies where it first developed. This course offered no module on literature; and literature figured implicitly in only one module (where the issue of realism versus modernism is discussed). Because of the ways that the syllabi of media, culture and communications degrees have been designed and described (and hence marketed), students have not expected – and have even been reluctant – to read any literature, and have generally found it irrelevant to what they had chosen to study. It is thus questionable to interpret the engagement with issues of textuality in teaching and writing in cultural studies as the dawn of a 'combined paradigm', since the emphasis of cultural studies is still largely on popular and media culture. While the method may be common, the analytic object is not.

This differentiation was made clear from the very beginnings of cultural studies. As early as 1966, Richard Hoggart began an article entitled 'Literature and society' by asserting two things:

> First, without appreciating good literature no one will really understand the nature of society; second, literary critical analysis can be applied to certain social phenomena other than 'academically respectable' literature (for example, the popular arts, mass communications) so as to illuminate their meanings for individuals and for their societies.[12]

The words of the founder of the Centre for Contemporary Cultural Studies legitimate techniques of literary analysis as operative in the analysis of popular culture while, by the same token, the object of cultural studies, which Hoggart had helped form, becomes 'popular culture' as against 'academically respectable' literature. While acknowledging the significance of literature in the understanding of society, Hoggart at the same time set it apart from 'popular culture', the study of which he advocated.

Literary versus popular in the self-representation of cultural studies

However, the reason for the marginalisation of literature in cultural studies cannot exclusively lie in the ideological role it has been made to play in societies where it has been equated with 'high' culture. This process must be motivated by other reasons.

In fact, that ideological placing of 'literature' can be contested, along at least two lines. First, it is difficult to regard 'literature' and 'popular culture' as distinct essences; and second, the 'literary' and the 'popular' have in fact from time to time fulfilled quite similar ideological functions. The shifting definitions of what should be considered a part of a 'great literary tradition' or 'canon' across history point to the difficulty of attributing an 'essence' to literature which would in turn legitimate its identification with 'high' culture. To quote Terry Eagleton: 'a piece of writing may start off life as history or philosophy and then come to be ranked as literature; or it may start off as literature and then come to be valued for its archaeological significance.'[13] The precariousness of the division between 'high' literature and 'popular culture' is further demonstrated by C W E Bigsby when he alludes to the process through which a 'popular' work can be transformed into 'high' art by reference to familiar terms of literary criticism and vice versa. The possibility of this transformation makes Bigsby observe that the classification of a cultural form as 'high' or 'popular' culture is in fact 'a matter of critical appropriation'.[14] Furthermore, as notions of 'the unity of the text' and 'authorialism' – which have been variously used to sustain the legitimacy of a literary canon – have been questioned, so has 'literature' become even more difficult to define. And as to the term 'popular culture', the fact that it has been invariably used as a cliché obscures its various and contradictory definitions which, as Tony Bennett acknowledges, include: what remains when high culture has been defined; that which is well-liked by many people; mass (manipulative) culture; or an authentic creation of the people.[15]

On the other hand, literature has not been the sole means by which nationalist and aesthetic ideologies have been promulgated. Peter Burke has shown how popular culture was 'discovered' as the founding myth of nationhood,[16] rather as English literature was constructed as emblematic of the national heritage. Even in aesthetic terms, both 'popular' culture and 'high' literature derive their value in connection with the Romantic movement. The turn to popular culture has been explained as ensuing from the Romantic reaction to Classicism.[17] Similarly, it was the Romantic movement that bequeathed to us the modern, restricted notion of literature as the 'creative and imaginative';[18] a definition which formed a ready ground for literature's equation with 'high aetheriality'.

It follows from all this that notions of both 'high' and 'popular' culture are recent constructions, whose apparent opposition is revealed as arbitrary once we consider their similar conditions of emergence and use. Besides, literature's common identification with the bourgeois ideology of the 'pure aesthetic' ignores the extent to which this aesthetic has also historically offered a possibility of a critical rupture (also shared with some 'popular' cultural forms) with the same utilitarian bourgeois ethic that helped 'produce' literature as generically (and hence historically) autonomous.[19]

Given the instability of the division between 'popular' and 'high' culture and the implication of both in ideologies of power, the choice of the construct 'popular culture' as the privileged object of cultural studies and the consequent marginalisation of literature point to a specific politics of representation of the new discipline, which is played out in quite contradictory terms. On the one hand, the establishment of the study of popular culture through the academic institutionalisation of cultural studies rests on the conviction that 'high' culture is no better than 'popular' culture, rendering this distinction irrelevant. Instead, the anthropological definition of culture as 'a whole way of life' was initially taken up as an unpolarised alternative. On the other hand, by privileging the study of 'popular culture' and excluding literature as 'high culture', cultural studies in fact reinforces this 'high'–'popular' distinction. This contradiction, peculiar as it seems to the genesis of cultural studies, is, I think, paradigmatic of both the absurdity and the necessity of such categories and distinctions in the process of self-representation. The fact that literature is marginalised in cultural studies by being identified with 'high' culture can thus be seen as an inimical condition of the possibility of cultural studies coming into its own. Cultural studies premises its *raison d'être* on reproducing by exclusion the symbolic primacy of 'high culture' so that it can define itself against it.

The popular and the 'real'

To the extent that cultural studies emerged out of the discipline of English,[20] the boundaries between the two were dangerously faint. To draw them more firmly, the project of cultural studies had to be defined not just against literature (by repressing it), but also in terms of explicit assumptions about the nature of what it had chosen as its principal object, namely 'popular culture'.

In 1989, Stuart Hall published a paper entitled 'The emergence of cultural studies and the crisis of the humanities'. This may be cited as a key statement on the object and objectives of cultural studies in Britain, for it reads as a kind of retrospective manifesto of the birth of the project back in the 1970s. Hall specifies as follows one of the 'practical ramifications' that the development of cultural studies had:

It was not possible to present the work of cultural studies as if it had no political consequences and no form of political engagement, because what we were inviting students to do was to do what we ourselves had done: to engage with some *real* problem *out there in the dirty world*, and to use the enormous advantage given to a tiny handful of us in the British educational system who had the opportunity to go into universities and reflect on those problems, to spend that time *usefully* to try to understand how the world worked.[21]

Here we can examine the premises on which cultural studies has based its predilection for popular culture. And the definition of these premises, though expressed in positive terms, in fact rests upon their (implicit) opposition to what literature has come to be thought of as. The object of cultural studies is such that students can 'usefully' engage with 'real' problems 'out there in the dirty world' as opposed to the 'pure', 'useless', 'unreality' literature is often accused of. The paradigmatic object is *popular* culture, whose usefulness and reality are somehow implicit in its popularity, whereas literature cannot claim much popularity within the contemporary cultural scene – and, being 'unpopular', is easily constructed as élitist. And further, even though cultural studies' predilection for popular culture would seem to entail an immediate engagement with women's culture associated as it had been with the 'mass' in modernist literary (and hegemonic academic) discourse,[22] this has not quite been the case. On the contrary, cultural studies can be seen as a primarily masculine project in two ways. First, the emphasis of early cultural studies on 'popular' rather than 'mass' culture with its roots in the (male) working class and youth subcultures did not leave women much space to be represented.[23] Second, the current prevalence of mass media issues in the work of cultural studies can be viewed as of a masculine character because of the media's intrinsic relation to technology traditionally associated with masculinity. In this context, cultural studies' emphasis on 'masculine' forms of culture seems to concur with the marginalisation of a field such as literature where women have made a difference as producers, and to suggest that cultural studies in fact shares with canonical, masculinised high culture a tendency to value men's work more and reserve for women mainly the status of passive consumer unworthy of serious study.[24] A certain form of élitism therefore has not been exclusive to traditional literary discourse.

In an article entitled 'Cultural studies and its theoretical legacies', Stuart Hall repeats that British cultural studies has to retain that political edge in its project which he calls (consciously borrowing from Edward Said) 'the worldliness of cultural studies'. He identifies this 'worldliness' with a certain 'dirtiness', aiming 'to return the project of cultural studies from the clean air of meaning and textuality and theory to the something nasty below'.[25] His concern to make theory and practice meet is registered in an (implied) reference to the reality out there which cultural studies is supposed to address and which literature, identified as it is with textuality, fails to do. Hall's 'above–below' model here does not just recall the 'high–low' opposition; it also implies that there can be an unmediated, 'text-free' way of understanding reality, which rules literature out. The conflation of a 'dirtiness below' with 'real' reality involves, too, a certain radical claim.

It is indeed this questionable address to non-valued things that 'really' matter because they are 'nasty' that helps cultural studies make a difference, ie that constitutes the identity of the cultural studies project. The place to which literature is then confined is a historically static and politically reactionary one. On the one hand, it is denied a political force by being relegated to the sphere of the imaginative and, on the other, its construction as pure aesthetics also sets it up as élitist, which legitimates, by contrast, the professed radical nature of cultural studies' preoccupation with the political, the low, the popular, in short with 'what is going on in the real world'.

If, borrowing from Bourdieu, we can define the production of academic discourse as a 'playing field', a field of objective relations among individuals or institutions competing for the same stakes,[26] then it would be possible – not least on account of the increasing fashionability of cultural studies – to extend what Bourdieu says about the dynamics of succession apropos the fashion field to the process through which cultural studies makes claims to 'distinction' within academia. For Bourdieu, the permanent struggle for dominance within the field is played out on the basis of conservation and subversion strategies employed by the established and the newcomer respectively. The newcomer seeks to overthrow the established in two ways: by subverting the values that legitimate the established, and by appealing to something already existing 'outside' the field (designated as 'the real'). This appeal to the 'real' on the part of the newcomer in the field, in our case on the part of cultural studies, is what legitimates its distinction within academia, its claims to dominance. However, even though the absolute values of the game might change, the structural positions of the game remain the same, hence the game is not destroyed. To quote Bourdieu:

> Someone who wants to achieve a revolution in the cinema or in painting says, 'That is not *real* cinema' or 'That is not *real* painting'. He pronounces anathemas, but in the name of a purer, more authentic definition of the principles in whose name the dominant dominate.[27]

In that sense, hierarchy is simply inverted in the game of succession.

Literature and critical education

To see cultural studies as having reproduced, in its development, a pattern of margins versus centre (by marginalising that in relation to which it was initially marginal)[28] is not to underestimate the political significance of introducing the study of popular and media culture into academia; nor is it to deny the (still?) strong tradition of a literary canon within some English departments. Here, I seek only to suggest how cultural studies remains blind to its own politics of emergence and dissemination while it simply thinks of itself as on the side of the radical, defined in opposition to and by repression of a supposedly 'high' literature at a time when literature is generally seen not to perform any useful, practical function.

A certain blindness, as the story of Oedipus has shown us, is necessary in order to assume an identity. However when it claims an exclusive identity for itself, cultural studies negates its own radical pretensions, in that the game itself is not destroyed; and by appealing to an already constituted 'real' as useful and important, it obscures its own part in producing definitions of both what is real and what is valuable. Contrariwise, the marginalisation of literature in the field of cultural studies not only constructs it as analytically and educationally unworthy; it also reinforces the ahistorical illusion of aesthetic autonomy and contradicts cultural studies' proclaimed concern with the historicisation of culture and the unmasking of 'unstated presuppositions'. Cultural studies presents us with the radical opportunity of a historical interrogation of different cultural forms through tracing their trajectory among other symbolic discourses and institutional practices. Consistent with its political project, cultural studies needs to acknowledge that the uses and meanings of literature have been historically determined and transformed, rather than consigning literature, by exclusion, to the symbolic position of the non-changing (and hence reactionary).

We may also ask whether it is really radical to premise an identity on claims to usefulness, popularity and realist representativeness when these notions both rest on and support a functionalist perspective which serves the reproduction of existing power relations only too well – especially so in a society which readily advocates these same values, and so often accuses the subjects and approaches of university education of lacking them.[29] After all, the popularity of media studies in the research and educational field opened up by the cultural studies project could be interpreted as a response to social and market demands currently made of universities to provide 'technical know-how'. To characterise the work of cultural studies as 'useful' is strangely resonant of the discourse of vocationalism on which several contributors to the present volume comment, a discourse already prominent in the British Government White Paper 'Higher education: meeting the challenge' of 1987. There the aims of higher education are specified as 'serving the economy more effectively' and 'having closer links with industry and commerce and promoting enterprise'.[30] Moreover this emphasis of cultural studies on the media, and especially its recent 'consumptionist' trend,[31] is in line with the currently dominant media and consumer culture which makes cultural studies so attractive to student populations, and which impresses upon literature the taint of an irrelevant quaintness.

Thanks to its engagement with the popular and its claims to 'realist representativeness', cultural studies has been placed at the centre of contemporary culture and increasingly of academia, while literature – seen as part of the tradition of the (once) 'high' culture – is pushed to its margins. If the noise of moving from the margins to the centre has deafened us so we have not heard the silencing of literature, it is now time we looked again at what literature has to offer as part of an educational project. To the extent that that project is critical, we might argue with Barthes for the significance of the inclusion of literature:

> For what the human sciences are discovering today, in whatever realm: sociological, psychological, psychiatric, linguistic, etc., literature has already known; the only difference is that literature has not said what it knows, it has written it. Confronting this integral truth of writing, the 'human sciences', belatedly constituted in the wake of bourgeois positivism, appear as the technical alibis our society uses to maintain the fiction of a theological truth, superbly – abusively – disengaged from language.[32]

By virtue of its freedom from truth-value judgements and its 'staging' of language, literature assumes a powerlessness to represent the real, and a power to 'represent the sovereignty of language',[33] that can ground a critique of all types of ideological discourse that claim to have a transparency of message and hence a direct relation to the real. At the same time, literature does refer to the real and is conditioned by the real as its shifting definitions and value across history testify. And, historically thinking, we may begin to identify its current value for that analysis of culture and of the real which is required of education if we consider the possible reasons why in the contemporary cultural space literature no longer quite fits.

Notes

1   Hall S, 'The emergence of cultural studies and the crisis of the humanities', *October*, Vol 53 (1989), p. 15.
2   Hall, 1989, p. 13.
3   Eagleton T, *Literary theory: an introduction*, Blackwell, Oxford, 1983, pp. 27–29. For an account of the establishment of English studies also see Brian Doyle's 'The hidden history of English studies', in Widdowson P (ed.), *Re-reading English*, Methuen, London and New York, 1982.
4   A first-hand informal search into the UCAS CD-ROM ECCTIS 2000 (in November 1997) attested to the following: a) of those 26 BA/BSc Courses that matched in tandem the subject areas of Cultural, Media and Communication Studies in Great Britain and for which there was a content outline available, in ten course titles 'culture' or 'cultural studies' featured together with communication, social and media studies, and only in three occurrences did it feature on its own; in the other 13 courses the titles included only media and/or communication studies even though in the course content 'cultural studies' and 'popular culture' was a

core specification; b) in the brief description of the 26 courses only five contained any reference to literature as an object of study while in another two there was reference to modules on 'literary codes' or 'literary analysis' as one of cultural studies' analytic methods.

Of course, there were numerous combined or joint courses which I have not included in the sample and in some courses there was the option of studying modules in English, history or other languages offered by other departments; but the overall trend was to concentrate on media, technology, social issues and popular culture with literature basically left to English studies.

5   One such history is Turner G, *British cultural studies: an introduction*, first published by Unwin Hyman in 1990 and reprinted by Routledge in 1992. The early 1990s saw a surge of publications offering histories of and key texts in cultural studies.

6   The first Reader, entitled *Cultural studies*, is edited by Lawrence Grossberg, Cary Nelson and Paula Treichler (Routledge, London, 1992). Soon afterwards, in 1993, the second Routledge Reader appeared, edited by Simon During with the telling title *The cultural studies reader*. Another publication representative of the 'key-text' approach so characteristic of textbooks is *Reading into cultural studies*, edited by Martin Barker and Anne Beezer and published (once again) by Routledge in 1992.

7   Easthope A, *Literary into cultural studies*, Routledge, London, 1991, pp. 65–74.

8   Easthope, 1991, pp. 74, 71–72.

9   Easthope, p. 74.

10 A much-cited statement of this argument is found in the collection of essays, *Re-reading English* (Widdowson, 1982), and especially in Widdowson's introduction entitled 'The crisis in English studies', pp. 1–14.

11 The Communication studies course I refer to was offered at Coventry University until Spring 1997; it was phased out at Mediterranean College, Athens in 1997–98.

12 Cited in Bigsby C W E, 'The politics of popular culture', in Bigsby C W E (ed.), *Approaches to popular culture*, Arnold, London, 1976, p. 24.

13 Eagleton, 1983, p. 10.

14 'It is, after all, worth recalling that the desire to create such distinctions is itself a recent phenomenon. It has been argued, for example, that while writers like Richardson, Cooper, Twain and Dickens . . . have been accorded classic status because of an achievement which is intimately connected with their popularity, this status has been defended primarily by reference to the familiar terms of literary criticism – irony, tragic consciousness, structure, etc. A similar paradox is apparent in film criticism which often praises avowedly popular films for reasons which are not merely totally unconnected with their popularity but which would seem to be inimical to it. Popular culture, then, can apparently be transformed into "high" art by a simple critical act of appropriation. Indeed so insecure are these categories that the popular culture of one generation can become the high culture of the next and vice versa . . .': Bigsby, 1976, pp. 16–17.

15 Cited by Jim McGuigan in *Cultural populism*, Routledge, London and New York, 1992, p. 65.

16 See Burke P, 'We, the people: popular culture and popular identity in modern Europe', in Lash S and Friedman J (eds), *Modernity and identity*, Blackwell, Oxford, 1992, p. 243. In this article Burke shows, among other things, how the study of popular culture, which is today associated with left-wing politics, was seen as a defence of traditional values against 'the assaults of modernisation' by conservatives in the nineteenth century.

17 McGuigan, 1992, pp. 10–11.

18 Eagleton, 1983, pp. 17–19.

19 For a thorough account of the history of the artistic field becoming autonomous by its identification with pure aesthetics, and of the premises and consequences of this process in relation to contemporary social and political fields, see Bourdieu P, *The rules of art*, Polity, Cambridge, 1996, especially Part I 'Three states of the field' (pp. 47–173).

20 It is significant that figures whose work has been seminal to British Cultural Studies, such as Raymond Williams, Richard Hoggart and Stuart Hall himself, had had formal training in English. Moreover, the cultural studies project has acknowledged continuities with the 'Leavisite' tradition, despite Leavisism's hostility towards the object cultural studies chose to take up. The emergence of cultural studies can thus be traced back into the field of 'English'. (On this, see Green M, 'The Centre for Contemporary Cultural Studies', in Widdowson (ed.), 1982.)

21 Hall, 1989, p. 17 (emphasis added).

22 Andreas Huyssen, for example, has convincingly argued that popular – in the sense of 'mass' – culture has been associated with women in modernist discourse ('Mass culture as woman: modernism's Other', in Modleski T (ed.), *Studies in entertainment*, Indiana University Press, Bloomington, 1986).

23 This is indicated, after all, by the relative delay in dealing with gender issues in relevant Birmingham Centre publications as is acknowledged in Chapter 1 of the first publication of the Centre to address women's issues, *Women take issue*, put together by the Women's Study Group (Hutchinson, London, 1978, especially pp. 7, 11).

24 It seems that the canonisation of any cultural form also tends to rely on gender terms. A telling example of this process in the area of literature is that of the novel. Celia Lury (*Cultural rights*, Routledge, London, 1993), among others, shows that even though the novel had initially been a form of popular culture in which women were both active producers and a significant part of the readership, it was transformed in the late nineteenth century into high culture upon the intervention of newly instituted bodies of professional (male) critics who praised novels produced by men much more. The implications of this historical example do not contradict the already mentioned fact that English was initially seen as the appropriate subject for female students newly admitted to university. On the contrary, the implied feminisation of English literature at that time reinforces the argument that what is associated with the feminine is already seen as having or acquires a secondary status and that women are relegated to consumers in two ways: first, at that time the valued subject of study, fitted for men was mostly the classics and not English, and second, women students of English could be seen as not choosing for themselves but rather as subjected to the formative force of the canon approved by and taught by primarily male critics and professors.

25 Hall S, 'Cultural studies and its theoretical legacies', in Grossberg *et al.* (eds), 1992, p. 278.

26 Bourdieu P, 'Haute couture and haute culture', in *Sociology in question*, Sage, London, 1993, p. 133.

27 Bourdieu, 1993, p. 134 (emphasis in original).

28 'We tried, in our extremely *marginal* way up there on the eighth floor in the Arts Faculty Building, to think of ourselves as a tiny piece of a hegemonic struggle': Hall, 1989, p. 18 (emphasis added).

29 Raymond Williams himself, at the 1986 conference of the Association of Cultural

Studies, urged upon his audience 'the paramount task of contesting the new educational utilitarianism', 'work experience' and so forth, 'a definition of industrial training which would have sounded crude in the 1860s' (McGuigan, 1992, p. 27).

30 'HE: meeting the challenge', HMSO, 1987, iv. For more details, see Rice J and Rice P, 'Future imperfect? English and the new vocationalism', in Brooker P and Humm P (eds), *Dialogue and difference: English into the nineties*, Routledge, London, 1989.

31 A consumptionist populism is one of the trajectories of what Jim McGuigan calls 'Cultural populism', which he traces through the development of cultural studies and defines as 'the intellectual assumption, made by some students of culture, that the symbolic experiences and practices of ordinary people are more important analytically and politically than Culture with a capital C'. The initial trajectory lay within a 'productionist', 'dialectical' populism concerned with the workings of hegemony (see McGuigan, 1992, pp. 4, 45–159, esp pp. 45–85). In a later article, entitled 'Cultural populism revisited', McGuigan further criticises the advent and prevalence of an exclusively consumptionist preoccupation witnessed in cultural studies analyses at the expense of political economy considerations (in Ferguson M and Golding P (eds), *Cultural studies in question*, Sage, London, 1997, pp. 138–154).

32 Barthes R, 'From science to literature', in *The rustle of language*, Blackwell, Oxford, 1986, p. 10.

33 Barthes, 1986, p. 10.

5 Relativism and utopianism: critical theory and cultural studies

Kate Soper

Many of the chapters in this volume offer retrospections on the history and ongoing practice of cultural studies conceived as a contribution to a political project of a broadly left-wing kind. My own particular engagement here is with the legacy of the early Frankfurt School theorists, and what it may still have to offer such a practice, though I shall be concerned throughout to relate any possible critical theory input or mediation to the questions about popular culture and aesthetic value which have been foregrounded in the more recent and specifically 'cultural studies' formation in the academy.[1]

There are, admittedly, aspects of the Frankfurt School's style and content which render it problematic and out of touch with contemporary critical perspectives, and in the following two sections I shall offer some comment on these. I shall proceed to argue, none the less, that the distinctive critical theory approach to questions of pleasure, sensuality and selfhood offers a powerful resource for current cultural critiques, particularly where these bear on gender and ecological issues. I shall also try to show that critical theory has kept open questions of hedonism and aesthetic value which have been suppressed or ignored in much postmodernist cultural criticism only at the cost of exposing that criticism to the charge of inconsistency and political vacuity.

Critical theory and British cultural studies

I have spoken of a critical theory 'legacy', but I am very aware that to date, there has been rather little in the way of direct bequest from the Frankfurt Institute to British cultural studies. Or if there has, it has been more by default or disownment, a patrimony rejected rather than exploited. One reason for this, noted by Tom Steele in his *Emergence of cultural studies*, lay in the wartime relocation of the Frankfurt School to the USA, since this inevitably diminished their influence on the emerging post-1945 left-formation in Great Britain.[2] Another factor, no doubt, is the philosophical illiteracy of British cultural studies, and particularly the lack of familiarity with several of the key influences, notably Kant, Hegel and Nietzsche, on the argument of the Frankfurt theorists themselves.

But third, and perhaps most important of all, any rapprochement between the two formations was discouraged by the increasing tendency of cultural studies to engage sympathetically with the forms of popular culture or entertainment which the Frankfurt theorists had deplored as the commodified and philistine products of the 'culture industry'. Whereas critical theory viewed popular entertainment as a means whereby the masses were co-opted into perpetuating the conditions of their own oppression, and saw 'high (modernist) art' as alone keeping open the possible promise of redemption, cultural studies drew on earlier popular traditions to contest aesthetic élitism and theories of mass manipulation. There are also of course significant differences between critical theory and cultural studies in their conception of 'culture'. As Fredric Jameson has pointed out, the idea of it at work in the 'culture industry' essays of Horkheimer and Adorno has very little, if anything, in common with the concept of 'culture' whose formulation in the work of Raymond Williams lays the foundations of a 'cultural studies' programme in Great Britain. Indeed, the 'culture industry' work offers not so much a theory of culture as a theory of an *industry*, argues Jameson: it is about the commercialisation of life, rather than culture in Williams's sense of a 'live system of meanings and values' which are constitutive of a sense of reality for most people in the society; and as such it is *Ideologiekritik* in the classical Marxist sense rather than *Kulturkritik*.[3]

Moreover, although many New Left influenced cultural critics have remained committed to a broadly socialist critique of commodification, and still aspire to radical social change, they do not subscribe to the monolithic critical theory conception of culture in terms of 'culture industry' ideological manipulation. On the contrary, they have problematised the anti-democratic, even authoritarian, tendencies of a 'Marxist' analysis so certain of the malleability of mass tastes, and so bent on preserving 'high art' from contamination with them – and, in line with this, have tended to look less to art than to the dissatisfactions bred of consumerism as the paradoxical source of a possible renewal.[4]

In drawing these contrasts, I recognise that there is some controversy about the extent to which the Frankfurt School may fairly be charged with cultural élitism. My own view is that this charge may not be entirely justified, and is certainly in need of qualification, though I am not going to pursue that debate here.[5] I also think it regrettable that so much attention came to focus on the 'Culture industry' essay, since this is one of the less sophisticated and considered pieces of writing to issue from the Frankfurt School, and seems in marked contrast to the nuance and sensitivity displayed by Adorno in other critical commentary.[6] However, what does seem clear is that the 'culture industry' analysis was quite widely *viewed* as 'élitist' by the New Left critics; and that it was essentially through a more 'democratic' and Gramscian corrective to the claimed élitism of the Adornian approach (whether or not this engaged explicitly with Adorno's writings themselves) that the distinctive 'cultural studies' perspective matured, opening itself in the process to constituencies and bodies of work previously ignored in the study of culture.

Critical theory, feminism and social movement politics

This brings me to a further important contrast and source of disaffection between critical theory and cultural studies, namely the difference in the extent and quality of their engagement with the condition and cultural representation of marginal and subordinate groups. The essential point here is that, unlike critical theory, the cultural studies formation developed under the influence of, and in tandem with, social movement politics, most notably in the first instance that of the women's movement. Since then, we have also seen the growth and consolidation of a varied and complex body of post-colonial theory in cultural studies; and when viewed from this perspective, the offering of the early Frankfurt School is indisputably and Eurocentrically disengaged from the cultural condition of the 'other' (although arguably no more abstracted than other formations on the left at the time).

In the case of feminism, the record is not quite so clear cut, since the critical theorists were on the whole more ready than others to acknowledge and explore the oppressions of patriarchy. This protofeminist engagement is evidenced, for example, in the work undertaken on the contradictory functions and needs of the family and its role in the formation of the authoritarian personality; in the discussions in *Dialectic of enlightenment* of the ways in which enlightenment proceeds only by way of the defeat and oppression of women;[7] and in numerous scattered references in other writings to the theft of happiness incurred for both sexes in male dominated society.

All the same, from where we have arrived now, the Frankfurt School discussion of these issues does indeed seem androcentric or gender blind in many respects. The utopianism, for example, associated with the critique of Enlightenment and its monogamic norms and bourgeois frigidities in texts such as *Dialectic of enlightenment*, and Herbert Marcuse's *Eros and civilisation* and *One-dimensional man*, typified the gender blindness of the 'free love' ethic of their time, which conveniently overlooked the asymmetrical positioning of the sexes in regard to sexual freedom, and disdained all talk of childcare, contraception and abortion. In this respect, its framework of thinking about sexuality was rather nonchalantly 1960s libertarian in precisely the ways that were to be challenged by Second Wave feminism when it emerged in the early 1970s.

More problematic, however, than this, we may argue, was the almost exclusive focus on the male child in the studies of the impact of the family on the formation of the ego; and the tendency to analyse Fascism and the rise of the authoritarian Führer as due to the weakening of the father's authority in the bourgeois family – in terms, that is, which from any contemporary feminist point of view, must have an awkwardly conservative and nostalgic ring to them.[8]

Also awkward, though raising issues that remain today of critical importance to feminists, is the Frankfurt account of the family as still offering, despite the extent to which its functions and forms of influence have been undermined in bourgeois society, a bulwark of some kind against the dehumanising effects of modernity: and as offering this in large part because of the caring and nurturing role of the mother. It is true that even as the woman was saluted as fosterer of human relations, the consequences of her economic dependence on the male and submission to the patriarchal family were also deplored.[9] But deplored less for their consequences for her as an individual needing more autonomy and self-fulfilment outside the domestic sphere, than for their conservative reinforcement of the male's ambition and his self-repressive pursuit of economic security: and the general tendency of these analyses of the social role of the family was always to present it in the framework of the contrasts between 'public' and 'private' realms and their respective 'productive' and 'reproductive' activities, and to acclaim it as the preserve of those countervailing values which were resistant to capitalist commodification and the cash-nexus reduction of all human relational and affective ties. Of course the family has functioned in the past, and to a significant extent still does function, as a haven from heteronomous activity; but its sentimentalisation as such is also bound to remain problematic for women given its tendency to endorse the existing gender division of labour and the domestication of women.[10]

Postmodernism, critical theory and the 'will to happiness'

Thus far, I have noted the reaction against an Adornian 'culture industry' élitism; and I have indicated some of the reasons why the Frankfurt school, both in its abstraction from issues of ethnicity and in its treatment of those relating to gender and sexuality, might seem to have rather little to offer a cultural studies perspective. But the fact that cultural studies has not to date been very extensively influenced by critical theory does not mean that there is no legacy of which it might avail itself in the future. I now want to turn to this somewhat more forward-looking dimension of the issue, and to make a case, in particular, for viewing some aspects of the argument of Adorno and Marcuse as offering a potentially enriching bequest.

My sense of the potential value of any such legacy is very closely related to my understanding of the current context of philosophy and cultural theory, so I want to begin by saying something about this. So far, I have focused primarily on the contrasts between the position of critical theory, on the one hand, and a New Left, Williams-influenced cultural studies formation, on the other. I have said very little about postmodernist developments. But it is clear that in order to complete the picture, one needs to take note of these, and in particular to recognise the impact in recent years of the ongoing dynamic of the anti-élitist impulse. For this has now propelled criticism into new theoretical perspectives and political commitments very different from its earlier, Gramscian forms. The poststructuralist critical position is one that rejects the lurking foundationalist Marxism of any theory of culture construed in terms of the concepts of 'repression' and 'ideology'. It questions the imperialising tendencies of liberal enlightenment, and prefers to emphasise the plurality and relativism of cultural values and aspirations. It has lent itself to a demotic elision of the distinction between art and entertainment, and in the work of some of its adherents offers a more or less unqualified validation of precisely those forms of cultural consumption which the Frankfurt thinkers found so pernicious an influence.

These are developments which the more orthodox socialist critics have simply condemned outright, accusing the postmodernist turn of collusion in the commodification and neo-libertarian ethos of contemporary capitalism. Other left critics have been more qualified in their reaction, but have none the less felt obliged to point to the impasse created by this postmodernist demotic drift: to point out that what has been lost through it is, as Jameson expresses it, 'the Archimedean point' of some 'genuine aesthetic experience' from whose standpoint the structures of commercial art may be critically unmasked.[11]

Readers will be familiar by now with this general line of critique, which can be put in more or less strongly worded form. To put it at its rudest and crudest, what has been lost is any aesthetic criterion for pronouncing most of the cultural products on offer from the video industry, and the vast majority of programmes put out on TV to be crap: a loss we may feel all the greater in that if anything since Adorno's day the crap has got crappier, the banality more banal, and the ugliness uglier. (Nor, we might add, for all the Lacanian media studies graduates going into the advertising industry, do its productions seem any less infantilising, sexually stereotypic and ecologically mindless than before.) The more guarded and academic version, on the other hand, is the one that talks about the problems attaching to the relativization of aesthetic value; of how, while recognising the inadequacies of the erstwhile academic pieties about intrinsic literary merit and the eternal verities of the text, one may yet defend the fairly obvious literary merits of Hardy or Dostoevsky over James Herriot or Jeffrey Archer; of how to present a given text or artwork as more or less progressive from a feminist or post-colonial point of view if all conceptions of the good life are deemed to be on a par; of how to argue that some cultural depiction of a given identity is false if the self is theorised as entirely the construct of discourse, and hence without a presence or truth to be distorted in its representation. And so forth, and so forth. But whatever gloss we put on it, the essential question posed here is one, I suggest, that returns us to the Frankfurt School legacy. It brings us back to this, because it is a question about the extent to which we can consistently dispense with any theory of media manipulation and co-option, any *Ideologiekritik*, any 'true'/'false' needs distinction, and still lay claim to be offering some professedly emancipatory engagement with cultural production.

I am not here suggesting that in the light of the impasse of postmodernist relativism we should simply repent of the sins of the past, and return forthwith to the fold of the 'culture industry' analysis. There can be no endorsement of that analysis as it stands. The postmodernist authentication of mass choice may have proceeded only at the cost of abstracting from the question of how far those choices are indeed truly autonomous, or how far they further the real interests of the choosers; and only at the cost of leaving the whole question of the role of art, its distinctiveness and possible political efficacy essentially unaddressed. But the Adornian emphasis on the manipulative dimension also had its costs, in that it denied mass responses any autonomy or authenticity, and failed to give proper recognition to popular traditions of resistance to capitalism and grassroots counter-cultural formations. So it is not a case of reverting to an unqualified Marxist-Modernist aesthetic. My point, rather, is that there is a dilemma for any cultural criticism which aspires both to be 'democratic' in its respect for mass taste, and progressive (green, feminist, anti-racist, socialist . . .) in its political aspirations; and that this is a dilemma which a postmodernist cultural theory should be prepared explicitly to address. What line, for example, does one take on the popularity of Teletubbies or the continuing high levels of demand for Barbie Doll and Action Man? – that it is a form of cultural snob-bishness to deplore these tastes, or that they testify to the power of the market to generate the most ideologically regressive consumer desires? (There is, one might argue, a third possibility here, which is to claim that they represent a parodic and potentially subversive commentary on our life and times; but insofar as this represents a critical position with continuing aspirations to social 'subver-sion', it is still operating with a 'true'/'false' needs framework of reference and thus far aligned with the critical theory perspective.)

Now, it would seem that the line of response to this sort of dilemma will very much depend on the view taken of the main political requirements of our times and of the prospects for their realisation. Importantly, that is, it will depend on whether it is thought that the need persists for an alternative – more economically egalitarian, socially emancipated, and ecologically rational – order of society. And 'need' here does not imply strongly consciously felt and articulated need, but need in the 'culture industry' sense of a potential for a happiness that is being distorted, denied or repressed for the majority of people by the global market economy, the consumer society and the machinations of the capitalist media. Those who remain convinced of this need will be much more likely to commit ourselves to what might be termed a 'critical hedonism' in their study of culture: a position of critical engagement with the actual in the light of a possible alternative happiness and pleasure in the future. Those, on the other hand, who do not really discern any such need, are likely to be altogether more complacent about the pleasures of the moment, and much less concerned either with sustaining, or with justifying, a critical dimension in the academic engagement with popular culture.

It may be objected, however, that it is one thing to recognise the existence of a 'need' for an alternative order of production and consumption, quite another to suppose there are realistic prospects of it being acted on; and that in the absence of those prospects, any theory of culture that continues to press on the 'critical hedonist' nerve is at risk of becoming vacuously idealist. This is indeed a major problem for cultural studies in our times, and many working in the field are increasingly sensitive to the impasse it appears to present. Yet it is in respect of precisely these critical difficulties that the early work of the Frankfurt School may have most to offer us today, since the position they sustained was one which combined what I have termed a 'critical hedonist' approach to actuality with a very high degree of articulated awareness of the potential idealism and self-subverting contradictions of their own critical position (or position *as* mere critics). On the one hand, they always kept open the promise of another happiness, and saw it as inconsistent to offer a critique of modern society if there were no human subjects aspiring to escape it and in a position to resist it; on the other hand, they were all too well aware that they were damning the society in question precisely on the grounds that it was systematically destroying the will to resist it, or to enjoy any system of pleasures other than that which it already provided. Even Marcuse, who on the whole took a more optimistic view of the tensions in question than did Horkheimer and Adorno, recognised that since the oppressed are not strong enough to liberate themselves, liberation is at once 'the most realistic, the most concrete of all historical possibilities and at the same time the most rationally and effectively repressed – the most abstract and remote possibility'. Of his argument in *One dimensional man*, he wrote that it would

> vacillate throughout between two contradictory hypotheses: (1) that advanced industrial society is capable of containing qualitative change for the foreseeable future; (2) that forces and tendencies exist which may break this containment and explode this society. I do not think that a clear answer can be given. Both tendencies – and even the one in the other.[12]

Poststructuralists do not fret out loud like this. I grant that there are many comparisons we may draw between a poststructuralist and early Frankfurt theorisation of the Enlightenment and subjectivity, of power and desire (and Foucault himself towards the end of his life acknowledged how close his own position was to that of the Frankfurt School). But where the critical theory position differs markedly, I would argue, is in combining its 'will to happiness' with explicit recognition of the social forms of conditioning that were rendering its aspirations ever more purely utopian.

Take, for example, Adorno's discussion of the problem of subjective freedom in *Negative dialectics* – where he argues that it is just as inadequate, and in a sense cruel, to insist on personal autonomy as it is to insist on cultural determinism:

> If the thesis of free will burdens the dependent individuals with the social injustice they can do nothing about, if it ceaselessly humiliates them with desiderata they cannot fulfil, the thesis of unfreedom, on the other hand, amounts to a metaphysically extended rule of the status quo . . . To deny free will outright means to reduce men unreservedly to the normal commodity form of their labour in fully fledged capitalism. Equally wrong is aprioristic determinism, the doctrine of free will which in the middle of commodity society would abstract from that society. The individual himself forms a moment of the commodity society: the pure spontaneity that is attributed to him is the spontaneity which society expropriates.[13]

Hence the importance, according to Adorno, of a dialectic that recognises both freedom and unfreedom: that can grasp the moment of unfreedom within the moment of Kantian freedom itself. In these and other similarly dialectical engagements with the relations between cultural repression and manipulation on the one hand, and the subjective capacity for resistance or escape on the other, Adorno confronts questions about agency and process which are largely evaded in poststructuralist argument and discourse theory. Foucault, for example, insists both on the constructed nature of subjectivity and on the subject's capacity for resisting that construction; he denies the objectivity of truth while yet seeking in the name of such truth to reveal the distortion in those discourses attaining to the status of knowledge; he is sceptical about a repressive understanding of power while yet inviting us to conceive its workings in terms of the manipulation of some seemingly 'natural' need and desire. In all these moves, his argument has clearly shared with critical theory many of its aporias around the issue of subjectivity. What Foucault, however, does not do and Adorno does, is make explicit the sites of tension at the heart of his own account of power and desire.

Or to come back to the hedonist dimensions of this difference: the early Frankfurt school have shown themselves to be pretty pessimistic about the prospects of any alternative to the 'false' Enlightenment of capitalist modernity. In the argument of Horkheimer and Adorno, in particular, the hope of emancipation fades to a mere glimmer, and by the time of *Negative dialectics,* Adorno can find little to keep it alight other than the fact that 'critical theory' is no more than that: it is just theory or critical criticism, and might still be surprised in its all-knowing pessimism by developments in reality itself. (For even the most pessimistic theory is subject to the 'critical' consideration that its pessimism is always immanent to the society in which it evolves. Absolute despair can in this sense never be quite absolute.)[14]

Yet the essential difference is that the critical theorists *are despairing,* in other words, always damn or lament the present in the light of the possible

other order whose emergence it is preempting. This ongoing 'utopian' engagement with the question of human happiness is again quite absent from
poststructuralist critiques (and arguably also differentiates 'early' Frankfurt from
the more procedural concerns with communicative ethics which have been
the central focus of Habermas' work). Whereas Foucault has denied he has any
concern for or belief in human happiness,[15] the early Frankfurt thinkers are
passionately committed to it, however despondent about its realisation.

In what sense, if any, are the aspects of the critical theory analysis and critique
which I have made central to my discussion above of direct relevance to the
current teaching of cultural studies? Only, perhaps, in the sense that the work
of the Frankfurt School keeps open an utopian horizon without which it is
difficult to sustain any kind of progressive critical engagement with culture.
A discriminating approach to the teaching of culture and the assessment of
new cultural formations would seem to require at least some gestural
acknowledgement of this horizon. It will need to recognise, too, that one cannot
beckon towards a future redemption without a degree of humanist commitment. The alternative, more positivistic celebration of pluralism clearly offers
a form of protection against the problematic naming of political commitments.
But, this position, too, will always run up against the problem of its own
critical credentials. Many students, and teachers, will have felt the sense of
impasse created in the academy by the value relativism of the prevailing
poststructuralist critical approaches: they are sympathetic to the anti-
hierarchical and democratising impulse of poststructuralist engagements, but
aware that these can offer no coherent justification for that impulse itself, and
are thus inherently self-subverting.[16] I have tried to indicate, in respect of this
kind of theoretical problem, how the dialectical conceptions offered in critical
theory, and the sophistication of its discourse on the tensions between
constructivist and humanist approaches to subjectivity, can offer something of a
corrective.

There is the related consideration that recent developments in media and
cultural studies, though promoted in the name of a postmodernising liberation
of the subject, may be directly colluding in the maintenance of the fundamental
structures of social inequality rather than encouraging any serious awareness of
these. In what sense, it may be asked, does a cultural studies approach remain in
any radical critical relation to the wider social context if the training it provides
in postmodernist theories is simply going into the creation of more compelling
advertising copy? In what sense can an 'identity politics' scrutiny of cultural
productions be considered emancipatory if it merely translates into
commodified and consumerist conceptions of personal empowerment, rather
than any more extended concern with the liberation of oppressed groups?
Teachers and critics who appreciate the force of these questions will also be
seeking to retain cultural studies as a forum in which reservations of this kind

can be voiced about the direction and use of their discipline, and critical questions raised about the human and ecological cost of current modes of consumption and conceptions of the 'good life'. Here, too, I have tried to suggest, the quest for an alternative, more genuinely utopian mode of being, which is preserved – however precariously – in critical theory, may have something to offer the critic and teacher.

I recognise, of course, that I am here advancing the claims of critical theory only in virtue of its more explicit recognition of the requirement that cultural criticism be grounded in some theory of need. I recognise, too, that any reference to a 'more genuinely utopian' mode of being is always open to the objection that it has no privileged rights of representation of what is 'good' or 'needed'. But the fact that any utopian discourse is challengeable in its claims is not in itself a reason to renounce the discourse. Indeed it is just as implausible to suppose that human cultures can flourish without any register of the place and time beyond themselves as it is to think one can ever 'truly' represent this political sublime. If viewed in this light, the promotion of what I have termed a 'critical hedonist' perspective in cultural studies is a legitimate exercise, and one to which certain themes or dimensions of the Frankfurt School argument may still have something to contribute today.

This is particularly so, I think, in the case of the counter they offered to dominant ideologies on consumption and work. The early Frankfurt thinkers certainly wanted to get past the pleasures of consumerism but not in the name of some new-found spiritual terrorism of the flesh. Both anti-consumerists *and* sensualists of the flesh, they espoused a form of hedonism which chimes in important respects with the arguments of environmentalists today, and sounds an important note of dissent to the ever more vocationalist and work oriented priorities of contemporary society.[17] This is reflected in numerous assaults on the stupidity and tedium of capitalist work routines, in the hymns to Baudelairean '*Luxe, calme et volupté*', and, most extendedly, in the second half of *Eros and civilisation* where Marcuse calls for the 'Great refusal' of the Promethean culture hero of toil.

> If Prometheus is the culture-hero of toil, productivity, and progress through repression, then the symbols of another reality principle must be sought at the opposite pole. Orpheus and Narcissus (like Dionysus to whom they are akin: the antagonist of the god who sanctions the logic of domination, the realm of reason) stand for a very different reality. They have not become the culture-heroes of the Western world: theirs is the image of joy and fulfilment; the voice which does not command but sings; the gesture which offers and receives; the deed which is peace and ends the labour of conquest; the liberation from time which unites man with god, man with nature.[18]

Of course, all this is shamelessly Romantic. But perhaps, for that very reason, all the more worth preserving as a counter-cultural voice at the present time. And perhaps the same may be said of certain aspects of Adorno's utopian vision: notably, its holistic aesthetic imagination. By this I refer to its noted capacity to see the totality in the particular: to conceptualise the spirit or being of the historical epoch in the most seemingly insignificant and mundane of its material effects; or, to put it a touch less abstractly, a capacity to discern the horrors of the whole in the design of the door handle. As he puts it in the arresting passage from *Minima moralia*:

> Technology is making gestures precise and brutal, and with them men. It expels from movements all hesitation, deliberation, civility . . . Thus the ability is lost, for example, to close a door quietly and discreetly, yet firmly. Those of cars and refrigerators have to be slammed, others have the tendency to snap shut by themselves, imposing on those entering the bad manners of not looking behind them, not shielding the interior of the house which receives them . . . What does it mean for the subject that there are no more casement windows to open, but only sliding frames to shove, no gentle latches but turnable handles, no forecourt, no doorstep before the street, no wall around the garden? And which driver is not tempted, merely by the power of his engine, to wipe out the vermin of the street, pedestrians, children and cyclists?[19]

Adorno does not tell us 'what it means for the subject' – thus exposing himself to the objection that it is much easier to put such questions than to answer them. But he does alert us here to our own failure sufficiently to consider the impact on our sensibilities of the more minor changes and routine innovations in our lives. What he recalls us to is the rapidity of our accommodation to new technical, environmental and cultural changes, and the extent to which this may be achieved only at the cost of reducing our responsiveness and sensual enjoyment – and reducing it in a manner that simultaneously deadens us both to the sense of the reduction itself, and to the loss entailed by it.

My advocacy of these possible contributions to the background 'political imaginary' of a contemporary cultural studies has been deliberately sketchy and elliptical. Cultural studies of its nature is an ongoing and historically located critical exercise which cannot afford to become too fixated upon any given theoretical outlook. Rather than argue that today we can find ready-made arguments or political agendas in critical theory, I have wanted to suggest that there are a number of utopian themes and elements which have been marginalised or ignored in recent criticism, but which might, if updated and mediated through forms of awareness contributed by cultural studies itself, infuse teaching and thinking in this mode with a renewed sense of purpose and political inspiration.

Notes

1 Some of the themes in this chapter will be discussed in my forthcoming contribution to the *New Formations* Frankfurt School special issue (drawn from contributions to the 1998 Salford University conference on the legacy of the Frankfurt School).

2 Steele T, *The emergence of cultural studies 1945–65*, Lawrence and Wishart, London, 1997, Chapter 5 on 'The Emigré Intellectual', especially pp. 106f. In this respect, Steele contrasts their history with that of Karl Mannheim, who remained in London.

3 Jameson F, *Late Marxism: Adorno or the persistence of the dialectic*, Verso, London, 1990, p. 144.

4 Cf. Jameson (1990), pp. 141–42.

5 See, for example, the qualified defence by Jay Bernstein in his edition, *The culture industry*, Routledge, London, 1991, pp. 1–25.

6 I think we need to recognise, too, the complexity of Adorno's argument on the relations between 'free will' and cultural 'determinism'. His position looks less élitist than is sometimes supposed if proper due is given to his account of the 'dilemma of unfreedom' to which the 'culture industry' reduces the masses – who, he insists, are either incriminated in the system through toleration of it, or denied the freedom to do anything by way of resisting it. Cf. my discussion below of Adorno's discussion of 'free will' and 'determinism' in *Negative dialetics*, trans. Ashton E B, Routledge, London, 1990, pp. 260–65. Cf. Wiggershaus R, *The Frankfurt School*, trans. Martin Robertson, Polity, Cambridge, 1994, pp. 604ff.

7 Theodor Adorno and Max Horkheimer, *Dialectic of Enlightenment*, trans. John Cumming, Allen Lane, London, 1979. See especially Chapters 2 and 3.

8 On the sociology of the family and the analysis of Fascism, see the following works by Adorno: 'Anti-Semitism and Fascist propaganda', in Simmel E (ed.), *Anti-Semitism: a social disease*, International Universities Press, New York, 1946; (with Frenkel-Brunswik E, Levinson D J and Nevitt Sanford R), *The authoritarian personality*, Harper, New York, 1950; 'Freudian theory and the pattern of Fascist propaganda', in Arato A and Gebhardt E (eds), *The essential Frankfurt School reader*, Blackwell, Oxford, 1978; *Minima moralia: reflections from damaged life*, trans. Jephcott E F N, NLB, London 1974; and see Max Horkheimer, 'Authoritarianism and the family today', in Ruth Nanda Anshen (ed), *The family: its function and destiny*, Harper, New York, 1949; 'Authority and the family' in *Critical theory: selected essays*, trans. Mathew J. O'Connell *et al.*, Seabury Press, New York, 1972; 'The lessons of Fascism', in Cantril H (ed.), *Tensions that cause wars*, University of Illinois Press, Urbana, 1950.

9 Horkheimer, 'Authority and the family', p. 118.

10 These and similar criticisms have been made by Nancy Fraser in her discussion of Habermas: see Benhabib S and Cornell D (eds), *Feminism as critique*, Polity, London, 1989. See also my review in *New Left Review*, 176 (1989) (reprinted in *Troubled pleasures*, Verso, London, 1990, pp. 197–227, esp. pp. 204–06).

11 Jameson (1990), p. 142; see also, for instance, the discussions of Eagleton T, *The ideology of the aesthetic*, Blackwell, Oxford, 1990, Chapter 14, and Sim S, *Beyond aesthetics: confrontations with poststructuralism and postmodernism*, Harvester Wheatsheaf, Hemel Hempstead, 1992, Chapters 1 and 11.

12 Marcuse H, *One-dimensional man*, Routledge, London, 1964, p. xv.

13 Adorno (1990), pp. 263.

14   Adorno (1990): see the 'Meditations on metaphysics', pp. 361–405; and cf. David Held's discussion of the similarities with Kant, and Adorno's feeling that 'Kant's' stress on the import of what lies beyond the mind must be saved', *Introduction to critical theory: Horkheimer to Habermas*, Hutchinson, London, 1980, pp. 221f.
15   'Now, I do not think that the notion of happiness is truly thinkable. Happiness does not exist – and the happiness of men exists still less' (Foucault interviewed by *La Fiera Litteraria*, September 1967, cit. in Miller J, *The passion of Michel Foucault*, Harper Collins, London, 1993, p. 173).
16   This impasse has been explored by number of commentators in recent times. Particularly helpful and nuanced discussion is to be found in Squires J (ed.), *Principled positions*, Lawrence and Wishart, London 1993.
17   Many arguments of Marcuse's on repressive desublimation and the transcendence of the Performance Principle are clearly illustrative of this theme. It also finds an interesting, if in many respects challengeable, reflection in Adorno's essay on Aldous Huxley's *Brave new world*: Adorno, 'Aldous Huxley and Utopia', in *Prisms*, trans. Samuel and Shierry Weber, Spearman, London, 1967, p. 99.
18   Herbert Marcuse, *Eros and civilisation*, Boston, 1972, p. 120.
19   'Do not knock', in Adorno (1974), p. 40. Cf. Adorno's remark that 'while the notion of society may not be deduced from any individual facts, nor on the other hand be apprehended as an individual fact itself, there is nonetheless no social fact which is not determined by society as a whole', in 'Society', *Salmagundi*, Nos. 10–11 (1969–70), p. 145.

6 Whither cultural studies?

Jim McGuigan

I ask myself an impossible question, Whither cultural studies? There are other questions that should probably be asked first, like, What is it? To find out what it is, part of the answer would involve addressing the question, Where has it been? If it were possible to answer these preliminary questions satisfactorily, that would still only provide a clue to where cultural studies is going. In the uncertain world in which we live, it is wise to rule out of order faith in prediction straight away. It may be feasible, however, to identify current trends but even that strategy presents great difficulties since cultural studies is now going down so many different avenues that it is impracticable to keep track of them all. Whether dispersal in its various forms results in cancerous fragmentation or healthy diversity is hard to say. Also, the claim to objectivity in the following account should be treated with some scepticism since it is quite self-consciously marked by my own situated experience of participating in the institutionalisation of cultural studies. Inevitably, whatever I say about the direction(s) of cultural studies is framed, consciously or otherwise, by where I would like it (them) to go and by my current anxiety specifically about a lack of direction or, rather, dynamism in Britain where cultural studies is said to have originated. I sense that the action has moved elsewhere.

Actual conditions

Two general points need to be made at the outset. First, any nostalgic belief that cultural studies has ever been coherent and unified, with a very clear sense of direction, is most likely the effect of hindsight. It is tempting to see coherence in the past and there is some justification since what became labelled 'cultural studies' was at one time local to Britain and in a very particular location there, the institutionalisation of New Left politics in certain enclaves of academia and higher education, which in itself was a much broader phenomenon than the constitution of this field of study. Even that national history has recently been disputed by James Carey (1997), an American, who says the term 'cultural studies' was first used in the USA in the early 1960s.[1] This is a pointless dispute. That left-wing intellectualism, on both sides of the Atlantic, became institutionalised in university humanities and social science departments where the politics of culture was to be an abiding preoccupation is an extremely pervasive phenomenon and it is very largely what allows the term 'cultural studies' to perform such a promiscuous function.

The second general point, and linked to the first, is that the development of cultural studies must be understood institutionally and not only in terms of the movement of ideas and successive waves of representational politics, which is to recall an argument made by Raymond Williams in 'The future of cultural studies', towards the end of his life. Williams was keen to contest Stuart Hall's account of the formation of cultural studies in terms of key texts and organising paradigms.[2] He wanted to remind practitioners of its origins in adult education, the actual conditions and agencies of its emergence in Britain, something which Tom Steele has recently documented.[3] Moreover, Williams urged a recovery of the popular educational project against the excessive theoreticism that had overcome cultural studies in some quarters and the crude vocationalism being advocated by the Thatcher government for education in general. As an old adult educationalist, Williams raised doubts concerning curriculum reification in the Open University's distance learning course on popular culture and clearly he was nostalgic about the negotiated curriculum of University Extension and Workers' Educational Association classes during the 1950s. What he would have made of the massification of higher education in the 1990s, especially in the ex-polytechnic 'new universities', and further exhortations to vocational relevance by a Labour government is open to speculation.

In this particular institutional context, cultural studies is most closely associated with media studies and communication studies. That is the context where I have been working until recently so I am predisposed to comment upon it. It is now generally appreciated that the demographic characteristics of students at old and new universities are somewhat different from one another. The old universities tend to cream off a larger proportion of school leavers with high 'A' level grades and from comparatively well-off backgrounds which they can afford to leave so as to go off to uni. A much greater proportion of students at new universities come from the locality and region. Significant numbers are mature in years and are seeking a second chance, typically and not just stereotypically, for instance, women in their thirties, whose own careers were hitherto subordinate to bringing up children who have grown old enough to look after themselves, and similarly aged men who have experienced redundancy or were without a previous career path. Because they are strapped for cash and have to work on the side, such students are, in effect, studying part-time. This is the adult education of the 1990s and, amongst other things, it is a salient characteristic of media and cultural studies in the ex-polys. Many such students may be disappointed by the career outcome of their studies. A degree in media and cultural studies is no guarantee of entry to professional employment or even a lowly job in the communications and cultural industries. However, these students may be less disappointed than those school leavers who were given entirely instrumentalist and unrealistic reasons for taking media and cultural studies, in the first instance, by careers advisors and others. Yet, on the more positive side, both kinds of student might, nevertheless, have experienced a form of contemporary education which is both relevant and intellectually demanding while actually helping them make sense of themselves, their places in the world and opportunities for action.

Media and cultural studies are popular subjects across the universities – and not only in the new ones – but they are by no means the most popular. Business studies and management courses are by far the most heavily populated. Psychology has also seen a spectacular increase in numbers. Yet, it is media and cultural studies that attracts the most attention, perhaps not surprisingly, from the media. I want eventually to comment upon that media attention which is usually hostile and make out a case for the educational – and not only vocational – value of media and cultural studies. To begin, however, I shall draw specifically on my own personal experience of becoming caught up in cultural studies, largely because I don't think there was anything peculiarly unique about my experience.

Discovering cultural studies

In the 1970s I studied sociology and literature as an undergraduate in what was then a 'new university'. On the sociology side of the degree there was an option in the sociology of literature. It might have seemed an obvious option to take for those of us on the joint sociology and literature programme but we were warned off doing so by the head of literature who thought it would have a damaging effect on our literary criticism: all that sociological jargon. This dramatised my growing personal experience of dissatisfaction with the disciplinarity that had already been attacked by the '68 generation, an attack propagated in books with titles like *Counter course*. Also, the influence of Marxist scholarship, which was going through such a huge revival at the time, followed swiftly by feminism, worked very strongly against disciplinarity. Then, I wound up at another university, an older one, as an SSRC-funded research student in sociology. Fortunately, the sociology department was very open-minded and didn't seem to care that myself and several other postgrads were uncommitted to a narrow definition of sociological disciplinarity. Our interests in Western Marxism and cultural analysis inevitably led us onto an interdisciplinary terrain. Although it was a good and permissive sociology department, I had the distinct feeling that I was in the wrong place. The place to be was Birmingham. I hadn't heard of the Centre for Contemporary Cultural Studies when I was an undergraduate but I soon did as a postgraduate. As each now classic edition of the Birmingham Working Papers came out we fell upon it eagerly. They really seemed to know what they were doing at Birmingham. It was only later that I discovered the coherence of Birmingham was more evident to outsiders than it was to insiders. As postgrads teaching part-time for the WEA, we would try out some of the Birmingham material which, at the time, did not go down so well as Hoggart, Williams and other strands of research from, say, the sociologies of art, media, work and deviance that we thought relevant to cultural studies.

Subsequently, after periods as a researcher at the Arts Council and script editor at the BBC, I turned up in the non–university sector of higher educa-tion and was very soon designing undergraduate courses in cultural studies. In the universities, it was still almost exclusively a postgraduate subject. Teaching in a college of higher education did not leave much time for research but we certainly thought we were at 'the cutting edge' with our courses. There was a sense then that everyone teaching cultural studies in a poly or a CHE was inventing cultural studies as a teaching subject and you had to be inventive because there was not much actual research to draw upon. There was an inspirational literature and journals like *Screen* and, more usefully, *Screen educa-tion* that are now given nodal status in historical accounts of the field, but these sources did not provide enough material for whole degree courses. New journals like *Media, culture and society* had not yet made much impact. *New Left review* was still a very major source of theorising but, mostly, too advanced for undergraduate reading material. In practice, we were applying theories to what was going on and it was going on so quickly that the academic publishing industry had not yet caught up. Material came from anywhere and everywhere. Student projects were original and when they were good they were publishable, if only there were the publishing outlets. We also swaggered around the place boasting that we were doing soap opera with the students mainly in order to upset the staff in the English department. They did not seem to know much about theory but we did and were doing something really popular with it. Those were the days . . . Cut to the present.

HEFC/RAE/TQA/Graduateness, etc

Then, the Tories decided we could teach double the numbers for half the money. An exaggeration, but it felt like that and still does. Communication/cultural/media studies had enjoyed a disreputable status, Mickey Mouse subjects taught by KGB agents with the aim of destroying the fabric of Western culture and civilisation (a curious conspiracy between Hollywood and Moscow) – but cheap. These were subjects that could be rapidly expanded. Simultaneously, the ex-polys were given a look into HEFC research funding. So, where are your publications? Some lucky ones even got a rating and some money. A mini-bonanza followed for the likes of Routledge. Next thing, research grants. Few media and cultural studies departments in the new universities had experience of pulling in such money, with some notable excep-tions such as Westminster, yet they had to try and catch up on that front as well. Funnily enough, even in this field, which had largely been developed in the old polys, most of the money from, say, the ESRC Media Economics and Media Culture programme seemed to go to the old universities that were also putting on undergraduate media and cultural studies by then. Although some ex-poly people may still feel aggrieved by the rigging of the game, in fact, there was a convergence happening. In some old universities it was becoming nearly as tough as in the new universities, with new managerialism and all that. The transition to university status for the ex-polys has had uneven results; and has been especially weak where second-rate academics have become third-rate managers, and models of business organisation have prevailed over properly academic and educational procedures and facilitation. Teaching quality assessment was another thing to deal with: media and cultural studies have just been done.

This wasn't what it was supposed to be about. One now reads articles by young Americans who go on about the 'anti-discipline' of cultural studies and are concerned with contesting standard accounts of the 'origins' of cultural studies (and being anti-academic in a very academic way in well-funded universities where students paying fees for their tuition is not a new and shocking idea).[4] But, it's not so far from the truth, historically. Cultural studies refused to define itself: hence, so much literature on what it is about. Some say this is normal for a new discipline – but, hang on, it wasn't supposed to be a discipline. Even now, in the straitened circumstances and madcap organisation under which many lecturers try to do their work, there is a reluctance to concede the point. You can give this a postmodernist gloss, of course, yet the fact of the matter is that we were, in a small way, part of the radical conscience of social democracy, trained to ask awkward questions, and beneficiaries of an earlier phase of expansion in higher education. In this, we were always dependent upon a certain patronage and, indeed, tolerance.

I have argued elsewhere that in the institutional realities where we find ourselves, we have to recognise that cultural studies is an academic field of study (not a 'discipline') and not a political movement.[5] It does, however, offer a space for what I would still call 'progressive' currents of thought and, to a lesser extent, practice; but its emplacement is, for better or worse, in universities either as a free-standing subject or as part of something else, such as literature or sociology. In consequence, cultural studies, whatever its particular emplacement, has to meet certain pragmatic requirements in both teaching and research in a British university system undergoing dramatic transformation from 'élite' to 'mass'. A case has to be made out quite specifically, however, for why media and cultural studies are worthy university subjects in ways that are not simply reducible to immediate vocational pay-off. That case would be fortified by the further development of coherent and mutually informing traditions of research that are seen, at least to some extent, as accumulative and not just constantly subject to high speed revision in response to sudden theoretical spasms.

There is another thing that should be said, in passing, about the development of cultural studies which branches out from the particular institutional context under discussion. This is the impact on literary study and sociology. Take, for instance, the influence of Terry Eagleton's *Literary theory* (1983), which has sold in the hundreds of thousands.[6] Cultural studies jived up lit. crit., first, by introducing Theory and, second, by installing issues of Identity, thus allowing literary study to do something not so very different from Leavisite education for life and without the old style moralism. In sociology we find a 'cultural turn',[7] which may tell us something about the postmodernisation of society but also tells us quite a bit about what entertains students who are less inclined to become social workers, and for good reason, nowadays. In fact, a great deal of sociology today is indistinguishable from cultural studies, something which is not entirely appreciated on the media studies end of the spectrum.

In the rest of this chapter I want to consider three matters: first, the codification of cultural studies in the kind of context that has already been outlined; second, the internationalisation of cultural studies; and, third, the educational rationale for cultural and media studies in circumstances where their practical utility is repeatedly called into question.

The cultural studies stor(e)y

With the institutionalisation of cultural studies there inevitably comes the codification of the subject. Textbooks get written; anthologies are compiled. This presents a tricky problem for a field in which practitioners have prided themselves on its ineffable quality and its indefinability in conventional disciplinary terms. We do need the textbooks and the anthologies, otherwise the subject is unteachable in conditions of mass higher education with huge pressures on library holdings that are only partly relieved by what can be snaffled from the Internet. I am to blame for some of these textbooks myself. Cultural studies is an institutionalised subject. How else could it exist? Undoubtedly, something may be lost, however, in the codification.

One of the main exponents of such codification in Britain is John Storey, who has written and edited a number of textbooks on cultural studies and popular culture that are a ubiquitous presence on new university undergraduate reading lists in media and cultural studies. His approach in, for example, *An introductory guide to cultural theory and popular culture* (1993) is to structure the text as a series of handy summaries of key concepts, key theorists and key books.[8] Now, this immediately runs the risk common to such 'essential' textbooks across the humanities and social sciences of thus enabling students to avoid actually reading the primary literature in the subject. Storey, however, supports his textbook with another one which is a selection of key readings in cultural theory and popular culture, presumably in order to avoid that very risk.[9] None of this, in itself, is objectionable. Yet, although Storey has deliberately put himself in a secondary position to primary scholarship in the field, by performing a disseminatory, popularising role, he allows himself to pontificate with a quite breathtaking authority about the subject as well. So, his textbooks not only provide the study material: Storey also tells his student readers exactly what to think about that material, an approach which is rather inimical to the open-ended and exploratory qualities that had made cultural studies different from the established disciplines where the dead-weight of tradition was laid, cyclically, upon the brains of the living. In addition to the questionable pedagogic strategy promoted by Storey, there is the problem of 'politics', to which I shall return.

Another of Storey's works is *What is cultural studies? A reader*, in which he compiles yet another set of key readings, this time texts that try to define the subject. In his introduction to that book, Storey points out that the traditional definition of a discipline requires the identification of its object, its method(s) and its history.[10] So, we are treated to brief discussion of the culture concept, mention of textual and ethnographic methods and the enduring message handed down through the history of cultural studies is extracted for us: 'we make culture and we are made by culture; there is agency and there is structure'.[11] I'm sorry, but I read that line in the voice of John Major rather than Karl Marx. Storey aims to have it both ways: he both simplifies and complexifies. He is not to be caught out by actually answering the question in the title of his book. After all, if you are postmodern, you should be able to live with undecidability. Storey knows what cultural studies is, but he won't tell us. What Storey is really interested in stressing in his introduction is that cultural studies is a *Political Project*. Now, that cannot be the definition of the field, surely? The Conservative party is also a political project. Is cultural studies like the Conservative party, then? There is a real problem here about the sense in which cultural studies is supposed to be political. For Storey, this has something to do with Marxism but not in any straightforward sense. Cultural studies is now 'post-Marxist', which among other things means it is as much concerned with gender and sexual politics as with class struggle. Moreover, Storey concludes his introduction by saying you can't be part of cultural studies and a racist. The politics of 'race' and ethnicity are also a distinguishing feature of cultural studies. Thus, cultural studies combines feminism, gay and lesbian politics, anti-racism and the traces of class politics and the critique of capitalism. Storey's account of cultural studies is curiously consistent with the right-wing American depiction of the field as a rag-bag of oppositional politics. And while most people in the field would subscribe to oppositional politics, so would many in other fields. In some ways, Storey is on safer ground when emphasising the study of popular culture as a distinguishing feature of cultural studies (together, I would add, with its more sociological view of culture in general) than when caught up in defining the field in terms of the politics of difference.

The political rhetoric of cultural studies is in danger of playing into the hands of its enemies by confirming their deepest prejudices. From within cultural studies, however, an important challenge has been posed by Tony Bennett's recycled paper in *What is cultural studies?* Bennett's 'Putting policy into cultural studies', originally published in the well-known collection edited by Grossberg, Nelson and Treichler (1992), calls into question the neo-Gramscian rhetoric of training students to become organic, counter-hegemonic intellectuals, cadres in a cultural war rather than workers in a cultural economy.[12] Bennett's own position, which I personally find too instrumental,[13] is to revise cultural studies as a tool of policy analysis that is oriented towards actual institutional processes; and towards producing cultural 'technicians' of governmentality rather than counter-hegemonic intellectuals or even cultural critics. In spite of its deliberately limited purview, there is a realism in Bennett's position that is entirely absent from the Storey curriculum for cultural studies in the ex-polytechnics. In Bennett's further elaborated position, the politics is retained but more modestly and the case for a closer relationship to actually existing occupational practices is spelt out.[14]

The national and the global

Cultural studies has now become internationalised, transnationalised and globalised. There are three distinguishable yet interrelated aspects to this development that I want to comment upon. The first is the diffusion of the nomination, 'cultural studies', which is only partly related to the migration of scholars and ideas. The second is the redefinition of past and continuing work in various different academic fields around the world as 'cultural studies'. The third is to do with developments in the 'real world' that undermine notions of national culture that were the focus of cultural study in the broadest sense and not just in the sense of 'cultural studies'. To survey each of these aspects in depth is beyond the scope of this chapter. At the risk of seeming narrowly nationalistic, my remarks are largely confined to the implications for research, scholarship and teaching in Britain.

In the Australian and North American literature on cultural studies you find a phenomenon called 'British cultural studies'.[15] Around 1990, one of those curious alterations of perspective occurred. It happens at moments when one's own ethnocentrism is suddenly cast into sharp relief or 'exposed'. The way mind-sets are shaped by our own positionality, which is constructed in so many different ways, is one of the abiding preoccupations of cultural studies in any case. It was reported back from abroad that what was going on in Britain regarding cultural studies was of interest in places like Australia and the USA. I remember, in the 1980s, being impressed by the codification of cultural studies as a teaching object/subject in the Open University's popular culture course but it never struck me then that it was peculiarly 'British'. But, I suppose, it must have been. This identification of cultural studies as 'British' was double-edged in its implications. It both suggested a nationally based coherence to the field which was of international merit, yet, also, suggested a field unduly circumscribed by that national base. Ex-pats had carried the 'message' to Australia, for instance, but soon a reaction set in against 'British cultural studies' as a postcolonial imposition. In response, a confident and extremely lively

'Australian cultural studies' emerged in a country that is much more self-consciously a nation, for reasons of historical subordination, than the multinational Britain which had been dominating rather than dominated historically.

The situation in the USA has been different. For a start, the USA lacks a sense of insecurity about its nationhood, which is one of the most troubling features of that country's role in the world. The USA has enormous powers of absorption. Something like 'British cultural studies' could be picked up, devoured, digested and defecated with great ease. The really significant thing about cultural studies in the USA is not, however, so much to do with what it learnt from Britain but with how the term 'cultural studies' was used to rename all sorts of past and present forms of scholarship and education: for example, in the trajectory in literary study from formalism through structuralism to a brand of poststructuralist and textualist cultural studies. Moreover, on the sociological side, that writers like Norman Denzin should see an affinity between the Chicago School of symbolic interactionism and cultural studies is quite justified.[16] Symbolic interactionism certainly influenced Birmingham. In fact, the subcultural research of 'the Birmingham School' in the 1970s could be described as a Marxified symbolic interactionism. So, cultural studies comes to name diverse currents of work: for instance, schools of Indian cultural studies have been uncovered.[17]

If I stress the Australian and US contexts here, it is to point up, as much as anything else, the parlous state of cultural studies in Britain. Surveying these developments some time ago, Graeme Turner noted 'the relative slowdown in Britain'.[18] And, he suggested this was to do with the institutional context, the impact of Thatcherism on the universities and polytechnics. Just as British cultural studies was becoming an export item its intellectual force was waning at home – due, I believe, mainly to diminishing resources, increasing pressures of teaching and, rather more diffusely, the crisis of socialism. Furthermore, it is now almost impossible to publish a book in media and cultural studies with any of the major publishers that has a specifically British focus. Such publishers function 'globally', which mostly means selling books and journals in the USA: every other market is 'peanuts', as they say, in comparison. For example, the Association for Media, Communication and Cultural Studies, the main professional association for the field in Britain, does not have a Journal of (British) Media and Cultural Studies. And, although a significant number of journals in the field are based in Britain, their purview is 'global'. I suspect, as well, that there is a schism opening up between British scholars of cultural studies who have substantial international connections and those who do not. And, if such a schism does exist, it probably corresponds quite closely to the great divide between old and new university departments.

I am all for the internationalisation/transnationalisation/globalisation of media and cultural studies insofar as these studies relate to actual trends in the world, trends that are so admirably charted in Manuel Castells's great work on 'the information age'.[19] We cannot understand the ascendant developments in communications and culture satisfactorily in narrowly nationalistic frameworks (including American ones), although national and local circumstances do remain of prime importance in the everyday lives of most people. I feel it necessary, however, to draw some attention to the specific problems of media and cultural studies as an institutionalised field of study in Britain on one of those rare publishing occasions when writing about specifically British matters is okay. Still, this requires a comparative dimension.

Educational purposes

In a similarly entitled chapter to this one, Ellen Messer-Davidow has declared that cultural studies in the USA is in trouble. The 'big tent' of cultural studies has been subject to a concerted assault upon its educational and political purposes.[20] This has been orchestrated by privately and lavishly funded right-wing organisations like the Madison Centre for Educational Affairs, the Intercollegiate Studies Institute and the National Association of Scholars. They have stressed a decline in academic standards and the undermining of Western Culture and Civilisation, trends that are said to be associated with the 'political correctness' of cultural studies and related activities in the American universities. This culminated in an attack on the National Endowment for the Humanities, the major source of public funding for 'disinterested' cultural research.

There has been nothing comparable to such an organised conservative backlash against media and cultural studies in Britain on grounds of 'traditional' cultural education. Both the British Academy and the Economic and Social Research Council have even given some limited recognition to media and cultural studies in recent years. Alleged trivialisation and incomprehensibility of language, though, are routinely lampooned in the still relatively few reviews of media and cultural studies books that appear in the national 'quality' press, usually representing stuck-up bemusement, however, rather than a political campaign based upon the defence of standards and eternal verities. The main assault has come, instead, from some journalists who cannot see any value in specifically 'media studies' from the point of view of vocational outcomes.[21] It is interesting that the more instrumentally disposed end of the broad spectrum of media and cultural studies should become the focus of critical attention in Britain. At the other end of the spectrum there are versions of cultural studies and film studies, mainly in the older universities, that make no instrumentalist claims and are, most typically, still caught up in the old struggle over what counts as knowledge with the 'traditional' humanities in more or less the same academic space as 'the enemy'.

In the ex-polytechnics, humanities and social science courses have been more generally, albeit often just rhetorically, 'applied' and 'practical' in orientation. Although there are several variations on the theme, there is supposed to be a relation between 'theory' and 'practice' in many media and cultural studies courses. On the problem of demonstrating that relationship, media and cultural studies are vulnerable, unlike, for instance, applied social science linked to producing qualified social workers. By and large, universities are extremely marginal to the certification of media professions. Training needs for creative and management posts have usually been met by the cultural and media industries in-house or, for technical employment, at sub-degree level. Moreover, many university departments simply do not have the up-to-date technology and facility for instruction in practical skills to, say, the standards of mainstream television. Some try to do the impossible or, rather, claim to do so on false pretences. More typically, an argument is constructed about giving students practical experience which does not aim to match high-level training. Such practical experience has characteristically been informed by 'theory': so, students may have sought themselves to subvert, for instance, mainstream television discourse in their video projects, or been required to do so by unrealistic lecturers. That is probably not so common now as it used to be. And, although a genre of 'video art' has derived from such education, there has developed greater humility about the discourses of mainstream television, the production of which can only be taught in a modest fashion in many departments.[22]

Complaints have been lodged against 'media studies' not only by the staffers of the 'quality' press and broadcasting but also by journalists and other media producers who have, for whatever reason, found themselves teaching practical modules on university media and cultural studies courses. At the Standing Conference on Cultural, Communication and Media Studies in Higher Education which met at Nottingham Trent University in January 1998, one such journalist/educationalist denounced her tenured academic colleagues for teaching useless theory and exploiting part-time and temporary-contract staff like herself who deliver the practical modules that students really want and need. In view of such spats, Tim O'Sullivan is right to argue that a 'middle way', a 'coexistence of theory with practice', must be sought between two one-sided responses, the first which merely asserts the superior value of an education based upon critical theorising over a reduction to 'training' and the second which succumbs completely to the demands of vocationalism.[23]

The fate of media and cultural studies in this respect must be seen in relation to recent debates about 'the postmodern university'. Universities are unavoidably implicated in the reproduction of certain kinds of labour power. No longer are they confined, however, under conditions of massification, to certifying entry to 'the professions'. A degree of any kind is no guarantee of election. In a flexible labour market even skills are not fixed assets. The preference that employers still show for graduates from older and well-established universities is to a significant extent to do with the cultural capital such graduates are said to possess, a discursive confidence and habitus acquired through élite education and a privileged background. The new universities, in this context, are inclined to concentrate on niches in the labour market. And, according to that strategy, media and cultural studies courses strive increasingly to meet 'the needs' of the media and cultural industries. Yet, still, job skills are most likely to be learnt on the job. 'Work experience', attachments and placements are probably the most efficient means of orienting students towards opportunities in their chosen labour markets, more efficient, I suspect, than much of the skills training on undergraduate courses. This and the development of high-level postgraduate diploma courses designed and funded in partnerships with industry sectors offer the best opportunities of meeting 'the needs' of industry. The vocational dimension should become much more realistic than it is at present and the promises concerning occupational outcome that are made by undergraduate courses should be modest and honest. Then, I believe, an argument can be made out for the value of media and cultural studies that is hardly ever made when a narrow instrumentalism prevails. We should argue – and, I believe, with considerable justification – that media and cultural studies courses provide a good education for living and working in the 'postmodern' world.

The argument here is broadly twofold. First, it involves a defence and renewal of the critical intelligence that is fostered by humanities and social scientific education generally. In such education at its best, students learn to think for themselves, to ask questions for which the answers are not already known, to investigate, to debate alternative perspectives, to develop an ethical good sense and criticise injustice. I am struck by the way in which engineering students in the USA are required to study 'culture', either still construed in some places as a 'civilising heritage' or elsewhere as inculcating a critical, multicultural awareness. This kind of 'liberal' education has been squeezed in Britain where narrow-minded and short-sighted instrumentalism is currently the order of the day. In my opinion, media and cultural studies are at a comparative advantage when it comes to encouraging the habits of critical thought among students. In a world of complexly mediated experience, where all objects are also signs and there are real uncertainties about how to live, to actually study these matters rigorously must surely have something going for it.

The second general point is that none of this is irrelevant to work. If it is the case that careers are becoming disaggregated, that there are no longer 'jobs for life' and a continuously learning attitude is a vital capacity for survival, then, the critical intelligence cultivated by even the most theoretical of media and cultural studies courses is useful indeed. In my admittedly biased experience, media and cultural studies graduates display an impressive street wisdom and everyday nous for coping with the ordinary dilemmas of late-modernity – and for finding employment. Lateral thought, discursive acuity, communicational technique, team-working competences, such qualities are cultivated routinely on the courses they have taken.

Notes

1 See Carey J, 'Reflections on the project of (American) cultural studies', in Ferguson M and Golding P (eds), *Cultural studies in question*, Sage, London, Thousand Oaks and New Delhi, 1997.
2 See Williams R, 'The future of cultural studies', in *The politics of modernism*, Verso, London and New York, 1989; and Hall S, 'Cultural studies – two paradigms', in *Media, Culture and Society*, Vol 2 No 2, 1980.
3 Steele T, *The emergence of cultural studies 1945–1965*, Lawrence and Wishart, London, 1997.
4 For example, see Wright H K, 'Dare we de-centre Birmingham? Troubling the "Origin" and trajectories of cultural studies', *European journal of cultural studies*, Vol 1 No 1, 1998.
5 McGuigan J (ed.), *Cultural methodologies*, Sage, London, Thousand Oaks and New Delhi, 1997.
6 Eagleton T, *Literary theory: an introduction*, Blackwell, Oxford, 1983.
7 See Chaney D, *The cultural turn – scene-setting essays on contemporary cultural history*, Routledge, London and New York, 1994.
8 See Storey J, *An introductory guide to cultural theory and popular culture*, Hemel Hempstead, 1993; and see also Storey J (ed.), *Cultural theory and popular culture – a reader*, Harvester Wheatsheaf, Hemel Hempstead, 1994; and *What is cultural studies? A reader*, Edward Arnold, London and New York, 1996.
9 Storey (ed.), 1994.
10 Storey, 1996, p. 1.
11 Storey, 1996, p. 11.
12 See Grossberg L, Nelson C and Treichler P (eds), *Cultural studies*, Routledge, London and New York, 1992.
13 See McGuigan J, *Culture and the public sphere*, Routledge, London and New York, 1996.
14 Bennett T, 'Towards a pragmatics for cultural studies', in McGuigan (ed.), 1997.
15 See Turner G, *British cultural studies – an introduction*, Routledge, London and New York, second edition, 1996 (first published 1990).
16 See Denzin N, *Symbolic interactionism and cultural studies: the politics of interpretation*, Blackwell, Cambridge, MA and Oxford, 1992.
17 See Sardar Z and Van Loon B, 1997, *Cultural studies for beginners*, Icon Books, Cambridge, 1997.
18 Turner G (ed.), *Nation, culture, text: Australian cultural and media studies*, Routledge, London and New York, 1993, p. 3.
19 See Castells M, *The rise of the network society*, Blackwell, Malden, MA and Oxford, 1996; *The power of identity*, Malden, MA and Oxford, 1997; *End of millennium*, Malden, MA and Oxford, 1998.
20 Messer-Davidow E, 'Whither cultural studies?', in Long E (ed.), *From sociology to cultural studies: new perspectives*, Blackwell, Malden, MA and Oxford, 1997.
21 See O'Sullivan T, 'What lies between mechatronics and medicine? The critical mass of media studies', *Soundings*, Vol 5 (1997).
22 See Holland P, *The television handbook*, Routledge, London and New York, 1997.
23 O'Sullivan, 1997, p. 219.

Part II

Cultural Studies and its Others

7   Teaching queerly: politics, pedagogy and identity in lesbian and gay studies

Andy Medhurst

> A row broke out yesterday over the appointment of Britain's first professor of lesbian and gay studies. Conservative MP Ann Widdecombe branded the move 'a phenomenal waste of public money'. She added: 'It would be far better spent giving young people academic and vocational training to ensure they get jobs. It is not at all clear to me what kind of job this would qualify someone for.' (*Sunday Mirror*, 5 July 1998)

It is always gratifying to know that you're upsetting the right people. If Ann Widdecombe, a politician so liberal-minded that she once presided over the shackling with manacles of a pregnant prison inmate to a hospital bed, finds the idea of Lesbian and Gay studies both perplexing and indefensible, then those of us involved in furthering the progress of this relatively new area of academic work can hardly avoid savouring a small glow of delight. This chapter, however, needs to move beyond extrapolated smugness. What I hope to try and sketch, sift and worry over in the next few pages is a set of concerns and questions brought into focus by the developing profile of Lesbian and Gay studies in contemporary British higher education.

My blithe usage of the term 'Lesbian and Gay studies' is not, of course, intended to imply that such an entity exists in any remotely settled or stable form. Some attempts have been made at definition, such as the claim by the editors of the dauntingly hefty *Lesbian and Gay studies reader* that:

> Lesbian/gay studies does for sex and sexuality approximately what women's studies does for gender. It intends to establish the analytical centrality of sex and sexuality within many different fields of enquiry . . . In particular, lesbian/gay studies focuses intense scrutiny on the cultural production, dissemination, and vicissitudes of sexual meanings.[1]

As the best available summary of the Lesbian and Gay studies project I have no quibble with that, mainly because of all the loopholes it offers. Its discourse of 'approximately' and 'many different' and 'vicissitudes' is hardly a language of rigid parameters, which is just as it should be for an area of academic work still only just starting to coagulate into coherence, an area which in other helpfully elastic formations has been called an 'interdisciplinary . . . field-in-progress' and 'an eclectic intellectual guerrilla [that] uses any serviceable means'.[2]

In the same paragraph as that last quotation, Sally Munt also suggests a parallel between Lesbian and Gay studies and cultural studies: 'both areas are committed to exposing the naturalising discourses that reinforce commonsense assumptions in everyday life, discourses that have oppressive effects'. This linkage (or perhaps even parentage, with Lesbian and Gay studies cast as one of the many constructively troublesome offspring of cultural studies) is a very appealing one, especially given the broad remit of the book for which I am writing this chapter. Yet it would be both gullible and premature to assume that cultural studies always sees questions of sexuality and sexual identity as priorities on its agenda. Open, for example, an otherwise excellent introductory reader in cultural studies and read this: 'cultural studies assumes that capitalist industrial societies are societies divided unequally along ethnic, gender, generational and class lines'.[3] Notice anything missing? Here, and in many other places, the cultural studies agenda is set entirely without reference to sexuality, and this is the chief reason Lesbian and Gay studies is a necessary intervention. Its fundamental purpose is to ensure that such exclusions are exposed, rebutted and redressed: it insists that the map of cultural analysis cannot be drawn without taking sexuality into account. Lesbian and Gay studies, then, is all about putting sexuality centre stage.

But rather than dwell too long here on terminologies and categorisations, I want to move on to consider what happens when you take questions of sexuality into a rather more everyday space: the classroom. The issues that action sets in motion are varied and complex, touching on difficult matters of identity and authority, protocol and pedagogy, politics and the academy, belonging and desire – matters so littered with pitfalls that the standard disclaimer of limitations which prefaces (or should preface) every academic essay is even more obligatory than usual. What follows has no delusions of definitiveness; it is partial, anecdotal, tentative, corner-cutting, self-centred, more-questions-than-answers and worryingly light on footnotes. I offer only one individual's reflections on his experiences of teaching as a queer, teaching queers and non-queers about queernesses, and teaching queerly.

Since this chapter has a close-to-solipsistic focus on my own teaching, a few words about the contexts of that teaching are necessary. I lecture in media studies at the University of Sussex, and take care to ensure that, where relevant, issues concerning sexuality have a place in all of my courses. This might, for example, take the form of using sexuality as the case study when lecturing on media representations of social and cultural identities. Most importantly in the context of this chapter, I am also fortunate enough to teach an option on an MA programme called 'Sexual dissidence and cultural change'. This programme, the first in Britain to have Lesbian and Gay studies as its core concern, is one of a menu of MAs offered by the English Literature faculty, since its co-founders in 1991 (Alan Sinfield and Jonathan Dollimore) were both Professors of English, but its syllabus is not confined to literary texts or approaches. It would not, I think, be unfair to call the MA a cultural studies course centred on sexuality; my option within it is called 'Queering popular culture', and attempts to introduce students to the intersections between sexual identities and popular cultural texts, activities and practices. It is methodologically eclectic, though I always stress the importance of students reflecting upon their own experiences and involvements. The option began life with a narrower focus, as 'Homosexualities, film and television', but was later renamed and broadened to include study of other cultural fields such as the press, fashion and popular music. It is also available to students on the University's media studies MA, and can, under certain circumstances, be taken by students on other MAs across the Arts and Social Sciences. The Sexual Dissidence MA, and my course within it, is the source of most of the reflections that follow, though in a later section I want to consider the advantages and drawbacks of fixing a 'sexuality label' to a course as opposed to dealing with matters of sexuality across a wider curriculum.

Who's queer here? Sexual identity in the classroom

The most basic level at which questions of sexual identity impact upon teaching is the sexual identity of the teacher. Queer teachers need to consider the strategies of how, when or whether to come out to their students. Personally I prefer to go for broke, giving an autobiographically rooted lecture on sexuality to two-hundred-plus students on a first-year undergraduate prelim course. Common-room gossip does the rest, alongside the carefully placed signifiers in those mini-biographies all faculty are obliged to write for incoming students' handbooks. As for the MA teaching, the sheer fact of participating in that programme is seen by many as an acknowledgement of homosexuality – although this assumption is far from appropriate, since options within the Sexual Dissidence programme have over the years been taught by heterosexuals and bisexuals as well as lesbians and gay men.

That last fact raises some interesting questions. After all, courses based (to simplify them horribly) on matters of identity have a history of being taught by those who inhabit that identity. It is hard to dislodge the belief that you have to be it to teach it, a belief which separates 'identity courses' from longer-established disciplines. Teachers of Latin are not expected to be ancient Romans, any more than teachers of chemistry are expected to be small piles of powder, but teachers of women's studies *are* expected to be women. Identity courses are most frequently taught from the inside outwards, from experience to analysis. Indeed, those twin terms are not, in the best teaching about identity, poles at either end of a linear journey, but interconnected discourses that comment on and strengthen each other. The rationale for this might be summed up as 'I can understand X because I belong to X', a rationale which then blossoms into the politicised pedagogy of 'because I belong to X and have used that experience to deepen my understanding of X I am better equipped to improve the lot of X' – and this means both the members of X in the classroom and, in more wildly grandiose moments of ambition, the members of X in society more widely.

This is hardly an unproblematic road to follow: it can imbue the crusading teacher with an excess of what might be called identity-righteousness, a zealous belief that his or her own take on identity must be drummed into students. Charlotte Brunsdon, in a characteristically sharp and purposeful critique of some kinds of feminist teaching, has made the point that the feminist academic, in her drive to communicate feminist knowledge, can overlook the bullying effect this can have on female students, 'who can experience a pressure to defer to (feminist) definitions and accounts of their own identity and experience . . . being a good girl, which so many female students want to be, can be profoundly contradictory and stressful for women with feminist teachers'.[4] So too for Lesbian and Gay studies: the queer teacher should always beware of dragooning students into deference, reducing them to cloned acolytes.

None the less, those of us involved in teaching about culture and identity can hardly deny our political agendas. Without them, without any sense that we want to help students to acquire the analytical tools for grasping the ideological make-up of the culture they live in, we would be doing nothing other than indulging in those parlour games of minor aesthetic differentiation that make up traditional arts degrees. Alan Sinfield has recently made a bid to establish the importance of intellectuals for sexual subcultures, seeing their role not as arbiters of taste or aloof dictators of the 'correct' line, but as 'claiming space for cultural work; space in which to . . . develop our own structures of understanding and recognition'.[5] To do this, as Sinfield's pointed use of 'our' underlines, we need to remain committed to the strategic use of shared identities. Brunsdon's warnings against force-feeding students the teacher's one true vision of what certain identities mean, a pedagogy that might be called the missionary imposition, are timely and wise, but it is important to note that she at no point advocates the erasure of identity from teaching. She still takes it as read, for example, that feminist teachers are women and that their impact on female students lies at the centre of a feminist pedagogy. In other words, the teacher of identity courses needs to speak from an experiential base as well as an intellectual one. What concerns her is that the teacher's use of identity should never fossilise into dogma. Identities exist (even if only as temporary labels or necessary fictions) but they are complex, contradictory and histori-cally contingent, never simple, easy or monolithically static.

Quite right: although a politicised sense of my homosexuality fuels much of my teaching, that sense, that politics, even that sexuality itself have changed over time. As a case in point, if I had been writing this piece some years ago, I would never have used the word 'queer' to describe myself. Now it feels right – despite my disappointments that the militant brand of early 1990s queer politics seems to have exhausted itself and notwithstanding my suspicions that the academic growth industry called Queer Theory is becoming unduly abstracted and abstruse – but in the next decade, who knows? In recent times, 'queer' has offered a way out of essentialism, providing an umbrella term to indicate those who, whatever their preferred sexual practices, feel the need to question and challenge the orthodoxies of normative heterosexuality. Consequently the fact that much of the Sexual Dissidence MA is not taught by lesbians or gays is less of an issue than it might at first appear – although honesty compels me to admit that I could not be so blasé about this if the programme was called Lesbian and Gay Studies.

These complexities around identity are further convoluted and intensified by the wide range of students I have taught on my MA option. As with all collections of students, those MA groups are marbled with the social variables of gender, ethnicity, class and age. The most immediately important variable, not surprisingly, is sexuality. Many, sometimes most, but never all, of the students I've taught on this course, identify as lesbian, gay or bisexual. Heterosexual women frequently take the course, but in seven years only one heterosexual male student has done so, and then only after its title no longer contained the word 'homosexuality'. I am not aware of any transsexuals taking the course, though this does not mean there have not been any. Students are not required to disclose their sexuality either to their peers or to me, but their affiliations tend to emerge due to the nature of the material studied and my emphasis on the importance of factoring in an autobiographical dimension to cultural criticism. Nobody is obliged to 'come out', although interestingly the students who most often make direct, defining statements are the heterosexual ones (and I can't help but smile a wry, queer smile at that pleasing inversion of the social norm). I suspect they do this because the class feels like a 'queer space', where what are usually minority sexualities are the taken for granted ones, while heterosexuality is, strikingly and instructively, required to label itself rather than impose that requirement on others.

It is also, invariably, a very international group, with Israelis sitting next to Austrians, Koreans debating with Croatians, Canadians and Greeks giving class presentations to Trinidadian, German, Taiwanese, French, American, Japanese, Malaysian, Italian and (of course) British colleagues. Given the varied and often conflicting conceptualisations of sexuality in students' home cultures, this internationalism can generate vigorous discussions. At times, the fact that contemporary critical theory has, for better or worse, become a globalised *lingua franca* can ease and smooth those discussions, offering a shared base from which to proceed, but equally as often the Anglo-American emphases of that theoretical literature are challenged by students whose backgrounds lead them to resent and resist its inbuilt hegemonies and homogenising assumptions. Another set of differences that matters is the intellectual history of the students. Their first degrees may be in literature, media, communications, politics, sociology, art and design, cultural studies, women's studies, anthropology – the list is lengthy. Again, this throws up differing perspectives that can gell, on a good day, into a productive interdisciplinarity.

Most important of all, there are the different motivations and investments that have led students to study this kind of material. The multiplicity of angles from which students arrive is perhaps the best riposte to the scaremongeringly homophobic caricatures of the field epitomised by former MP Terry Dicks' proposal upon hearing of the Sexual Dissidence MA that Sussex University should be shut down and disinfected, a remark which reveals him to be both a less equivocal Ann Widdecombe and a closet Foucauldian. Student diversity on the MA is also a vital safeguard against the monolith-peddling that concerned Charlotte Brunsdon: even if I were inclined to foist one brand of thinking about sexuality on to a group, the sheer variety of its constituent parts would render such foisting impossible. Consider the following sketches, each of which (all British, all with false names, and all unavoidably stereotyped) is based on composites of MA students I have taught in recent years.

Matt is a seasoned student politician, having run the lesbian and gay group at his previous university. Although more than bright enough to understand and apply the course's theoretical baggage, he worries about its hermetic tendencies and its inabilities to make connections to the world outside the campus. He works part-time for a gay newspaper, and while he understands why his colleagues there mock the excesses and pretensions of queer academia, he none the less wishes they would grasp that there might be more to homosexuality than clubs, drugs and wearing the right underpants.

Janet is a lesbian in her late twenties. She did her first degree at a small college in a rural area with no substantial lesbian subculture. One of the very few out students at that college, she constantly found herself at odds with the conservative English syllabus she was required to study. She wanted to study the Sexual Dissidence MA partly because of the course content, but primarily as a way of getting to Sussex and Brighton. Her interest in locating 'positive images' of lesbianism stirs little enthusiasm in some of her fellow students.

Sophie is a heterosexual woman aged twenty-one. An academic high-flyer, she is determined to carve out a career in university teaching and research, and has concluded that a stint of Queer Theory would enhance the marketability of her CV. Her interest in matters of sexuality is a mainly cerebral one, with a strong preference for psychoanalytic approaches, and she is irritated when seminar discussions veer into what she sees as loose, woolly, confessional areas. She finds it hard to stifle a smirk of disbelief when she hears people use quaint phrases like 'positive images' (imagine – at Sussex).

Sangeeta is bisexual and Asian. Determined not to let class discussions neglect issues important to her, she finds herself constantly intervening to point out the simplistic homo/hetero binary which keeps surfacing as well as the assumptions of whiteness. As a consequence, she feels hemmed in by this spokesperson status, since it sits uneasily with her postcolonialist belief in the inadequacy of identity politics, and annoyed that whatever she says might be pigeonholed as The Bisexual View or The Asian Perspective. She is still mulling over whether that pigeonholing is worse than letting those points go unmade.

Neil is a gay man in his early twenties, although he has only come out to a few people. In fact, signing up for this option is part of his coming out. His interest in the course is more interpersonal and social than academic (he is studying for an MA in an unrelated discipline but is able to take one 'outside' unit). The two most surprising things about the seminar group for him are first the fact that not all the students are gay, and second that those who are seem so confident in their identity that they make no concessions towards those who have found coming out a problem.

Lee is an unapologetically queeny gay man from a working-class background. His politics are often concealed by the sharpness of his camp one-liners. He finds it both easy and enjoyable to rile his fellow students by berating what he calls bourgeois gay lifestyles and by accusing shyer gay men of hiding behind what he calls a mask of masculinity. The women in the group warm to his attacks on male privilege but wonder whether his own persona might not veer towards misogyny.

Jo is a feminist who prefers not to define her sexuality, but is taking this course because she wants to see what, if any, connections might be made between feminist theory and work within Lesbian and Gay studies on lesbian issues. She remains sceptical as to whether gay male and lesbian matters can be usefully studied together, and finds it particularly dubious that her gay male tutor rattles on about the importance of letting experience inform analytical work but then has the effrontery to teach lesbian material.

Anna is a leather dyke who combines an assured grasp of theoretical complexities with a militant commitment to her particular subcultural fraction. This combination succeeds in terrifying the rest of the class, whose admiration for her togetherness is marred only by their fear of how she might respond to their less incisive comments.

Gordon is a gay man in his late forties. Having been involved in gay activism and community work for two decades (from 1970s gay liberationist politics to helping out at an AIDS awareness project), he is keen to know about current academic thinking on sexuality. Its jargon appalls him, though he finds many of the arguments stimulating. What upsets him, however, is the ageism of the younger students and their indifference to what he sees as their history.

James came out as gay five years ago, in between public school and Cambridge, but the more cultural theory he reads, the more distanced he feels from that label. Indeed, he finds any labels that imply group identity incompatible with the demanding and difficult business of theorising. Where his old self would say 'As a gay man', his new self feels compelled to write '"As" a "gay" "man"'. He would like to be more politically active, but is distressed by the simplification of philosophical principles that this would entail.

I could go on, but hopefully the point is made: identity is the trickiest business in a Lesbian and Gay studies classroom. Attempting to juggle the different trajectories and aspirations of students on that MA option is no easy task, although it may be worth recalling here that Richard Johnson once encouraged teachers of cultural studies to foster 'the development in a group or class of a degree of self-consciousness about its own interactions' until 'part of the object of study lies in the structured interactions of the group or class itself'.[6] Written almost two decades ago, those words still have a relevance and resonance today: when students in my class wrangle and tussle over the meanings of *Roseanne*, lesbian chic and the Pet Shop Boys, such texts are, partly, only pretexts for engaging with how they understand themselves, their peers and their cultures. Lesbian and Gay studies is, among other things, a chance for reflecting on our queer selves. However there are dangers if we linger too long at that mirror. Paul Gilroy has pointed out that an over-emphasis on concepts of identity and selfhood in cultural studies can become narcissistic and depoliticising, a dangerous shift where

> politics gives way to more glamorous and avowedly therapeutic alternatives . . . an inward turn away from the profane chaos of an imperfect world . . . a problematic gesture that all too often culminates in the substitution of an implosive and therefore anti-social form of *self*-scrutiny for the discomfort and the promise of public political work.[7]

An equally stern critique of the dangers of identity politics, albeit from a very different perspective, has come from the lesbian separatist writer Sandra McNeill. In a telling anecdote of how a rigidly applied notion of identity politics can lead to 'a points-count system, where the oppressions were added up', she recalls a meeting 'where one discussion was settled when a woman said "Speaking as an Irish woman, I think X". Her opponent in this discussion had replied "Speaking as an incest survivor, I think Y". Naturally, Y was the course of action decided upon.'[8] Both Gilroy and McNeill make vital points: identity politics can become a navel-gazing distraction from hard political work, and/or it can stand in as some mutated parody of politics where a league table of victimhoods replaces difficult ideological choices. Identity, once it becomes a reified, essentialised, fetishised end-in-itself, can be a block to further thinking, a blanket that smothers subtleties and contradictions, a banner waved so furiously that it obscures the fuller view. So why continue to work with it at all?

The simple answer is that we cannot do without it. Identity is still, for all its reductiveness and limitations, the entry point into Lesbian and Gay studies. A sense of shared belonging, albeit one felt with differing degrees of allegiance and distrust, is what leads the vast majority of students into my MA classroom – even poor, tortured, Baudrillard-battered James, try as he might to footnote himself into infinity and scare-quote himself out of existence. Perhaps shrewd, careerist, she'll-go-far Sophie hasn't been drawn to Lesbian and Gay studies out of any experiential connections or existential need, but the field wouldn't be there, ripe for her picking, if we queers (with all our contingent alliances and squabbling spats) hadn't put it together to address some questions about our relationships with identity, culture and politics. Identity is never where the story ends, but I remain convinced it is where it begins – which is why the teacher's identity has to be one counter in the game.

Queer – there or everywhere?

The biggest luxury afforded by the Sexual Dissidence MA is that teachers and students alike can take it for granted that sexuality is a topic worth studying. On less specialised and privileged terrain, that validity cannot be assumed, it must be fought for and won. Those campaigns are important, since it would be both ironic and tragic if the slow emergence of Lesbian and Gay studies backfired, leaving the investigation of sexuality academically ghettoised into a small number of élite and discrete programmes, and thereby absolving other courses of the responsibility to take those issues on board. Thus, much as I have enjoyed teaching and learning from my MA groups, it is that first-year lecture I give which often feels both more necessary and more influential. This is not due to its content (it skims superficially over complex areas with a shameless-ness matched only by this chapter), but because of the audience. It is heard by a broad cross-section of students, many of whom later tell me they have never before heard a lecture from an unabashedly queer perspective, rather than a self-selecting minority of sexuality-attuned postgrads. In media terms, that lecture is Saturday prime-time BBC1, as opposed to the after-midnight Channel 4 ambience of a Sexual Dissidence class. What it lacks in subtlety (which is plenty), it gains in reach.

This distinction, between discussions among the specialised few and introductions for the unaware many, is hardly unique to Lesbian and Gay studies. It is a distinction that can become a dilemma: where should we best concentrate our energies if we want students to engage with difficult cultural and political debates? Although I do not deny relishing the chance to strut some queer polemic in front of those first-years (and the fact that a handful of homophobes annually walk out of that lecture is almost as heartwarming as the fact that a smattering of queers have felt prompted to come out because of it), I'm also conscious of the dangers of tokenism, of being the 'queer week', neatly shepherded by the timetable into one-fifteenth of the course. Pragmatically, I know that's preferable to no fifteenths at all, but it would be foolish to suppose that some students at least aren't able to tick sexuality off their mental checklist, before proceeding to tuck away another aspect of identity politics in the following session ('third week of March, that'll be race then'). The way beyond this laundry list approach, perhaps, is to pursue an integrated agenda, where numerous questions of cultural identity are all always held in play, and here is one reason to defend the label 'Cultural Studies', which for all its vexing bagginess has the potential to do just that – unless, as in that troubling John Storey quote I used earlier, sexuality somehow melts off the page.

Another reason to maintain a commitment to incorporating the study of sexuality in wider curricula is that hiving it off into discrete courses enables students to avoid it altogether. Worse, and most poignantly of all, this can specifically disadvantage queer students, who might be too unsure (closeted, undecided or just plain bashful) to sign up for an option which boasted sexuality, or worse still homosexuality, in its title. I once offered an undergraduate variant of my MA course on queer popular culture, which ran for two under-subscribed years before folding. Several queer students later told me they would have loved to do the course, but didn't want to be identified as doing so in a public sphere of noticeboards open to the eyes of prurient peers. Incidents like this strengthen the case for an integrationist approach: insisting on the relevance of sexuality in more general courses can both empower students who locate themselves in sexual minorities and enlighten those belonging elsewhere.

At the same time, however, the growth of Lesbian and Gay studies as a distinct area is a gain to be cherished, since it offers a designated space, even a haven, where queer scholars can develop their own agendas. If it is, for the time being at least, a primarily postgraduate space in Britain, then so be it. Some of those postgraduates have already begun to find themselves teaching in mainstream curricula, productively queering them wherever they can. Specialisation versus outreach should not be a choice of either/or but a matter of whatever, wherever, whenever possible. When I co-edited an introductory textbook in Lesbian and Gay studies (*Lesbian and Gay studies: a critical introduction*, 1997),[9] one of the first and most important decisions taken was to split the volume into two halves, one detailing queer contributions and interventions in existing academic disciplines and traditions, the other mapping the emerging concerns of lesbian and gay thought. Play the system *and* plant your own turf – evolve *and* secede. Subcultural spaces are crucial for any minority, but the conversations can become boring when you only talk to variants of yourself.

Disciplinary desires

Briefly, and not without trepidation, I think it's appropriate to conclude with the question of desire. One of the exalted buzzwords of queer theory, 'desire' is uttered countless times in the Lesbian and Gay studies classroom. Yet it also has another, less uttered life. Agony columnists are always advising bright but unattached readers to seek romance through evening classes, so if Cupid can score in a room devoted to Intermediate Portuguese or Six Victorian Novelists then imagine his potential strike-rate in a class where queers talk to queers about fist-fucking, cottaging and lesbian SM. Facetiousness aside, a sexual dynamic is not a rare occurrence in sexuality discussions, although this is rarely acknowledged. Such coyness is only circumspect: lurking just out of sight in most reactionary attacks on Lesbian and Gay studies is that perpetual figment of the homophobic imagination, the predatory queer preying on younger, more vulnerable minds. When the Sussex MA was first announced, a radio commentator on the story wondered aloud to his listeners if there were going to be any practicals.

Irritating and predictable as such jibes are, they do illuminate one of the reasons why Lesbian and Gay studies matters. Like other academic enterprises arising from identity politics, Lesbian and Gay studies refuses to sever the intellect from the emotions, insists on keeping the body in the picture. Studying sexuality can become an awfully arcane and dessicated process, especially in the airless, bloodless heights of Queer Theory, but at the root of it all are bodies, emotions, feelings, desires. Small wonder that beneath and around the sober weekly progress of some Lesbian and Gay studies classes other narratives are woven, much as residential conferences attended by academics in the field do not stay purely discursive after dark. To say this is of course to risk invoking another dangerous myth, that of the hypersexual homosexual, and it is not my intention here to suggest that students attend these courses with overridingly carnal motivations, but it would be disingenuous in the extreme to pretend that eroticism plays no part at all.

It may even be the case, as bell hooks has provocatively argued, that all teaching and learning situations contain a potentially passionate dimension, a dimension that has damagingly been lost through a stress on objectivity and neutrality. Her advice: 'To restore passion to the classroom or to excite it in classrooms where it has never been, we must find again the place of eros within ourselves and together allow the mind and body to feel and know and desire'.[10] Heady, brave, risky words, fragments of a language that queer teachers, mindful of workplace homophobia and sensitive to issues of power and exploitation, are particularly wary of speaking. Yet if any intellectual project is equipped to think through and beyond those difficult boundaries, surely it is Lesbian and Gay studies. Maybe one day, until then perhaps we must content ourselves with the pedagogy that dare not speak its name.

Notes

1 Abelove H, Barale M A and Halperin D M, 'Introduction', pp. xvf., in Abelove, Barale and Halperin (eds), *The lesbian and gay studies reader*, Routledge, London, 1993.

2 See Dinshaw C and Halperin D M, 'From the editors', in *GLQ: A Journal of Lesbian and Gay Studies*, Vol 1 No 1 (1993), pp. iii–iv; Munt S R, 'Mapping the field', in Medhurst A and Munt S R (eds), *Lesbian and gay studies: a critical introduction*, Cassell, London, 1997, p. xiv.

3 Storey J, 'Cultural studies: an introduction', in Storey (ed.), *What is cultural studies?*, Arnold, London, 1996, p. 3.

4 Brunsdon C, 'Pedagogies of the feminine', in *Screen tastes: soap operas to satellite dishes*, Routledge, London, 1997, pp. 172–89, p. 184.

5 Sinfield A, *Gay and after*, Serpent's Tail, London, 1998, p. 159.

6 Johnson R, 'Cultural studies and educational practice', *Screen Education*, Vol 34 1980, p. 16.

7 Gilroy P, 'British cultural studies and the pitfalls of identity', in Curran J, Morley D and Walkerdine V (eds), *Cultural studies and communications*, Arnold, London, 1996, p. 37 (emphasis in original).

8 McNeill S, 'Identity politics', in Harne L and Miller E (eds), *All the rage: reassessing radical lesbian feminism*, Women's Press, London, 1996, see p. 55.

9 Co-edited with Sally R Munt: see note 2.

10 hooks b, 'Eros, eroticism and the pedagogical project', in McRobbie A (ed.), *Back to reality: social experience and cultural studies*, Manchester University Press, Manchester, 1997, p. 80.

8 Teaching women's studies: whose experience?

Jane Elliott

Emerging from the teaching and researching of women's studies are many important contradictions and controversies. For example a major concern among teachers and researchers is 'how do we represent women whose experiences we do not share in our teaching and writing?' It has been argued that no woman should attempt to speak for another woman's oppression. This view is based on the recognition that in speaking on behalf of less powerful women, the more privileged white, academic feminist becomes part of the process of 'Othering' in which the experiences of the former are colonised by the latter.[1] In attempting to theorise another woman's experience there is a danger, or even inevitability of misrepresentation. However, there is also the possibility that if we do not discuss 'other' women's experiences, those lives will be ignored. Much of the debate has focused on writing and research and it is my purpose, in this chapter, to discuss the issues in the context of teaching as the issues are also of relevance to the classroom, the questions of power and privilege being ever present. Moreover, for several students, the classroom may be their first point of contact with many of the debates. I focus on the teaching of women's studies in higher education and adult continuing education, although the issues are clearly of relevance to many areas of the curriculum such as cultural studies and more conventional areas of knowledge. In examining the issues, I am concerned with both the misrepresentations and the ignoring of the lives of women who do not share the privileges of many of the women who research and teach women's studies.

The (mis)representation of experience

Women's studies represents a form of experiential learning based on the notion that the genesis of any theoretical understanding of women's lives is experience. While this relationship between understanding and experience is a necessary one, the result is that many of the feminist ideas represented in published work have been those emerging from the experiences of comparatively privileged women. It has therefore been suggested that we are possibly too concerned that we should not speak from the experience of others.[2]

This is an issue of power and privilege: some women are more powerful and privileged than others and different women experience oppression in different ways.[3] My concern is with the issues associated with more privileged women attempting to speak on behalf of their less powerful sisters and to theorise a common experience of patriarchy. The notion, associated with some early 'Second wave' feminism, that under patriarchy all women share a common oppression of greater significance than issues which may divide them, is problematic. Mary Daly, for example has been criticised for denying the specific oppression experienced by black women by subsuming their experience into that of more privileged white women, thus obscuring the realities and diversities of women's lives and power positioning between women.[4]

The problem is at least two-fold: either we misrepresent the experiences of 'other' women or we ignore those experiences. In the first case we develop inadequate theories, based on false assumptions about many women's lives. We may also become part of the colonisation process, identified by Edward Said, in which histories are written by powerful outsiders.[5] In the second case our theory is limited because it only addresses the lives of certain groups of women and the experiences of most women remain invisible.

This discussion focuses on problems involved in attempting to theorise the experiences of black women. I note that the term 'black' is problematic: it may refer only to specific groups such as Afro-Caribbeans, or it may refer to all non-white people. Whilst I use 'black' to refer to non-white people in recognition of their common experience of racism, I am aware of pitfalls involved in generalising all black experience on the basis of one group of black women.[6] I focus on black women first, to problematise my experience of working within an all white women's studies' tutor team and second, because black women's feminist writings such as those referred to here have been particularly influential in alerting white feminists such as myself to the problems of colonisation and exclusion within feminist writing. However, many of the issues are also relevant to, for example, middle-class women discussing working class women's lives or heterosexual women discussing lesbian women.

White feminist writing has been criticised for presenting stereotypical images of black women which reproduce racist constructions of black women. As Barrett and McIntosh note, representations of black women in white feminist work include, for example, 'the docile "victims" of arranged marriages': many feminists have thus accepted the stereotypical myth of the passive Asian woman.[7] These assumptions are sustained by media representations which perpetuate racist notions of black women and mask the realities of their lives. This might support the view that we should not attempt to write about the lives of 'other' women. However, if we accept this position, we are only able to write about a very limited range of experiences.

Misrepresentation also occurs if black women's lives are absent from white feminist accounts, especially when white women attempt to generalise the lives of all women from the experience of privileged, white women. What emerges is a racist perspective and inadequate theory.[8] As Lugones and Spelman put it:

> But if, say an empirical theory is purported to be about 'women' and in fact is only about certain women, it is certainly false, probably ethnocentric,

and of dubious usefulness except to those whose positions in the world it strengthens.[9]

There are several ways in which 1970s feminist theory and practice failed to incorporate the voices of black women. First, the Reclaim the Night marches, organised in opposition to male violence against women, were seen by some as racist as they often marched through areas in which many black people lived and demanded better policing, ignoring the fact that many black women's experiences of police agencies may be more negative than those of many white women.[10] The fact that marching in such areas may confirm racist stereotypes of black men as rapists and muggers was also disregarded.[11] The lessons drawn are not that feminists should ignore male violence, but that action against male violence must be inclusive of all women and sensitised to issues of racism.

Second, 1970s feminist writing which critiqued 'the family' neglected the different experiences of many black women from which an alternative theory of the family could emerge. Frequently, black women had to struggle to preserve their families against the effects of state undermining including immigration controls. Moreover, for many black women, the family supported their struggles against racism. As Flax argues, feminist attacks on the family have served to denigrate the ability of many black women to uphold their family units despite negative circumstances.[12] Clearly some black women do experience oppression and violence in the family or exploitation as unpaid workers but any theory of the family must incorporate a diverse range of family experiences, some more positive than others.

We need, however, to attempt to identify some common experience among women. As Ramazanoglu argues, while we must consider women's diversities, we need 'a sense of sisterhood' as a basis for feminist politics.[13] Possibly we can argue a universal oppression in the sense that we are all subordinate to the men in our own class or race, while we are not necessarily subordinate to all men. We can argue for a shared oppression in terms of, for example, male violence. While more privileged women may be in a better position to escape from violent relationships, women from all social classes and ethnic groups experience male violence. This could be a unifying experience for women.

The question raised is 'What are the implications for the women's studies classroom?' In a tutor team comprising only white women, can we ensure that black women's experiences are represented adequately? Can we avoid the misrepresentations and silencing of black women's voices, a feature of much white, feminist writing? I now turn to a consideration of these issues.

The women's studies classroom

The problems outlined are particularly relevant for the women's studies classroom which will inevitably reflect the dilemmas present within feminist theory. As I have already noted, much of the debate focuses on the representation of the 'Other' through research and writing and issues of central importance for feminism are being examined.[14] Yet, the problems are similar within the classroom situation. The teacher in higher education and continuing education classrooms has authority in similar ways to the authority held by the writer and researcher. However, at least in the classroom, the 'reader' has the immediate opportunity to challenge the teacher, a possibility which is rarely available to readers of academic books. The resolution of the problem depends in part on our perception of the teacher/student relationship. If we believe that the teacher speaks with an authoritative voice there is the danger that her perspective will become the received wisdom. If, however, there is the possibility of developing a relationship based on Freirean and feminist lines (that is, relationships which are non-hierarchical in which we recognise that the teacher is also a learner and the student is also a teacher), there is the possibility that the issues can be examined in a genuinely exploratory way.

Freire argues that education can never remain neutral: it must reflect a particular view of the world. Education may instil conformity into the young through a process of 'domestication'. Alternatively an 'education for freedom' can be achieved. This 'education for freedom' actively facilitates a political consciousness through new forms of education. Central to this education is a transformed teacher/student relationship whereby the teacher becomes the learner and vice-versa:

> The teacher is no longer merely the-one-who teaches, but one who is himself [sic] taught in dialogue with the students, who in their turn while being taught also teach. They become jointly responsible for a process in which all grow.[15]

Hence the roles of teachers as knowers and students as learners become obscured.[16] This approach is particularly appropriate for a non-hierarchical feminist pedagogy.[17] In adopting this notion of education within the women's studies classroom, an environment which is conducive for the sharing of a range of experience within a non-hierarchical relationship between student and teacher experience can emerge. It implies that a wider range of voices can be heard and validated equally within a classroom.

It is likely that this Freirean process is more feasible within an adult education context than within the conventional higher education classroom. This is because there are greater liberal and radical traditions within adult education.[18] These traditions have been informed, in part, by a closer relationship with all sectors of the community, and in particular those social groups who are under-represented in higher education. This radicalism is also evident in the fact that in the early days of women's studies, more courses were established in the adult and informal post-compulsory education sectors than in the more formal higher education institutions. Hughes and Kennedy suggest that adult education provides the most flexible educational approaches for adults, and in particular women. Associated with both the liberal and radical approaches has been a recognition that the experience and knowledge of the student is validated.[19] While it is important that these traditions are recognised, it is also true that they have not necessarily facilitated a reflexive exploration of issues such as racism or sexuality. Nevertheless, there is clearly an ethos and tradition which can help to facilitate such an inquiry.

However, we should not be tempted to see this Freirean perspective as a panacea for the problems I have outlined. In reality, regardless of attempts by some tutors to challenge traditional authority structures, the teacher–student relationship is almost always hierarchical and does involve power relations in which, for example, the tutor becomes an assessor of student achievement.[20] This has always been the case within mainstream higher education; and it is increasingly the case in adult education as a result of the funding policies of the 1990s which insisted that the bulk of adult education programmes should be accredited. While we may attempt to devise more liberal forms of continuous assessment such as group assignments, this does not take away our role as assessor of students' work. For many students, there is the expectation that the teacher possesses a body of knowledge to be imparted. Within this kind of reality, the teacher's attempt to reflect 'other' women's experiences may be more problematic in that assertions which may not take into account the voices of less privileged women are less likely to be challenged. Nevertheless, while we may note the limitations of a Freirean model within the current system of higher education in Britain, it is important that we do not jettison the vision of how things could or should be.

It is important also that we recognise the dangers, as in reality many tutor teams are made up of women who are predominantly white and relatively privileged.[21] If we were to argue that they should not attempt to theorise on the basis of any experience other than their own, there is the danger that courses will continue to reflect a narrow range of interests which is ultimately more damaging than the misrepresentation of experience. Even if we were to be successful in broadening the social base of our tutor teams, there will always be a wealth of experience remaining outside of the institution. How, for example, could a tutor team reflect the diversity of black experience? There is also the argument that by the very nature of their positions within the academy, all women teachers have become privileged in relation to many women. This privilege, albeit possibly newly acquired, is likely to influence our interpretations of experience. Nevertheless, it is preferable that experiences are presented, albeit inadequately, as opposed to being ignored. At least students then have the opportunity to examine and challenge the validity of the tutor's assertions.

However it is not sufficient simply to examine a wider range of experience than those often reflected in tutor teams. Women's studies programmes must also consider issues of power. This means moving away from models of power which assume a simplistic notion of patriarchy in which all men dominate all women. Hence we need, in what is likely to be a painful process, to explore how those who are oppressed within one set of relationships may act as oppressors in other circumstances: how white middle class women may be oppressed in relation to white middle class men, while at the same time oppressing black women. And, in what is an equally painful process, we need to consider how white women are positioned in relation to black men. We need to examine bell hooks's assertion in relation to American society (which is equally relevant for discussion of British society) that white women have 'the right to assume the role of oppressor in relation to black women and black men'.[22] Finally, if we are white, we must evaluate critically our 'whiteness' and its implications for our identities. This all requires that we re-evaluate and challenge our own assumptions and as tutors, we have to be skilled at dealing with discussion which some may find potentially threatening.

In a feminist theory module, 'Interpreting women's lives', I have included sessions on black feminist theory. I had two key aims: first, to highlight the experiences of black women in Britain, and second, to examine some of the issues raised by black feminists. In relation to the first aim, we explored women's experience of racism in Britain and looked at research on black women's lives in terms of educational achievement and participation in the labour market. In particular, Heidi Mirza's work on black girls in a London comprehensive school challenges the stereotypical assumption that black girls are underachieving at school.[23] In terms of the second aim, we examined some of the concerns put forward by black feminists. For example they have questioned the assumption that women share a common oppression and have highlighted the divisions between women which may be more significant than the common conditions.

The first time I taught the sessions, I felt a nervousness about the possibilities of misrepresentation, misinterpretation and over-generalisation. I was also aware that consideration of issues around race and the questioning of our own prejudices and racism, coupled with a recognition of the ways in which white women have benefited from the exploitation of black women, can be very painful. After the sessions one student admitted that prior to the classes she had felt concern that these issues were to be examined in an all white group. This was a perfectly valid concern in that it is debatable as to how far an all white group can challenge its own racism. Moreover, can a group of white women reach an understanding of why many black women may identify primarily with black men rather than white women? However, after the classes, all the students felt that they had been worthwhile and were a necessary and integral part of any feminist theory programme. I am mindful, none the less, of the dangers of complacency: positive feedback from a student group does not necessarily mean that there was no distortion of experience in the sessions. For example, if there had been black students or tutors present, different issues would have been raised and many of our assumptions would have been open to challenge. Possibly, I would have had to address more directly the legitimacy of my own knowledge and my authority as a teacher.

Emerging themes

When teaching the module a second time, I undertook more detailed discussions with the students about their feelings in relation to the module. Three themes emerged which form the basis of the rest of the discussion. First, we considered whether or not there should be separate sessions focusing on black feminist issues or whether the questions should be incorporated into all sessions. Second, students raised the question of the problems for white students in writing assignments on black feminist issues. Finally, we discussed the kinds of texts which are helpful to students in exploring black women's experience and related theoretical issues.

Should there be separate sessions?

Much of the discussion around whether or not the issues of black experience and related feminist theory should be explored in separate sessions was reminiscent of feminist concerns regarding the dangers of simply 'adding on' women's issues to the mainstream curriculum rather than incorporating the feminist challenge into the curriculum as a whole. In our discussions, we concluded that black women's issues should be considered in separate sessions and be incorporated into the rest of the course. In theory, there should be no conflict between the two approaches as throughout the module students are encouraged to explore different elements of women's experience, for example sexuality, violence and employment, in the context of a growing awareness of feminist theory. Thus, the separate sessions on black women's experience and black feminist theory should provide the conceptual tools to enable students to analyse all aspects of women's experience, with the sessions allocated specifically to black issues forming part of a larger process of awareness raising. The danger, however, with this approach, is that the assumption might be made that the specific sessions have dealt with the 'race issue' and the class can therefore move on to new themes: this would clearly not be adequate. Nevertheless, this is perhaps less likely than the possibility that in opting for an approach which relies totally on incorporating the issues into the rest of the module, the black women's experience and theory may simply be ignored or dealt with more superficially.

Written assignments

An important influence on my decision to explore the problems of representation in the teaching of women's studies was the publication of *Representing the other*, edited by Sue Wilkinson and Celia Kitzinger and published in 1996.

Here different writers explore the difficulties involved in representing the experiences of women whose experiences we do not share in feminist writing. As a tutor, I had not anticipated the discomfort students might experience in writing about 'other' women's lives, yet this emerged quite forcefully in the evaluation discussion. Two distinct viewpoints emerged: one was the feeling among some white students that they would not be qualified to write about black women's experience, they could be open to challenge and might be seen as condescending; the second perspective was that writing such an assignment presented the opportunity to research into the issues in more depth.

In some respects, the two viewpoints reflected an important tension within women's studies, with the first view reflecting the experiential nature of the field and the second view reflecting the academic element of women's studies. This tension also raises the question of the nature of the written assignment in a women's studies programme. Elsewhere I discuss the problematic relationship between the experiential nature of women's studies and traditional academic approaches which are more abstract and suggest that exploration of these relationships can be integrated into the curriculum.[24] The ways in which experience can be discussed in assignments; the need to distinguish between one's own experiences and those of other women; the dangers of misrepresentation and generalisation; and the relationship between theory and experience are all questions which can be debated and can encourage students to examine ways in which they may write about other women's experiences.

There is no simple solution to the dilemma which, to students, is a real one and which also is relevant to all students in terms of representing experiences which are not their own. For example, many black students may also feel discomfort at the fact that throughout the educational experience they have been expected to write about the lives of white people. The tutor needs to ensure that there is an open atmosphere in which the students can discuss their concerns honestly and in which they are not fearful of criticism in their assignments. Moreover, students should be encouraged to understand that an exploration of these concerns is, in itself, a learning experience.

Relevant texts

One way of ensuring that at least some black women's voices are heard on a course is through access to their texts. Set readings for 'Interpreting women's lives' included *Ain't I a woman: black women and feminism* by bell hooks and *Young, female and black* by Heidi Safia Mirza. Clearly, the students referred to many texts but I have chosen these in order to give brief examples of the ways in which texts were used to focus on particular questions.

hooks focuses on black women's experience in America and highlights the difficulties in achieving a common sisterhood among women when, she argues, both the early twentieth century suffrage movement and the second wave women's movement of the late twentieth century were racist and excluded many black women. Nevertheless, she still advocates a feminist politics:

> It is a contradiction that white females have structured a women's libera-tion movement that is racist and excludes many non–white women. However, the existence of that contradiction should not lead any woman to ignore feminist issues.[25]

This text provides a valuable starting point for discussion regarding our own racist assumptions and ways in which the women's movement in Britain may have revealed similar racist tendencies. Students indicated that hooks had raised new questions for them and had provided a valuable insight into black women's problematic relationship with the women's movement.

Mirza's text was used in a very different way: first, while drawing on American, Caribbean and British sources, it is written in a British context and second, as mentioned earlier, it aims to challenge the myth of black girls' underachievement. The book raises important questions as to why the high achievement of young African-Caribbean women is not reflected in their posi-tion in the labour market. Mirza maintains that an important contributory factor is the experience of schooling which, she argues, curbs young black women's career aspirations. Another important question raised within the class was why public perceptions of young black women's educational achievement is so stereotypically negative. What are the processes in our society which have allowed the perpetuation of this distorted perception?

In the evaluation session, students questioned the nature of the texts used in the module: they pointed out that the texts had all been theoretical and analytical works and that the issues could also have been explored through the use of literary texts such as Alice Walker's *The color purple* and Maya Angelou's autobiographical writing; and films such as *Bhaji on the beach*. This was an important point: the use of film and literature would raise different questions, in particular in relation to representations of black women within black art and the relationship between these representations and reality. Moreover, in an interdisciplinary field such as women's studies it is important that we draw on a wide range of texts. In future classes, I will therefore present a wider range of materials including both film and literary texts.

Conclusions

In this chapter I have attempted to raise some issues of concern for the teaching of women's studies. In many respects the problems are irresolvable: any solution will be inadequate because it is both impossible to construct tutor teams representing all experience and impossible to ensure that the wide range of women's experience is examined adequately within the women's studies classroom. By the very nature of the higher education system a member of the tutor team is likely to be comparatively privileged. However we need to recognise that the tutor is only one of the resources available to students: other resources will include feminist writing which will reflect a wider range of experience than any tutor team; and the students, themselves, who may also represent a wider social base than tutor teams (although this is more likely to be the case within adult education which actively targets students from groups which have been previously under-represented in higher education, than in conventional higher education classrooms). We also need to remember that many of the problems associated with academic feminism emerge from the valid tradition that theorising should arise out of personal experience, while the context in which that experience is theorised may be ensuring the hegemony of the experience of more privileged women. Often, emerging theories have claimed to be of relevance to all women but have, in reality, only spoken for the more privileged feminist. It is the duty of the women's studies tutor to find ways of exploring the experiences of a wide range of women and ensure that these form an integral part of our theory.

Discussion with students strengthened my view that ultimately we may have to dare to get it wrong rather than ignore crucial elements of oppression, although we may simply be opting for the lesser of two evils. However, in accepting that the more privileged woman in the academy can attempt to speak for 'other' women and in fact that it is her responsibility to do so, we may well at the same time be sustaining the power relationships existing between groups of women in the wider society. The question needs to be asked as to why there may be no black women or other less privileged women in an institution who can speak for their own experience. What kinds of role models are we offering our students? Just as an academic institution employing predominantly male researchers and teachers can be said to be reproducing the gender relations of the wider society, so are institutions employing predominantly white teachers and researchers reproducing the racial hierarchies of the wider society. However, we must have faith in our students' abilities to question and challenge us.

Acknowledgement

I thank Christina Brannigan, Jennifer Castle, Esperanza Gomez, Lois Poynting and Bev Richards, students on the 'Interpreting women's lives' module. My discussions with them helped me to clarify many of the classroom-related issues.

Notes

1 Wilkinson S and Kitzinger C, *Representing the Other: a feminism and psychology reader*, Sage, London, 1996.

2 Barrett M and McIntosh M, 'Ethnocentrism and socialist-feminist theory', *Feminist Review*, Vol 20, 1985.

3 It is useful to differentiate between 'Other' and difference. I use the term 'Other' in Carabine's sense that 'Other' is socially significant and reflects a relationship of power in which the 'Other' is relatively powerless. Difference is not necessarily socially significant and does not reflect a power relationship. Jean Carabine, 'Questioning representing the Other' in Wilkinson and Kitzinger (eds), 1996.

4 See Bulkin E, 'Racism and writing: some implications for white lesbian critics', *Sinister Wisdom*, Vol 13 No 3, 1980, p. 22; and Ramazanoglu C, *Feminism and the contradictions of oppression*, Routledge, London, 1989.

5 Said E, *Orientalism*, Routledge, New York, 1978.

6 Bhavnani K-K, 'Talking racism and the editing of women's studies', in Richardson D and Robinson V, *Introducing women's studies*, Macmillan, London, 1993.

7 Barrett and McIntosh (1985); the phrase quoted is on p. 24.

8 See bell hooks, *Ain't I a woman: black women and feminism*, South End Press, London, 1982.

9 Lugones M and Spelman E, 'Have we got a theory for you! Feminist theory, cultural imperialism and the demand for "The Woman's Voice"' in Tuana N and Tong R (eds), *Feminism and philosophy: essential readings in theory, reinterpretation, and application*, Westview Press, Boulder, 1995, p. 502.

10 Bhavnani K-K and Coulson M, 'Transforming socialist-feminism: the challenge of racism' in Evans M (ed.), *The woman question*, Sage, London, 1994.

11 Stacey J, 'Big white sister . . . sexuality and racism in the women's movement', *Women's Studies Occasional Papers*, No. 7, University of Kent, 1985.

12 Flax J, 'The family in contemporary feminist thought: a critical review', in Elshtain J (ed.), *The family in political thought*, Harvester Press, Sussex, 1982, p. 229.

13 Ramazanoglu, 1989, p. 174.

14 See Wilkinson and Kitzinger, 1996.

15 Freire P, *Pedagogy of the oppressed*, Penguin, Harmondsworth, 1972, p. 53.

16 Elliott J, 'Women's studies and adult education: a shared agenda?', in Bryant I (ed.), *Proceedings of the standing conference on university teaching and research in the education of adults: vision, invention, intervention – celebrating adult education*, Southampton, 1995.

17 See Higgins K, '"Making it your own world": women's studies and Freire', *Women's Studies International Forum*, Vol 5 No 1, 1982, pp. 97–98; and Weiler K, 'Freire and a feminist pedagogy of difference', *Harvard Educational Review*, Vol 61 No 4, 1991.

18 Elliott J, 'Teaching women's studies in adult education', *Adults Learning*, Vol 6 No 10, 1995. For further discussion of Freirean issues see Elliott J, in Bryant (ed), 1995; and Elliott J, 'Locating women: theorising the curriculum', in Benn R, Elliott J and Whaley P (eds), *Educating Rita and her sisters: women and continuing education*, NIACE, Leicester, 1998.

19 See Hughes M and Kennedy M, 'Breaking out – women in adult education', *Women's Studies International Forum*, Vol 6 No 3, 1983; and also Benn R and Fieldhouse R, 'Notions of community for university continuing education', in Elliott J, Francis H and Humphreys R and Istance D (eds), *Communities and their universities: the challenge of lifelong learning*, Lawrence and Wishart, London, 1996.

20 Elliott, in Bryant (ed).

21 Although we may argue that women teaching in higher and adult continuing education may be comparatively privileged, it is important to remember that women often form the less privileged academic staff within higher education institutions.

22 hooks, 1982, p. 123.

23 Mirza H S, *Young, female and black*, Routledge, London, 1992.

24 Elliott, 'Teaching Women's Studies' (cit., in *Adults Learning*, 1995).

25 hooks, 1982, p. 195.

9 Cultural studies and cultural practice: an interview with Eddie Chambers

Nannette Aldred

In an article in the Oxford Art Journal in 1991, Jonathan Harris argued that

> when cultural studies became Cultural Studies [where higher case letters indicate its academic entrenchment and legitimisation since the early 1970s], as many fronts were lost as those that were won. The terrain of 'High Art' slipped away to those from the traditional disciplines of the Humanities – including Art History – while 'popular culture' (also defined in a narrow and selective way) became the 'object' of Cultural Studies research and teaching . . . which . . . actually negated the political and analytic thrust which a work like [Williams'] *Culture and Society* represented. It was the bringing together, the tracing of relations, the identification of patterns, that Williams offered as the basis for understanding the interaction of the culture as a whole and the social relations as a whole, within a particular society at a particular time.[1]

The article continues that instead of considering marginalised and absent popular cultural forms rather than High Art, Williams argued for their integration: to consider cultural formations. This call to integration offers a way of considering aspects of Black symbolic practices other than the more usual association of Black culture with popular music and dance often within a subcultural analysis.

In the recent spin of 'Cool Britannia' the visual has come to the fore in fashion, publishing (including electronic publishing), design, advertising and fine art. The new British artists work with the vernacular in ways that ensure a wider audience for their work, appropriating images from pornography, fashion and the popular history of art; using advertising as part of their repertoire both in terms of images and of promotion. This renaissance is happening within BritArt and, as Paul Gilroy has pointed out, 'architecture, aesthetics and art have recently re-emerged as politically significant issues'. Gilroy argues:

> Black artists are now in a position to attempt a more ambitious project than simply filling in the spaces that racism left blank in the history of art. They are already working to re-compose an understanding of English culture; their creativity needs to be complemented by a re-reading of that cultural history which places the idea of 'race' at the centre rather than the margin. The visual arts will play a key role in this because of the tremendous vitality of black fine art during the last decade . . . .[2]

Taking his analogy from music Gilroy talks about 'two-tone' in relation to cultural practice and in dialogue with Stuart Hall he has taken the notion of hybridity to conceptualise Black culture in the diaspora or 'Black Atlantic'. However, there is a conceptual gap between dominant BritArt and Black British arts and analysing that gap calls for a consideration of the different histories of black and white art production and support in postwar Britain.[3]

Stuart Hall has noted that the Black community

> is one area where alternative practice is theoretically informed by what happened in the 1980s . . . It's an area where cultural politics has very deep roots and resonances: where a lot of political issues are also issues about identity and representation. This was the first generation that entered higher education, art schools and the polys, where they encountered a lot of new ideas. It has been extremely valuable for me, because my own work on ethnicity and race has been as much informed by the work of people who are actually producing creative work as by those who are theorising about it. I'm excited about the forms in which a lot of that theorising now takes place in artistic practice.[4]

The main body of this chapter will take up this theme in the form of an interview with Eddie Chambers, the artist, writer and curator who was curator-in-residence at the University of Sussex in 1995–96 (funded by History of Art at the University of Sussex and the South East Arts Board). Hall could be describing Chambers in the quote above; Chambers was one of a group of young artists who were all living or studying in the Midlands around Wolverhampton (and sometimes known as the Wolverhampton Black Artists) in the early 1980s. They started to organise their own exhibitions in order to get a showing (like later BritArtists would do, in the spirit of entrepreneurialism). WBA were later associated with the Pan-African Connection and Art for Uhuru – who organised the First National Black Art Convention in Wolverhampton in 1984. Chambers's curating began with 'Black Art an' done' at Wolverhampton Art Gallery in 1981. Subsequent exhibitions included 'D-Max A Photographic Exhibition', 'Black Art Plotting the Course', 'Let the Canvas Come to Life With Dark Faces', 'Diverse Cultures' (curated for the Crafts Council with Dr Nima Poovaya-Smith), 'History and Identity: Seven Painters', 'Four x 4' and 'The Dub Factor'. He has also had many exhibitions of his own work in England, Ireland, Scotland and Wales. These have included 'The Black Bastard as a Cultural Icon', 'The Slaughter of Another Golden Calf', and 'Marcus Garvey, The Blackest Star'. His work was included in the major Hayward Gallery exhibition 'The Other Story – Asian, African and Caribbean Artists in Post-War Britain'. In 1986, in conjunction with the Watershed Media Centre, Bristol, he researched, collated and assembled an exhibition of local Black History, called 'Black Presence'. These events were part of the highly political moment following the 1981 riots and marked a turning point in the Black art movement.

Chambers's description of the discussions about the denotation Black art can be followed in detail in his *The artpack: a history of Black artists in Britain* (1988). More recently Paul Gilroy has discussed the importance of the joint identity of Black and British and (by implication) artist (and male or female and straight or gay), rather than the single position of the dominant identification of artist or Black artist.[5]

Chambers made the transition from artist to commentator and curator acknowledging that critical context, distribution and access are essential to the cultural process. In addition to his exhibition work, he has written a large number of articles and catalogue essays about artists in the United Kingdom and the United States.[6] He recognises that visual cultural practice in the form of art exhibitions is about creating audiences or publics as well as producing cultural texts. As art history in the form of attendance at 'blockbuster' exhibitions like those programmed at the Royal Academy, the Tate and the National Galleries in London becomes more popular as a leisure pursuit, critical questions need more urgently to be asked about who is shown, who omitted and why. In a context where most galleries show little of contemporary or historical art from outside western traditions and where the work of Black artists has been systematically ignored (the late 1940s and early 1950s were more promising in showing 'Commonwealth' artists), the burden of representation for any single show or artist is considerable, especially given the lack of historical documentation of the work. In 1989 Eddie Chambers established the African and Asian Visual Artists' Archive (AAVAA). This was the only research and reference facility in the country exclusively concerned with documenting the history, presence and work of British-based Black artists. In 1992 he left AAVAA to concentrate on exhibition curating. Recent exhibitions have included 'Black People and the British Flag', 'Eugene Palmer', 'Us an' Dem', 'Home and Away', and 'Phaophanit & Piper'. His most recent exhibitions were 'Frank Bowling: Bowling on Through the Century' (which had a six gallery tour) and 'Tam Joseph: This is History'.

Eddie Chambers was appointed curator in residence at a very opportune moment for a new part time degree in cultural studies which was part of the provision offered by the Centre for Continuing Education at Sussex. The design of the degree took into account both the socio-economic environment of the region and its dominant industries (which are the 'cultural industries'). Within the array of options, students can take critical vocational strands by taking one year courses in arts management and/or multimedia design or digital arts (all of which provide vocational expertise and address regional needs, especially around curating and engaging in critical debate about the cultural industries). By introducing the arts management, multimedia and digital arts options into the degree we wanted to address questions of cultural policy and encourage students to recognise that the cultural industries are clearly organised industrially in specific ways and are part of the general productive system. On the other hand, the goods they manufacture . . . are unlike the products of other industries in that they play a pivotal role organising the images and discourses through which we make sense of the world . . . we need to conceptualise the relations between the material and discursive organization of culture without reducing one to the other.[7]

The presence of a curator in residence as a resource on which we could draw was particularly appropriate for adult students on this degree as the majority of them were interested in art and art history rather than having a knowledge of popular and youth cultures. By approaching visual art through an analysis of its institutional and financial support, its relation to capital (both cultural and economic) and the relationship between a society and its symbolic practice, and doing so in the social location of a gallery, cultural studies encourages us to probe into visual culture in terms of the social organisation and the structure of power in which it occurs. The students had already worked in the local art gallery, completing a gallery worksheet that had been jointly written with the education department of the gallery. The questionnaire encouraged them to consider the institution itself, its architecture as a means of suggesting a certain reading of its type of social space, and the difference between the ethnographic galleries and the fine art galleries in the hanging and selection process and their presentation of information.

Before their session with Eddie Chambers, the students had read Paul Gilroy's *There ain't no Black in the Union Jack* (1987). This was particularly appropriate as Chambers's exhibition called 'Black People and the British Flag' had been on that theme.[8] In addition, as a Black artist, he could raise questions of what the students thought of as 'their' culture and how invisible Black Britishness could be. The sessions started with a discussion around slides from the Flag show informed by the students' reading of Gilroy's book and moved from a discussion of the works to the conceptualisation of the exhibition and issues around cultural policy and ended with an (often moving) recognition by the students of the invisible and unacknowledged assumptions of their own positions as mainly white students, especially in relation to the authority of the big, main galleries (exhibitions at the Royal Academy in particular). The sessions with Eddie Chambers were a learning experience for me as much as the students and resulted in some deep discussions which considered race, ethnicities, cultural policy and accessibility and were also critical reflections made by a practitioner in the field.

The following year I met Eddie and asked him about the residency: the interview covers issues of art and institutional practices, the relationship between culture and education, identity and marginality (as exclusion and self-defined dissidence), and questions of audience and community.

Nannette Aldred: I am interested in the way in which you have moved from being an artist to the more overtly educational role of a curator and in particular your position of curator-in-residence at the University of Sussex. I suppose a significant part of your decision was your recognition of the lack of opportunities for Black artists working in Britain and that lack is not just about a lack of exhibiting opportunities but also the lack of a critical vocabulary to discuss the work. I'm interested in the way that you have raised questions about the larger cultural and educational contexts.

Eddie Chambers: Well there is an evolution within my work as a curator because I come from what might be termed 'a position of opposition'. That is to say, opposition to the invisibility of Black issues and agendas, and opposition to the oppressive workings of the status quo. It is this sense of 'opposition' that is my background in terms of my attitude towards Black culture, my work as a curator, an artist and a writer of art criticism. But that notion of 'opposition' is something that has at times I have to carefully consider, in terms of its application and relevance. There is an ongoing tension within my work because I want to remain faithful to my original vision of art, of what art can do and how art should operate but at the same time I have to be very mindful of the positions of the artists that I work with. A number of the artists I work with have no overt or explicit interest in notions of 'opposition' being associated with their practice. A number of artists that I work with want to be part of the 'normal' scheme of things, to be accepted as 'artists' in their own right – not necessarily as 'Black' artists or 'politicised' artists. There is an ongoing tension in my work between creating exhibition opportunities that slot into the dominant scheme of things and being true to activities that function in a much more, dare I say, confrontational kind of way.

NA: That epitomises the difference between your work as a 'private' art practitioner and somebody who works in a public cultural space. There is a debate that runs through your work concerning the dilemma between saying this is Black art as a category and it belongs in this world and wanting to work with and change the dominant institutions.

EC: These tensions do exist and they are difficult to accommodate and resolve within my curatorial practice. While I want to remain true to what one might call a 'Black' agenda, I also want to work with artists in an unfettered and unconstrained way. I don't always want to be seen as a 'Black' critic or curator of Black artists' work. I sometimes want to work without the sometimes constraining prefix of 'Black'. That was what was so good about the residency at Sussex University. It was not advertised as in any way being a position for a 'Black' curator, so that meant that during my time at the University working with students, I could raise their awareness of the conditions of Black British art and artists without it necessarily being the issue that dominated all of our weekly sessions. But I also wanted to ensure that students realised that sometimes, manifestations of Blackness were an essential part of a Black artist's practice. Within my weekly sessions, I also had to try to strike a balance between exposing students to work that personally interested me – that is, work with clear social and political narratives – and other artists' work that did not necessarily interest me as much.

I also wanted to make the students aware of some of the tensions and problems that might need to be considered when curating exhibitions. For example, some artists steer clear of anything that they think will locate them in a clumsy or heavy-handed way. A number of Black artists will steer clear of any kind of exhibition that they think is a 'Black' show. That is, 'Black' in a pigeon-holed or 'ghettoised' sense. I personally have major problems with this type of position, but I wanted to make it clear to the students that curating group exhibitions, particularly shows that one might regard as 'issue-based', might be a fraught or problematic process. For me as a curator, my consideration of and sensitivity to these issues is something that has developed over a period of time. Ten to fifteen years ago it was relatively easy to take the previously mentioned notions of 'opposition' and use these as a sort of universal yardstick for exhibition activity. Now, I don't think the curating of Black artists' work can ever be that straightforward. Numerous issues must always be considered. After all, the presence of Black artists in this country – just like the presence of Black people in this country – indicates a process of maturing and development. Back in the mid- to late-1970s, the presence of Black people like me was a 'new' presence. We, as British-born, British-raised, Black youngsters, were simply not a presence until the mid-1970s. People like me, the children of Caribbean immigrants emerged as a distinct new body of 'British' people not much more than 20 years ago. I would argue that for Black British youngsters, there was a greater sense of alienation and dislocation in the late 1970s and early 1980s than there is now. We have had to learn to grow and mature as 'British' people. Not as exiles in a strange land but as British people, at home in a country of which we are citizens. There are ways in which the 'Black community' has evolved significantly since I have been involved in the arts and I need to acknowledge that debates about the 'mainstream' and the 'margins' have changed fundamentally.

NA: Because of the work that people like you have been doing?

EC: Possibly, but these debates have involved many different commentators and activists. I believe that Black identity is the centre of the gravity in terms of Black creative expression, and that the ways in which we regard Black identity have changed fundamentally. In some ways these changes have been prompted or encouraged by individual thinkers and activists like Stuart Hall and other people who were major influences. But I suppose you could also argue that there have been some changes that are much less identifiable in terms of the things that drive them. For example, 16 or 17 years ago there were riots all over the country, in so-called Black 'inner-city' areas. Those riots were not necessarily prompted by the actions of individuals. They were general, communal expressions rather than the initiatives of one or two people. Those riots are not happening any more. How do orchestrations of shifts of culture and politics happen? What has happened to all that tension and energy?

NA: Are you suggesting that some of the anger has been dissipated through educational and cultural acceptance?

EC: There is a very good quote from Stuart Hall from an ICA publication on Black British Cinema. He said that 15 years ago he didn't have to think about or care that there was no Black in the union jack. But now, with the political and cultural landscape having shifted so much, it was now imperative that he (or we) took very seriously our stake as citizens of the country.[9]

NA: Do you think that it is necessary now to engage head-on with the image of the Union Jack as you have in your exhibition, *Black people and the British flag* – that it is no longer appropriate to be outside and ignore the dominant culture?

EC: I think what has happened is that some of the ideas, positions and assumptions that we as Black people were historically making about our presence in this country have outgrown their usefulness and can no longer serve us. We have had no choice but to actively consider the ways in which Britain defines and presents itself. When my parents came here it was considered that people like them came for no more than five or ten years, to save some money and then go back to the Caribbean. So they were, in cultural and political senses, 'living out of a suitcase'. In other words, not putting down proper roots or building a confident stake in the society. Obviously, Caribbean immigrants were not to know the extent to which their plans would change or remain unfulfilled, but taking the 'suitcase' analogy further, instead of 'living out of a suitcase', Caribbean immigrants really should have been looking to 'move into a house'.

By the time it started to dawn on Caribbean immigrants that many of them were here to stay, more or less at that precise moment, along came Rastafarianism and its attendant culture. In the mid- to late-1970s Rastafarianism, in its deep and profound appeal to young Black Britain, was heavily steeped in the notions of Black exile and displacement. Rastafarianism and the potent brand of reggae music that it influenced preached and encouraged a sense of Black Britain being in righteous exile. That thinking, that sense of alienation, impacted on the development of the British Black community. Just like our parents before us, I think it took young Black people a while to realise the implications of the fact that they were here and here for good. There is much evidence that we are coming to terms with this sense of being British, and I think that part of my work is identifying a cultural space for an expression of that 'Black Britishness'. By working as a curator I can create a space for the articulation of that identity.

NA: How important is the idea of that difference and identity being grounded in actual material conditions? You can't change history but how we understand it can be changed, as can current conditions. Does this alter the need for something called Black art? Does your project feed into the larger question of what is art as much as what is Black art?

EC: My main strategy in terms of curating is to create a visible space to show the work of the artists that I work with. In the early 1980s I was primarily interested in a sense of audience and community. My concern was that the work of Black artists be characterised by certain things; that this work in turn was oriented towards a Black audience and directed to the Black community. Now those concerns have gone out of the window – not because I no longer believe them so much but because other considerations have come into the scenario. It brings me back to what I mentioned earlier about Black artists having the right to be seen as 'artists' in an unconstrained sense of the word, and Black people in this country having the right to be seen as 'British' – in the most positive and progressive senses of the term. I suppose it is a matter of shifting priorities and contributing to a sense of place and visibility for Black artists. After all, it can't possibly continue to be the case that certain artists are excluded from the scheme of things simply because they are Black. I want to do what I can as a curator to facilitate the placing of Black artists' work within the wider scheme of things. The crux of this means abandoning, or setting to one side a sense that Black artists' work should primarily be aimed at Black audiences and that by extension, all sorts of British audiences are important. Whether this process has meant an abandoning of Black audiences is an uncomfortable question that remains. However, I should also add that too often in the past, Black artists, in exhibiting their work primarily to Black audiences, have had their work categorised or dismissed by the art establishment as being 'community art'. To answer your question, about my curating feeding into the larger question of what is art as much as what is Black art, I like to think that I may be making my own contribution to wider debates about the work and the role of the artist.

NA: There is evidence to show that galleries are offering more and more educational work and that growing numbers of people are attending continuing education courses in art. Students are interested in even conceptually difficult work like much produced under the BritArt banner. Is there evidence of a similar growth of interest in the artists and exhibitions that you work with?

EC: I think for Black artists, work that you might call 'conceptually difficult' is something from which they have been discouraged. This discouragement has been voiced by a number of Black art activists who were anxious to build bridges between the Black artist and the Black community. This process meant two things. First, as I've said, discouraging certain types of practice and second, building exhibition projects around the principle of 'accessibility'. The Black-Art Gallery in Finsbury Park were particularly keen to ensure that Black artists stayed on a literal, figurative and accessible path.[10] In the 1980s, for Black artists there was a strong sense of the need to connect audience with artist. 'Creation for Liberation' was a body based in Brixton who from 1983–87 organised four open submission exhibitions of the work of Black artists from all over the country. For CFL, the sense of 'community audience' was very important. Ideologically there was a massive gulf between my own attitude to art practice and their attitude to art practice but what CFL and myself had in common was a sense of the importance of Black audiences for Black artists' work. As I mentioned, there was the Black-Art Gallery in Finsbury Park, funded by Islington from 1983 until about 1990 and one of their central ideological planks was that the need for Black audiences should be acknowledged. Those concepts of audiences were very much of the 1980s.

But that was then and this is now. Some of the Black artists who are currently getting the most play are those whose work has no inevitable entry points. Their work is complex and challenging. I think the existence of these Black artists in high profile exhibitions is ample evidence of the ways in which Black British artists are maturing and developing and taking up rightful places within the 'mainstream'. These artists provide evidence of a type of wider artistic convergence, in which their work is in no way at odds with the work of many of the so-called 'BritArt' practitioners.

On the other hand, on a slightly tangential note, the Black press has histori-cally consistently let down Black artists. There are a number of Black papers and I believe they have a strategic role to play in informing Black people about the visual arts. But they have failed to fulfil that potential. Of course, there is the journal *Third Text*, which claims to offer 'third-world perspectives on contemporary art and culture', but it exists for a particular audience. Its subtitle is not going to endear it to many Black people, in fact probably the contrary! There was a magazine called *Artrage* which was took a 'multiculturalist' view of Black people's involvement in the arts, it came along in the 1980s and went in the early 1990s. I mention these things because there is much work to be done in encouraging Black people to take a greater interest in the visual arts.

NA: What difference do you think that work like yours has made in the way that art and art history is taught in higher educational art institutions?

EC: One thing that I do think has happened is that there is now a tangible body of material for academic and art history researchers to draw on. I know of several people who are doing PhDs on Black British art. That is very significant because the work of Black artists is now being recognised as a legitimate area of academic interest. Obviously, there have always been students doing BA and some MA dissertations but, until quite recently, nothing beyond that. There now exist significant bodies of material for researchers to draw on. I think increasingly the work of Black artists is being discussed and taken seriously as there is more archival and contemporary material to draw on. That certainly wasn't the case when I was a student. Then it was difficult to find the material to justify one's academic or professional interest in Black artists' work. But as usual, things are not as simple as they may at first seem. Now, instead of academia dismissing the existence of Black artists as a serious study option, I think that things have gone the other way for Black art students in particular, in that sometimes these Black students feel themselves to be under pressure from their tutors to make work that addresses, in skewed and prescribed ways, their Blackness. Sometimes now tutors say to Black students why don't you look at the work of Sonia Boyce and Keith Piper, which is good on one hand but on the other hand why should these students look at the work of Boyce and Piper just because they are Black? No Black student should ever feel themselves being racially pigeon-holed. But this sort of thing is happening, largely due to the familiarity with which some Black artists are now widely regarded.

Much of this regard, this familiarity has only come about quite recently. No one in academia used to be the least bit interested in the work of Black artists. It was only when people like Paul Gilroy, Stuart Hall and Kobena Mercer started to write about Black artists that the work of Sonia Boyce and other Black artists started to take on what you might call a mainstream respectability. When thinkers and writers like Gilroy and Hall started saying things like 'Black artists' work is interesting and important because it animates and interrogates ideas about "British" history and "British" identity, sexuality and so on . . .', it really helped to have those views expressed by academics of such standing, who were able to offer fresh ways of looking at the work of people like Boyce and Piper. Now the work of Black artists has become a legitimate area of interest – there is, I believe, someone at the Courtauld Institute doing a PhD about the history of Black art (or artists) in Britain (I don't know exactly which) and that is very significant, because there is no way that the Courtauld would have accepted that topic ten years ago.

NA: There is more acceptance in the academic community but the artists are not necessarily doing any better and the people that you would like to reach, the audience of ordinary Black people, are still doubly excluded. First, in not having a sense that art might belong to them rather than have nothing to do with them; but also because it has been further removed by being appropriated by institutional practice and then becoming part of the dominant culture, with some audiences still excluded.

EC: Yes, I think that those are very valid observations. As a curator I would really like to do some work with artists who would be keen to circumvent the whole art gallery system. But as I mentioned near the beginning of this conversation, the reason that a sense of 'community involvement', for want of a better term, hasn't been properly addressed by many Black artists is in part because of the professional aspirations of the artists themselves. Because what they most aspire to is the 'gallery' exhibition. Of course, lots of artists have gone through the 'community route' in terms of gallery outreach work, but fundamentally, gallery outreach work does not indicate or constitute an attachment to genuine communication and engagement with art itself. Genuine interaction between gallery and audience must involve some pretty basic and pretty fundamental questions about the role of art itself, the role of the artist, the role of the curator and the role of the gallery. Gallery 'education' work tends not to seriously raise these questions. Furthermore, artists and curators aren't usually interested in what happens within the art gallery beyond the private view. In Bristol we used to have a thing called Art on Tour that toured small scale exhibitions to sports and community centres, schools, libraries etc. It was a very good initiative but it did nothing to challenge the art gallery system. As long as there is a hierarchy of galleries that worships the sanctity of the white cube, and as long as serious artists want nothing more than white cube exhibitions, the gulf between art and audience will remain.

NA: Are those two things exclusive? What about a gallery like the Whitechapel that offers the 'white cube' but also with educational and public information events always programmed alongside?

EC: I think that the Whitechapel is a good model and one of the things I was able to do at Sussex was to invite Jane Sillis, the head of education down to talk about the integration of 'art' and 'education' into the gallery programme. Unfortunately education departments tend to be lower in the gallery hierarchy. They tend to be seen as a type of support or auxiliary service but that is, I believe, completely wrong. Education departments in art galleries – which in most cases just means a full or part-time education officer – are simply 'told' what the forthcoming exhibitions are, rather than having an input into the exhibition programme. Art galleries still tend to work within an ideology of art speaking for itself and the exhibition as an opportunity for the artist simply to make work in whatever media they use, rather than the exhibition being seen fundamentally as an opportunity for a dialogue with the public.[11]

NA: Art and educational institutions still marginalise certain sorts of activities. Do these margins provide you with spaces to challenge certain assumptions and allow different sorts of work to go on?

EC: The consistent factor in my work is a strategy for challenging and opposing racism. My curating is all about challenging the culture of invisibility or a culture that renders the work of Black artists of no consequence. This strategy is also present within my writing, and it is my art criticism that helps me to be true to my vision.

NA: *The ArtPack* was written as an educational resource . . .

EC: I don't know whether it worked in those terms but it was a first attempt, and quite a muddled attempt in some ways; but prior to that there was nothing that illustrated in colour the work of Black artists in Britain. It now sounds ludicrous because we're talking about ten years ago, but before *The ArtPack* there was nothing in print, in colour that included examples of the work of Black artists. In terms of what *The ArtPack* tried to do there were some aspects that were successful and I'm pleased to have been involved with it. On another note I feel I ought to mention that I have some problems with much of the material produced for an educational, school, context. I also have trouble with some of the ways that gallery education departments work, because education officers tend to want to fix meanings for work being exhibited. They tend to think that gallery audiences are only comfortable if the 'meanings' behind the exhibits are clearly 'explained' to them. But, at the risk of sounding postmodern!, I really do think that readings and meanings are allusive things. They depend on the viewer, on their own cultural and material histories. Meanings and readings can never be fixed, inflexible or emphatic things. And I think it is wrong to attempt to 'explain' art to the general public. Art should be something about which each of us makes up our own mind.

Going back to *The ArtPack*, I should have added that we also wanted to include a personal commentary about the emergence of Black artists in 1980s Britain. Not something that had a fixed or authoritative air about it, but something that took the form of personally expressed opinions, that adequately indicated that the writer had a familiarity with the history in question and its attendant debates. To me that was very important.

NA: If people are publishing more work about Black artists then that is going to provide material for better informed discussion and will allow dialogue between the tutor and students. What are your views on that?

EC: It's about presenting, in relatively easily accessible forms, informed arguments and opinions. What has happened in the last ten years is that there are now two or three centres where Black art archives, catalogues and articles are collected so that the researcher or interested gallery-goer can get a range of views on the work of Black artists. Access to these archives will I believe lead to more informed opinions being expressed about art and artists.

NA: So, even though there are no more exhibition spaces, there are spaces where people can reflect on arts practices. What have been gathered together are the educational resources that empower people to go out and encounter work in an informed way, so that people can ask their own questions about the invisibility of Black art. Once people have access to the information then they can start asking their own questions and finding their own answers. There are so few exhibition opportunities for all artists, so would you say that access to education and ideas are important?

EC: Absolutely, that is why in September 1988 with the assistance of the Arts Council and the Gulbenkian Foundation I set up the African and Asian Visual Artists Archive. I'd been documenting exhibitions and collecting material before then but when I set up the AAVAA that was the opportunity to promote the issue of archiving Black artists' work. I left the archive after four years and it is now in the library at the University of East London. Importantly, two or three other archives have been set up. So the work of Black artists, at least in London, is anchored around several research centres and the accumulative effect of that is very significant because to me, it is equivalent to having a couple of Black art galleries. Chelsea College of Art and Design also has a library that has a lot of relevant material. It is a very good collection about Black artists and it's turning into a major resource. Liz Ward, one of the librarians there has done a lot of work in the area and has been personally committed to the archiving of Black artists' work. I pass material on to these archives whenever I can. I also pass material to the National Museum of African Art Library at the Smithsonian Institution in Washington – the librarian there, Janet Stanley, has done a lot of work on the archiving of African artists' work. I send her material that relates to the work of diasporic Africans living and working in the UK.

Now that these archives exist, the manifestation of Black artists' work is changing. I should also mention that the Institute of International Visual Arts (the body that helped to set up my residency) also has a rapidly developing archive at their office base in central London.

NA: There are primary resources and there are also books like *Black Art and Culture in the Twentieth Century*.[12] That moves the debate into the Tate Gallery and mainstream publishing.

EC: Yes, but we still have to be careful. For instance, Paul Gilroy had some involvement with a show at the Tate Gallery that touched on issues relating to Black artists' work.[13] The exhibition was in a small side room and the accompanying brochure contained some very troubling art historical inaccuracies. I think that it is important to be rigorous. I think it is important that the history of Black artists working in Britain is always respected and treated as a proper and serious study. The Tate show, 'Picturing Blackness' was a shoddy and sloppy affair.

NA: How important is it that non-western art is now on the curriculum, in that it questions the dominance of the western tradition – offers new ways of seeing?

EC: You mention non-western art but to me the concept of non-western art is very problematic because it suggests all art is other to anything that can fit into the western tradition. I do have some problems with that approach and I think that it tends to dislocate the work of Black artists, from contemporary art, it locates the other in spaces that ultimately give Black artists' work a limited, rather than a wider currency. I think that the presence of 'non-western' art on any given curriculum is only a good thing if it properly challenges the bogus frames of reference that the west has created to look at 'non-white' art from around the world.

Returning briefly to the residency that I did at Sussex, I thought it was a very good model because I wasn't there in a 'racial' capacity, as I mentioned earlier, and the students didn't (as far as I could tell) register me in a 'Black' capacity. They simply related to me as a Curator-in-Residence and considered that I had experience in a field in which a number of them were interested in working. To me, because it was what one might call a 'deracialised' context, what that meant was that different issues of race could be animated in ways that were non-objectified. If you teach African art or non-western art as a module it will attract certain 'Africanists' or people who are inclined towards Africanism and at the same time other people won't be interested in it because they think it is not for them. When I talk about 'Africanists', I'm really talking about people who objectify Africa and its art, its culture, its people, its history. I think it is very important that as many Black graduates as possible choose academia as a career option, because if there are more Black people working in university departments then issues of 'race' can be sensitively and properly considered. I'm not suggesting that Black academics are only useful for their abilities to animate or address questions of 'race'. But I do believe that Black academics, whether or not they teach anything to do with Blackness, can be a very important presence on any given campus. Of course, at the moment, there is an insufficiently wide range of people working in art and art history in strategic or key positions in higher education departments and until there is more diversity reflected in the teaching faculty then the introduction of things like non-western art and the work of Black artists is going to be quite problematic.

What the residency allowed me to do was plot my own course in terms of my interaction with the students, there wasn't anything rigid about it. That fluidity was its strength, one week I might be talking about publicity, writing catalogues and organising exhibitions, then we'd go to a gallery and talk to a curator and artists or have a visiting speaker from a gallery or a gallery education officer, like Jane Sillis, whom I mentioned earlier. That flexibility allowed more interactivity with the students, asking students what they thought, what they wanted to discuss.

NA: So you could be responsive to students' needs and interests?

EC: I think at first they were hesitant in working like that. I was particularly pleased about the exhibition we organised at Bexhill,[14] and through that whole process they were encouraged to have faith in their own opinions. I thought the residency worked because of the level of debate and dialogue. I wanted them to reflect on what had gone wrong as well as the successes – to feel that they shouldn't be easily satisfied. I believe in the curator as activist, as someone who has personal and strong opinions who is trying to make a statement. What the art world believes in is the dispassionate statement: only balanced interventions as safe. I think that is the wrong way to curate exhibitions, because certain positions are masquerading as objective and inevitable. I was asking the students to be aware of how things were hung, what decisions had been made about the labelling of works, and their positions.

NA: Do you see curating as a political intervention?

EC: Yes, very much so. When I did my Flag exhibition the Director of Visual Art at the Arts Council got hot and bothered about some of things that I wrote in the essay, not because she necessarily disagreed with them but she thought the art catalogue wasn't the appropriate forum for expressing those sort of opinions. I think curators should express opinions about the work that they engage with, which isn't the usual view in the art world. I wanted to impress on the students that, in my view at least, they had every right to express their opinions through any exhibition that they might curate. Because everything is an expressed opinion, even if it does not present itself as such. I couldn't possibly think that, for example, the way that exhibits are displayed in Brighton Museum is any less 'political' than the ways in which some of my exhibitions seek to animate social issues.

NA: The strength of the residency seemed to lie in the fact that it was an opportunity for students to think about these important issues which are not part of the curriculum and are not examined at the end of a learning programme. It allowed students to be part of the process of determining their own learning. It seems that you were not engaged in training in the sense of training people to become curators. You were able to open up questions about curating and to encourage people to think about what that meant. Did you find the residency useful in terms of your own practice?

EC: Yes, I did, because it made me reflect on my own work and articulate why I do what I do and consider what my aims were. The students were receptive and different from the usual people I talk to professionally.

NA: The seminar that the cultural studies students took with you was different from the rest of your work as Curator-in-Residence because I had asked you to focus particularly on the relationship between the presence of Black British people and the gap between that presence and cultural representations of Black Britishness. The students were interested in the history of art but had not necessarily asked the question 'whose history' until that day. Have you any comments to add about that particular teaching that you did?

EC: The opportunity to talk with your students was a fascinating and useful one because it offered me another way of discussing the work of Black artists in general, and my 'Flag' exhibition in particular. In talking with the History of

Art students, we tended to avoid debates about culture, identity, history, nationality and other overtly social issues. I didn't have a problem with this, but it was a breath of fresh air to be able to discuss some of these issues in direct and candid ways within your session. I have an active interest in issues and debates that are not ordinarily located within 'art' or 'art history' contexts, so I greatly enjoyed my time with your students. Obviously, with them having read stuff by Paul Gilroy – plus whatever other ideas and debates they were previously familiar with – I knew that I was not just introducing your students to unfamiliar debates. We were able to throw around some established arguments and debates, which was useful to me, as much as it may have been useful to them. In any case, the major issues of how we see ourselves, in relation to how the country defines itself, are questions and debates that have an almost dynamic resonance. And as for the British flag, like it or loathe it, we cannot ignore it or assume it is an uncontested entity. On a personal level, I was gratified that so many of your students expressed considerable disquiet, insecurity and uncertainty about identity positions that I was perhaps assuming were fixed in ways that were antagonistic to my own positions. But this was not the case – I think we all found ourselves contributing to a debate in which our respective positions crisscrossed and overlapped. That was good.

NA: Our students benefited tremendously from the time with a professional worker who could critically engage with questions of cultural policy and national identity. Thank you for considering that as part of your residency and for taking the time to talk to me for this book.

Notes

1 Harris J, 'Alterity, metaphor and foundation: around the edges of a paradigm', *Oxford Art Journal*, Vol 14 No 2, 1991.
2 Gilroy R, *Small acts: thoughts on the politics of black cultures*, Serpent's Tail, London, 1993, p. 79.
3 For more information see Himid L, *The thin black line*, ICA, London, 1985; Araeen R, *The other story: Afro-Asian artists in post-war Britain*, Hayward Gallery, London, 1989; Chambers E, *The ArtPack: a history of black artists in Britain*, London, 1988; Owusu K (ed.), *Storm of the heart*, Camden Press, London, 1988; Aldred N, '*Postwar British art: a short history of the I.C.A.*' in Sinfield A and Davies A (eds), *The culture of postwar Britain* (Routledge, forthcoming).
4 'Interview with Stuart Hall: Culture and Power', *Radical Philosophy*, 86, 1997.
5 Gilroy, *Small Acts*.
6 These have been published widely in magazines such as *Race Today*, *Africa World Review*, *Circa*, *Creative Camera*, *Ten.8*, *Third Text*, *Artists' Newsletter* and the *Greater London Arts Quarterly*. Eddie Chambers is a regular contributor to *Art Monthly*.
7 Murdock G, 'Cultural studies at the crossroads', in Gray A and McGuigan J (eds), *Studying culture: an introductory reader*, Arnold, London, 1993, p. 87.
8 Gilroy P, *There ain't no black in the Union Jack*, Hutchinson, London, 1987; Chambers E, *Black people and the British Flag*, 1987.

9 'Now not only do we care, we *must*', Hall S, 'New ethnicities', in Mercer K (ed.), *Black film, British cinema*, ICA documents: No 7, Institute of Contemporary Art, London, 1989.

10 In 'A statement on Black art and the gallery', those responsible for running The Black-Art Gallery made the following comments: 'It is essential that Black artists aim to make their work "popular", [sic] – that is expression that the wide community can recognise and understand . . . it [Black Art] cannot afford to be élitist or pretentious'.

11 Eddie Chambers has recently become a consultant for Fabrica Gallery in Brighton (a gallery promoting understanding of contemporary art) which is introducing a quota system as a demonstration of its commitment to the work of artists of African and Asian origin.

12 Powell R J, *Black art and culture in the twentieth Century*, Thomas and Hudson, London, 1997.

13 *Picturing blackness in British art, 1700–1900*, 29 November 1995–10 March 1996. I should like to thank Cherry Gillingham, one of the students on the BA in Cultural Studies, for the work she did on this exhibition. I should also like to express my thanks to all the students on the course during that first year for all their insights and challenges in this (and other) seminars.

14 *Behind the Beach Hut*, de la Warr Pavilion, Bexhill on Sea, 27 September–26 October 1997.

10 A postcolonial pedagogy: questions of difference and the 'ethical horizon'

Christina Lupton and Heiko Henkel

When we began writing this chapter we wanted to make what we thought of somewhat naively as the simple point that postmodern or culturally relative approaches to learning were not ideology free but that they involved a real activity of subject-formation. By 'subject-formation' we refer here to the way in which even theories of culture which are associated with deconstructing, rather than constructing, ideal societies have certain ends in mind when it comes to their idea of who the 'free' student/subject is to be. In this case, we were thinking specifically of postgraduate humanities-based education in first world universities. But clearly our argument in this chapter applies to many forums where education programmes use the language of student-empowerment and dialogue to suggest that they are engaging with students in their 'difference'.

Fundamentally our sense remains that the basic principles of an 'open' and reflexive learning environment call for highly culturally specific skills. While we agree, basically, that such a learning environment is a good one, we also feel that it is necessary to point out just how specific – how ideologically laden – it really is to assume the 'freedom' and critical voice of the student as means rather than ends. To present such a classroom as obvious, natural or completely enabling of individuals as they stand is – we feel – to misrepresent what it really does.

So much for our simple point. As we began to think of ways to make it, we found ourselves in territory where the concepts of relativism already had well established lines of conflict with older models of socialist, progressive education. This concept of subject-formation we introduce is obviously one which has been used confidently as part of a socialist pedagogy, but is much less easily 'owned' in the new paradigm of liberatory, liberal education. And, roughly speaking, at the end of the 1990s most of us recognise (either regretfully or with some hope) that we are at a juncture where the idea of a left-wing political project is increasingly aligned with notions of difference rather than with the collectivity of a universal perspective.

Postcolonialism appears here as a way of naming the commitment to 'difference' which characterises one side of this divide. As a point in history, the postcolonial has been defined as an interregnum; a time when the logic of humanism, the European Enlightenment and essentialisms generally ceases to make sense, and when we begin to reassess – and deconstruct – these Eurocentric formations. As an academic practice, postcolonialism has been where, as San Juan puts it:

> We are advised to invent new relational logics, new concepts of communal border crossing and transnational habits, inaugurated and sustained in multiplicity . . . we are not allowed to generalise, much less totalise . . . Appeals to Enlightenment metanarratives of progress and liberation are not tolerated in this realm of deconstructive free play.[1]

In effect this has meant literature, history and geography courses where texts are read as having excluded or stereotyped the colonial 'Other', and where at all levels of historical and current analysis an effort is made to introduce to Western academic practice the sense that there is always, and inevitably, an other story to the one told in terms of rationality.

For Cornel West, this turn results in what he calls the 'New cultural politics of difference':

> The distinctive features of the new cultural politics of difference are to trash the monolithic and homogeneous in the name of diversity, multiplicity, and heterogeneity; to reject the abstract, general, and universal in light of the concrete, specific, and particular; and to historicise, contextualise, and pluralise by highlighting the contingent, provisional, variable, tentative, shifting and changing.[2]

Yet radical education has historically equipped itself politically with many of the exact certitudes and collectivities which West's new politics rejects. It is hardly surprising, then, that its encounter with these contemporary theorisations of 'difference' has been a difficult one. Most people involved in teaching literature or cultural studies today can attest to an all too apparent friction between the commitment to education for social change and the climate of relativism which has either challenged this commitment, or transformed it into something so defensive of individual differences that it becomes difficult to see where the basis for any ethical horizon might be.[3] Marjorie Mayo and Jane Thompson's collection *Adult learning, critical intelligence and social change* is indicative of how many of those who remain wedded to some vision of socialist progress feel that they do so in spite of postmodern and postcolonial theories of subjectivity, identity and history. In their article 'Challenging the postmodern condition' (which appears in Mayo and Thompson's collection) Paula Allman and John Wallis speak for many in adult education when they suggest that the very relativism which West celebrates as 'the new cultural politics of difference' is actually 'the impasse for radical education'.[4]

The postcolonial classroom

The aim of this chapter is to bring to the foreground certain elements of ethical intention within postcolonial theories of difference which might make less of this impasse. Such elements suggest that postcolonialism involves principles more political and collective than are at first apparent. By making them visible, we hope to begin a more candid account of what postcolonial education really does in terms of forming subjects and societies. In turn, we want to suggest that radical education actually has a history of commitment to difference from which more relativising approaches to pedagogy do not veer as sharply as they may first appear to. Our 'line' – to put it simply – is that 'pedagogy' and 'postcolonialism' can be concepts related not only by tension, but also by continuity.

One of our reasons for highlighting this continuity is the specificity of our own perspective – a perspective importantly shaped by the particular historical moment at which we enter this debate. Growing up in the 1970s and 1980s, we are both the inheritors of Marxian commitments and children of the postcolonial present, speaking from a time when neither the politics of 'difference' nor the urgent need for agreement can be denied. Difference as a political imperative is not as 'new' for us as West's formulation suggests – cultural diversity is not so much an achievement struggled for, or a ghost which haunts a 'new world order'; it is, as it were, our formative experience. When we look to a 'politics of cultural difference' we do this because it now seems clear to us that any contemporary project must take this question of difference on board as its necessary and enabling condition. Yet as people writing very much from within this 'condition', it also seems clear that we cannot afford to interpret the climate of relativism as the postmodern hubris which Wallis and Allman suggest it is.

Throughout this chapter, we use the idea of pedagogy in broad terms. At one level we are interested in raising the somewhat instrumental question of how cultural difference might actually be 'taught' in tertiary education. At another, however, pedagogy also serves as a heuristic device. It is the challenge of the classroom which leads one's concepts most thoroughly into crisis, opening up, in turn, new ways of seeing. Unlike purely theoretical discourses which celebrate the politics of difference, the pedagogical situation cannot deny its political implications and responsibilities. To think through the postcolonial commitment to the partial and the relative in terms of teaching is therefore to put its claims to tolerance and intervention most directly to the test.

To be fair, most critics of cultural relativism in the realm of pedagogy take issue with a poststructuralist effect, rather than a notion of postcoloniality itself. The difference here is important, and it is worth distinguishing between the two in order to clear some space for thinking of postcolonial experience as grounded outside French philosophy. To over-simplify: structuralist, and then poststructuralist philosophy exposes the way in which the subject is centred through language rather than essence. The decentering of this subject is a process which involves denaturalising the systems of meaning (seen as having the structure of language) which produced its centrality. This process is conceptually dependent upon the idea of difference in revealing the relational element of this subject position. The result, for the projects which deconstruction can aid, is that our selves, our identities and our struggles can then be understood as the effects of a shifting and provisional field of meanings rather than as fixed or independent of the positions they appear to differ from.[5]

But these poststructuralist contributions have occurred very much as a decentering (of canonical formations and the subject of the West) from within. It is largely a philosophical event which still takes place – as Enlightenment discourse – in the élite spaces of the West.[6] It significantly introduces the category of 'the Other' as a philosophical imperative; a lacuna in our own formations, but even as it does so, the 'oppositional manner' of this form of criticism may conceal the fact that it remains solidly within the European culture that produced it.[7]

In citing poststructuralism like this, we can see postcolonialism as a much more explicit attempt to bring this voice of 'the Other' in: through 'third world literature', through emphasising histories of the colonised, through critics and teachers who have in one way or another a foothold outside 'the West'. Here, challenging Western formations of authority implies two things. On the one hand, it involves recognising the ways in which what seems most natural within 'the West' is often complicit with imperialism – which is where postcolonialism as a field of study has benefited from the poststructuralist erosion of the Western subject. On the other hand, the idea of postcoloniality takes this project further by insisting on the real need for the 'voice' of difference to occupy the space left by the 'deconstruction' of Western literature, geography, philosophy and history.

In her article *The position of the critic in post-colonial studies*, Anne Zimmerman argues that a successful postcolonial practitioner would be defined by her part in a process of reciprocity and her preparedness to 'interact with the subaltern without desiring to impose his or her view on them'.[8] (Here the 'subaltern' refers to those subordinated populations oppressed by colonial/postcolonial regimes in various ways.) Without much extrapolation it can be said that the success of 'postcolonial' teachers would be judged along the same lines: they would be able to engage groups of students from 'different' and subordinated backgrounds in a discussion where meanings could circulate without one 'Western' version of events having to function as a yardstick. This is obviously the biggest challenge for any kind of postcolonial practice and its apparent impossibility haunts the range of progressive discourses which postcolonial theory has to offer. Yet the challenge of engaging with students and texts from non–Western cultures 'without imposing our view on them' also provides an urgent case for suggesting that the contours of an educational practice which reflects the 'politics of difference' would need to go beyond (and militate against) any simple training in deconstruction.

There are many examples of what this 'real' postcolonial classroom might look like. The British university today increasingly solicits international students, many of whom come from former colonies, and most of us need not look far afield to see how complicated, rich and ironic the teaching of and to and across 'cultural difference' can be. This is not least of all because the presence of 'postcolonial subjects' challenges continuously any definition of 'difference' or 'otherness'. For example, in the context of the multicultural classroom, there are unlikely to be clean lines dividing racial and ethnic groups: 'new ethnicities' and identities will almost certainly be ones which defy reduction to class, ethnic descent, or cultural heritage. There will be Indian–Austrian students who speak four languages and move in an intellectually and economically privileged world and there will be students who claim that their blackness has never been an issue for them because they're just British, but who are eager to talk about the exclusion they have felt as a gay woman reading Jane Austen.

The postcolonial classroom

The very complications of this setting bring out two elements of the postcolonial which are important to this chapter. First, they show how issues of race and difference are now 'on the table' in international universities, and therefore in the formation of any vision of radical education for the future. The question of cultural difference is not something to which European visions of utopia can simply adapt; it is now constitutive of the audiences and students to which such visions must appeal. This is not to suggest that the diversity displayed in a 'postcolonial' classroom lends itself easily to images of a happy 'melting pot', for it obviously also marks one of the sites where factions and misunderstandings can make such an appeal most hazardous and ambiguous.

The relationship between the classroom and the world is, of course, complex, and a discussion of the multicultural classroom does not in any simple way stand in for a discussion of the postcolonial world at large. But these classrooms are a clarifying example of a larger cultural and economic problematic: many of the approaches and strategies characterising the notion of a postcolonial pedagogy address the general problems which international agencies, 'development' organisations, and non-governmental organisations (NGOs) at all levels face as advocates of difference who do not want to 'impose their view' on the communities they co-operate with or 'help'. Here pedagogy, as much as policy making in a larger context, illustrates the difficult translation of the celebration of difference into a concrete social project.

The second element of the postcolonial that the international classroom brings to the foreground is the collective nature of the forums within which this 'new politics of difference' gets spoken of. For, however much it is evident as a venue for difference, the postcolonial classroom is no simple trope for global diversity. In all its diffusion, this classroom has to be read as a limited sample of the great range of socio-economic and cultural positions which make up the spectrum of possibilities in the postcolonial world-order: raising the question of difference here, in the liberal democratic setting, is already radically distinct from addressing the problems of economic inequality or dependency which make up so much of the 'difference' between 'first' and 'third' worlds. The instance which the international humanities-based classroom provides therefore limits the scope of the 'politics of difference' to a realm where many of these basic questions of privilege have already been answered at an individual level.

Here, the setting of the postcolonial classroom serves as an important suggestion that institutionally posed questions of difference inevitably involve questions of common ground; of similarity. The very limitations of the classroom sample point to the postcolonial classroom in the international university as a site as important for negotiating sameness as it is as a venue-for-difference: sameness of language, of privilege, of mobility can be seen as characteristic of the international student community's structure, as much as the differences which give that community its form. However irreducible the differences which characterise the postcolonial student constituency are, they make their appearance in an environment where the agreements between parties in that dialogue are also what lend something like 'postcolonialism' its potential to bring about change.

This sort of recognition of collectivity, though, tends to be very far afield from what education for 'difference' generally promotes as its own agenda. One of the more systematically pedagogical distillations of the 'politics of difference' has been the Critical Pedagogy movement in the United States.[9] Under the banner of pedagogy, Peter McLaren, Henry Giroux and others combine the importance given to difference with a more traditionally radical form of commitment to what they call 'critical democracy'. In this avowed political move they attempt to weave the possibilities of radical schooling into the project of creating a democratic public sphere.

In practical terms, what the advocates of Critical Pedagogy emphasise is a classroom which would encourage critical awareness among students of their own conditions, empowering them to voice their own diverse experiences. The curriculum designed to encourage this, Critical Pedagogy suggests, is a situational one which takes its cues from the students' own agendas. Giroux uses the idea of a 'border pedagogy' to suggest a process where the modes of knowledge/pedagogy would themselves be open to challenge and reinvention from both sides. The emphasis here is not specifically on issues of race or imperialism but Giroux does engage explicitly with the term postcolonial to describe his project. In effect, what Giroux promotes is the alliance between scholars who are dedicated to making the relationships of western/imperial power visible and those moving away from a centre/periphery model of authority in the classroom.[10]

This form of radical pedagogy which claims an ethical alliance with postcolonial theory includes the work of the American feminist bell hooks. In *Teaching to transgress*, hooks, like Giroux and McLaren, describes an open, communicative classroom in which students are highly self-reflexive, in which self awareness sits alongside awareness of power structures, and in which the teacher actively facilitates the emergence of individual positions. As hooks describes it, this classroom dialogue is often a painful one, where both students and teachers are expected to take part in a paradigm shift that comes directly from their willingness to engage with one another's different and partial position.[11] Through their insistence on difference at this level hooks, Giroux and McLaren are advocating what might be called a 'postcolonial pedagogy' which is rooted in a political project; a juncture, perhaps, where radical education seems able to work with the tenets of postcolonialism.

The problem, though, is that the advocates of Critical Pedagogy only reach this juncture by downplaying the sense that they are heading anywhere specific; they would certainly deny that they expect their students to be any particular sort of people, and they are highly resistant to any teleological reading of the dialogic process. This is epitomised in their selective treatment of the work of Paulo Freire. Both Giroux and hooks depend heavily upon a version of Freirean education in which the didactic element of Freire's programme for change is downplayed.[12] This all but denies that while Freire's programmes were designed to emphasise the world the students already knew and to use this world as the basic 'text' (ie not to impose views 'from above'), they were also designed to initiate the process through which the student placed themselves in history and began the struggle against hegemonic social relations.[13] 'Besides being an act of knowing,' said Freire, 'education is also a political act. That is why no pedagogy is neutral.'[14]

Dialogue and difference

The suggestion in Giroux and hooks's use of Freire is that the distinction between a socialist and a postcolonial education can be roughly measured as the distinction between education with a political objective and education as an open-ended dialogue. But there are ways in which Freire's teleology is inextricably wedded to dialogue, and there are ways in which dialogue, as Freire himself points out, is nothing if not a political principle.

Historically, after all, socialist education is no stranger to the perspective of the student as different. In England, the history of adult and workers' education is also one where a real emphasis on the student as an individual, and on the validity of working class experience, has been foregrounded in socialist terms. The work of Raymond Williams, Richard Hoggart, and E P Thompson has all veered radically away from the conservative, nineteenth-century view of the working class as 'empty vessels' into which learning had to be poured.[15] Since the work of Raymond Williams and the rise of cultural studies in Britain, even national culture has been understood as having the dimensions of a postcolonial society, with different forms of cultural experience all being valued in a non-hierarchical sense.

As class analysis has been modified by an emphasis on experience (itself problematic in the Marxist lexicon), adult educators have increasingly prized dialogue as the necessary condition for these differences and experiences to be expressed, and seen critical awareness as being developed through the valida-tion of individual, working class experience/culture. In his essay 'The role of the teacher', Hoggart expresses these tenets in the formula that the teacher should form part of a 'critically alert' group, where all members are part of a learning community and where his/her responsibility is often to remain in the background and let the students express what they already know.[16] The classroom he describes is not very different from Freire's:

> It is important to stress again the value of starting and indeed *the absolute need to start from where the people are*. This is always a double process; it is partly an understanding of what pupils or students are really saying and so of the texture of their lives, the better to understand the connections which can be made and developed from; it is partly a process of self examination by the teacher and this is quite a difficult process in which we strip ourselves of the protection given by those academic or pedagogic styles which give us the edge over members of the class.[17]

And yet, in terms of their place in a larger context, the classrooms which Freire or Hoggart describe *are* very different from the ones which Giroux and McLaren advocate as representative of a 'critical democracy'. Throughout British cultural studies, the experience of the working class student may be valued as part of a whole culture – may in some sense be the ideal experience – but this distinc-tion is also one which must at some point be written out of the ideal society. Given that class distinction has eventually to be seen as the problem of differ-ence, the categories of experience dividing those students from their teacher or from each other are not the categories upon which an ideal society depends. While differences in individuals' cultural experience are acknowledged, in the end it is these individuals who will come to share some sense of their com-munity and of their common purpose which succeeds their histories of differ-ence; they will understand the same world.

It is this kind of 'sameness' which postcolonial theories of education leave out of their versions of Freire or cultural studies. Admittedly, Giroux and hooks may actually support this socialist political objective in many ways. But in the version of Freirean education which they promote as being better suited to the multiracial/postcolonial classroom, such an objective appears very much beside the point. The very absence of such a utopia is what gives their use of Freire its definitive postcolonial 'swing'. In Giroux or hooks, the teleological certainties of Freire's early Marxism are replaced by an emphasis on the processural elements of dialogic education. Although these educators remain concerned with what sort of world unfolds outside the classroom, there is a far greater reluctance to assume Freire's responsibility for who the student/subject should be in that world. Rather than being points of recognition in the process of optimising 'the individual', differences of race/gender/ethnicity are seen as operating indefinitely and therefore working against any one concept of the 'free' individual. In this move, in spite of their heavy debt to Freire (and to British Cultural Studies), most 'postcolonial' educators have teased out the open-endedness of Freirean education while criticising the universalising tendencies of Freire's view of subjectivity. Giroux, for instance, has celebrated the defiance of hegemonic closure which can be found in Freire's later work as the better version of his earlier emphasis on a clearly defined view of 'the peasant'; and Gregory Jay and Gerald Graff, in a less benign attempt to expose Freire to the climate of relativism, have accused Freire of working with too deterministic categories of oppressed and oppressor.[18]

There is no doubt that at some level this move away from the single emancipatory path (upon which Freire's original formulation depends) is crucial to a wider postcolonial setting and it is a move which Freire himself supports in his later work. But the ease with which these postcolonial versions of the dialogic seem simply to slide the idea of the critical subject away from the context of any culturally specific objective misleadingly suggests that the older emphasis on subject formation and an exclusive emancipatory project can be simply left out of the 'new politics of difference'. The benefit of this illusion, an important one for the postcolonial educator, is that possibility of claiming that we no longer 'impose our views' on those we teach. This new claim is shaky though, because it depends on the idea that dialogue can operate purely as a method without defined outcome or interlocutor. This is a premise which denies the ways in which the postcolonial notion of dialogic education does depend upon its own form of the ideal society and of the free subject.

Critical democracy

What is clear so far, is that the tendency is for those who see themselves as proponents of a 'postcolonial' educational practice to vehemently defend the classroom which is open to culturally different texts/bodies/voices 'without imposing its view on them'. But this is, perhaps, too glib a definition of what a postcolonial classroom actually needs to involve. To begin with, we need only look at the specificity of an international university to see what subject positions such an environment affords and precludes. At the most basic level, even educators like hooks are not suggesting that students cease to write essays, construct arguments, and refer to a theoretical/literary canon. These boundaries, if nothing else, set up the differences between the natives and non-natives of the university world. And as Bourdieu and Passeron argue, the codes which govern this world are highly implicit and often misleading in their claims to simply represent 'reason'.[19]

Although those talking about teaching with the idea of difference in mind do usually rely more on the classroom discussion or the non-conventional written assignment as their proof of a new form of inclusion, they often risk taking the apparently 'open' learning environment as a guarantee against 'illegitimate' subject formation. bell hooks, for instance, rarely refers to her students' written work, but depends heavily on the idea of her classes as supportive and critical communities. This is one of her descriptions of a class:

> Working with a critical pedagogy based on my understanding of Freire's teaching, I enter the classroom with the assumption that we must build community in order to create a climate of openness and intellectual rigor . . . what we all ideally share is the desire to learn: to receive actively knowledge that enhances our intellectual development and our capacity to live more fully in the world. It has been my experience that what one needs to build community in the classroom is to recognise the value of each individual voice. In my classes students keep journals and often write paragraphs during class which they read to one another.[20]

Without discrediting the value of the community which hooks describes here, one can point to the sort of subjects her classroom privileges. Students for whom principles of 'knowledge', 'openness', 'acceptance of difference' are second nature are obviously going to fare far better in hooks's terms than those who do not feel comfortable sharing such forms of knowledge. In celebrating the individual who has, or can be given, access to the forum of democratic speech, hooks claims to be enacting the kind of pedagogy which is equally open to different voices. But in normalising the category of individuals who are keenest to co-operate with this classroom style, hooks also implicates the category of students who do not speak like this – and here the criteria for celebration draw specifically on a certain (liberal, western) culture of knowledge.

For the student who comes to bell hooks's class demanding to be 'taught', or wanting to be silent, or wanting to be the sort of individual who separates her own experience from her academic work, there are still positions which hooks's 'dialogue' disallows. These are arguably easy positions to dismiss because they are also probably the ones we see as least desirable. But they are sufficient for pointing out at the most basic level that 'critical democracy' discriminates between the sorts of 'free' individuals it supports. Such discriminations will often involve backing those from certain cultures and classes over others. As examples, the common assumptions that 'good' students in a liberal university will argue with the positions of those they read, or will be willing to draw on their own experience in making sense of their academic journey, operate as part of a liberal norm rather than as universal precepts. And well might such ideals be defended.

But, as Chandra Mohanty points out, even the notion of 'irreducible contingency' can and should itself be seen as an ideological project, with its own power of cultural and social prescription and its own power to shape the individual.[21] On our part, this is no accusation: acknowledging that an ideological choice underlies 'the politics of difference' is fundamental to our suggestion that socialist and relativist approaches to teaching have some compatibility of structure. However, it is precisely the fact that the 'politics of difference' does involve a set of ethical imperatives which means that its project of dialogue can also go wrong: acknowledging that it has objectives also involves acknowledging where they are yet to be realised.

The idea of dialogue, in other words, is no easy guarantee of radical difference. On the contrary, once institutionalised, the idea of the dialogic can and often does work against real differences. Various critics have drawn attention to ways in which the rhetoric of the multicultural, multiracial university can stabilise forms of inequality and exclusion. S P Mohanty, for instance, describes the institutional discourse of pluralism – particularly in the United States – having created a legitimate space for programmes and departments in women's studies and Afro-American Studies while also depriving these causes of their oppositional position. Others point to the way in which discourses of difference have failed to change the basic structuring of what is accepted and condoned in academic terms. Gita Rajan argues that the 'Other' who is now allowed – even invited – to speak in the academy is also only able to do so under certain governing conditions:

> The movement and inscription of differences has become commonplace in the academy. Yet if a multicultural body, either textual or material, has to enter this arena of discourse, it has to transgress a series of concentric circles to speak the truth (can one dare say truth?).[22]

Even when the positions which are expected of the student/teacher who is representing some sort of cultural difference serve as positions of dissent, the process of assimilation which underlies this invitation to speak 'from the centre' tends to be one of rigorous 'westernisation'.

What these criticisms point to – from various directions – is the sense that it is not enough to announce differences as being simply 'out there', waiting only to be affirmed or brought out in the right sort of dialogue. It is, rather, a matter of choosing which sort of utopia we want to defend. If it is to be one where disagreements and differences flourish, we are still dealing with an ideal outcome, not with an easy statement of reality. Like the classrooms of more pronounced ideological intention, critically democratic classrooms are ones where certain ideals operate and where institutional and social realities consistently fall short of them. The idea of the dialogic is not, as Critical Pedagogy tends to suggest, a possible substitute for the Marxian or Freirean commitment to a culturally specific view of freedom. We are still, at base, defending the need for change in a certain direction.

While it may seem all too markedly clear, it is worth stating how difficult the *activity* of cultural relativism really is, especially in educational terms. The actual changes which would need to take place, just so that a broad range of 'postcolonial' students could feel equally at home in the exchange of views around the seminar table, are no less than enormous. They are also changes which we can, with some optimism, think of as having had an enormous impact in the last 20 years.

In this light, the calls for radical postcolonial dialogue may well be best introduced as specific 'ethical horizons'. Given some acceptance of such horizons, notions of agreement and collectivity can become valid in the name of difference. The important effect of the foregrounding/ backgrounding move here is to allow the figure of ideological intention back into the pedagogical equation in a way that makes it productive to plural notions of subjectivity.

This is not to refute the possibility of a dialogue which does not impose its view on 'them' as an ultimate objective. But given that it is clearly no easy feat to begin with difference as a 'fact', it is important see that this desire for ultimate individuality is a project of utopian dimensions. This postcolonial project, moreover, still has a largely western/democratic model as its ideal. This is an ideal which is neither easily realised nor already universal: its existence is therefore still as reliant upon the collective imagination as on the expression of the culturally different.

Henry Giroux claims: 'I don't care what positions the students take. I want them to be able to justify whatever position they do take so they come out with a clearer sense of what they believe in and the effects that might have.'[23] What we have wanted this chapter to suggest is that the opposite is necessarily true. Giroux *does* care what positions they take – if only because he defines his classroom as a place where there is a commitment to different positions being equally recognised. This seemingly modest goal of an educational dialogue must, if it is to be achieved, be underwritten by a whole set of agreements between members of a society that these are ends worth achieving. For example, it means people willing to work together – from different positions, but with a spirit of agreement that should, and largely *already does*, underwrite the language of these postcolonial commitments. Here a postcolonial practice has to come to terms with the fact that it is working towards something more than the obvious. Culturally speaking, no notion of critical democracy is obvious or universal. Nor is the setting of a liberal university. But given that these are often among the most valuable settings that we have to contribute to the 'new cultural politics of difference', it is important to find ways to frame them as *options* which we want to defend.

Although a move towards a postcolonial pedagogy would certainly involve policy changes at curricular and methodological levels, it would also require a perspectival shift in how we presented education as critical democracy. The reality that needs to be acknowledged is that when we gather under the roof of academic institutions in the name of representing difference, however far we travel from around the world to do this, whatever thresholds of marginality we cross, we are gathering as representatives of more or less one ideological project. However far this community can be extended, its terms of consensus are going to be evident and important as terms of inclusion and exclusion. Were we to argue only that this dialogue we are involved in is unceasingly open to differ-ence, we would have to read the evidence of this process of exclusion and inclusion as a simple accusation. Yet by restating the commitment to difference as one which is culture-specific, and indeed also class-specific, it may become possible to be less defensive about not yet having brought it into reality.

In a postcolonial setting, this awareness of ourselves as practitioners of specific critical, democratic – sometimes even still socialist – ideals is increas-ingly important. Taking this language of the postcolonial seriously also means finding ways to acknowledge that which seems all too obvious to those outside the academy: our own sameness as participants in this dialogue for change. And this involves finding ways to own the reality of this sameness in ways that we can formulate positively, in terms of the institutional and social possibilities that we have at our disposal in the academic community.

Reflecting on 'sameness' is also a way of staying answerable to those we teach. This involves what we suggest should be the primary criteria for a postcolonial pedagogy: that we should choose practices and curricula whose rationale could be laid out in terms that we were able to defend, and which could be understood and contested 'from the outside'. For if we are to really consider the question of the 'Other' 'without imposing our view on them', it will have to be as the Other who is not already included in our preallocated spectrum of different positions, and who may well challenge the very liberal precepts which we have set up to include her.

If we see the postcolonial as the material instance of cross-cultural educa-tion, then we need to discover in its formations the best way to keep on teaching and speaking without losing faith in our limited roles. In this chapter, we have suggested that there are three elements to this, all of which have origins to be found in both radical/Marxist and postcolonial paradigms. The first is to recognise the degree to which postcolonialism itself inherits a cultur-ally specific pedagogy, and therefore an ideological project. The second is to recognise the degree to which its conditions of success are not yet realised, and to rethink the sort of material changes which will create these conditions in terms of a collective, rather than an individual commitment. The third is to enact this project in educational terms we are prepared to own, so that when we discuss culturally different texts we can be clear about the reasons for our ways of doing so, and the processes of subject formation which enter into the reading practice we encourage.

We began with Allman and Wallis' claim that postcolonialism presents an impasse for radical education. The aim of this chapter has been to reapproach this impasse by bearing in mind that, like radical/Marxist pedagogy, the politics of difference also involves an ethical horizon. Here the insistence on difference and the insistence on sameness, or universality, cannot, finally, be seen in opposition. Rather they become fluid in what we have described as the foregrounding and backgrounding of both difference and sameness in the two paradigms. Through this relationship between difference and community, where any celebration of difference needs also to be read as the language of a political and therefore collective project, it is possible not only to avoid Allman and Wallis' impasse but also to emphasise the notion of responsibility in diffuse landscapes of cultural difference.

If there is an element which is radically postcolonial here, it is that there will be those for whom our notions of subjectivity and freedom are radically different; a question of an audience that we can no longer predict. But this is less the moment to lose faith in our own positions than to be clearer than ever about what they are. What we owe to those who are speaking from outside this democratic convention is not a new element of uncertainty, through which we are only ever in danger of wielding – again – the weapon of the ethical universal newly encoded as our understanding of difference, but the commitment to staying answerable to a form of opposition which is not part of our scripted inclusions. This is something we can only encourage by being attentive to our own project of encouraging difference and equality as an ethically defensible goal and recruiting as many students to this cause as possible.

Notes

1 San Juan E, Jnr, *Beyond postcolonial theory*, Macmillan, Basingstoke, London, 1998, p. 2.

2 West C, 'The new cultural politics of difference', *October*, 53, 1990, p. 93.

3 We are indebted to Ato Quayson for the term 'ethical horizon', which he introduced during a discussion at the 'New Directions' conference at the University of Sussex in 1997.

4 Allman P and Wallis J, 'Challenging the postmodern condition: radical education for critical intelligence', in Mayo M and Thompson J (eds), *Adult learning, critical intelligence and social change*, NIACE, Leicester, 1995, p. 26.

5 Homi Bhabha, in 'The other question', has argued that deconstructive theories cannot do the work of representing the Other. Gayatri Spivak makes this same point repeatedly of deconstruction/poststructuralism, invoking it as a strategy for questioning existing formations rather than claiming it is sufficient in naming new ones. See 'Feminism and deconstruction, again: negotiations' in Spivak G, *Outside in the teaching machine*, Routledge, New York and London, 1993, pp. 121–40.

6 This is not to forget that academics from many non-Western backgrounds form the core of Postcolonial and Poststructuralist theorists, but to suggest that these scholars are generally well centred as part of 'Western' formations.

7 See Said E, 'Reflections on recent American "left" literary criticism', *Boundary 2*, Vol 111 No 1 (Fall, 1979), p. 13.

8 Zimmerman A, 'The position of the critic', in Doring T, Schafer U and Stein M (eds), *Can the subaltern be read? – the role of the critic in postcolonial studies*, Goethe-Universität Frankfurt am Main, Frankfurt, 1996, p. 79.

9 See Giroux H A and McLaren P L, 'Radical pedagogy as cultural politics: beyond the discourse of critique and anti-utopianism', in Zavarzadeh M and Morton D (eds), *Theory/pedagogy/politics: texts for change*, University of Illinois Press, Urbana, 1991.

10 See Giroux H, 'Paulo Freire and the politics of postcolonialism', in McLaren P and Leonard P (eds), *Paulo Freire: a critical encounter*, Routledge, London, 1993, p. 178.

11 bell hooks, *Teaching to transgress: education as the practice of freedom*, Routledge, New York, 1994.

12 Interestingly, Wallis, Allman and Rajan all also use Freire to exemplify their ideal pedagogy, pointing to the degree to which his models are open to partially serving both Marxist and postcolonial perspectives.

13 See Freire P, *The pedagogy of the oppressed* (trans. Ramos M B), Penguin, Harmondsworth, 1972.

14 Freire P and Shor I, *A pedagogy for liberation: dialogues on transforming education*, Bergin, South Hadley MA, 1987, p. 13.

15 See Steele T, *The emergence of cultural studies 1945–65: cultural politics, adult education and the English question*, Lawrence and Wishart, London, 1997; and also Steele's contribution to the present volume.

16 Hoggart R, 'The role of the teacher', in *An English temper: essays on education, culture and communication*, New York, 1982.

17 Hoggart, 'Role of the teacher', p. 39 (emphasis added).

18 See Giroux, 'Freire and the politics of postcolonialism'; Jay G and Graff G, 'A critique of critical pedagogy', in Nelson G and Barb M, *Higher education under fire*, Routledge, New York, 1985. In response, Freire has pointed out the extremely naive position of those who fail to see that such categories continue to operate: see Macedo D and Freire P, 'A dialogue: culture, language and race', in *Harvard Educational Review*, Vol 65 No 3, Fall 1995.

19 Bourdieu P and Passeron J-C, 'Introduction: language and relationship to language in the teaching situation', in Bourdieu *et al.*, *Academic discourse: linguistic misunderstanding and professional power*, Polity, Cambridge, 1994. See also Brian Street, 'Academic Literacies' (unpublished paper).

20 hooks, *Teaching to transgress*, p. 40.

21 Mohanty C, 'On race and voice: challenges for liberal education in the 1990s', *Cultural Critique*, Vol 14, Winter 1989.

22 Rajan G, 'Is my body proper? Postcoloniality in the classroom', in Rajan G and Mohanran R (eds), *Postcolonial discourse and changing cultural contexts*, Greenwood Press, Westport, 1985, p. 144.

23 Giroux, p. 16.

11 The value of theory in defining culture in Northern Ireland

David Butler

In cultural studies we make our own pedagogies, but not under circumstances of our own choosing. Politics – of the academy and society – affect curriculum design and institutional development in particular ways. Theory, too, is context specific. This chapter considers the political uses of cultural theory and its applications in Northern Ireland (NI).

Media and cultural studies are worthwhile doing because cultural forms are socially meaningful. Intended to identify how culture contributes to the reproduction of 'relations of domination', with the eventual purpose of indicting these, 'British cultural studies', as this project has come to be called, is left-politics by theoretical means.[1] Against economistic models, where culture must be regarded as an effect of the base, for 'cultural materialists' since Raymond Williams, a culture – the arts of all kinds, beliefs and labour, traditional and emergent social practices – *represents* the values prevailing in and circulating through the economy, polity and civil society at any given time. Moreover, these conventions 'are profoundly worked and reworked in our actual living relationships. They are our ways of seeing and knowing, which every day we put into practice, and while the conventions hold, while the relationships hold, most practice confirms them.'[2] Which is to say, meanings are made *in* culture.

The audacity of recent trends in cultural theory has been to reject, then reverse the foundationalist presumption of structured correspondence between cause–effect/context–text relations. In poststructuralist writing, texts absorb contexts, expanding the category of 'discursivity' to fill out the cognitive and sentient limits of human thought and activity. From Foucaultian premises, Judith Butler goes so far as to argue that there 'is no gender identity behind expressions of gender; that identity is performatively constituted by the very "expressions" that are said to be its results'.[3]

Living and working in NI, one does not need to be convinced that discourse 'has the capacity to produce what it names'.[4] There was a surreal quality to the television pictures of confrontations at Drumcree church and on the Garvaghy Road in Portadown, in July 1996. On that occasion, like the year before and again subsequently, sectarian culture begot sectarian activity. It was culture, specifically the triumphalist customs and atrophied iconography of Orangeism, that moved thousands of Ulster protestants to several days and nights of mutinous disorder – a province-wide blockade of arterial routes, air and sea ports, and the obstruction of movement in and out of major towns and villages – until the initial decision to refuse permission for the march was overturned. Can anyone doubt the 'reality' of these discursively constituted cultural expressions? The Conservative government's response was to value loyalist belligerence and the nationalist residents' opposition to compliance with it as equivalent claims, from which a consensus could not be achieved. On the basis of this relativist equation, prime minister Major justified police capitulation to demotic clamour as a pragmatically centrist solution undertaken to safeguard public order. What this sophistic manoeuvre ignored, of course, was the absolute 'fact' that balance is unattainable where there is material asymmetry as between interests and identities in conflict.

Cultural materialist and conventionalist or poststructuralist approaches are not mutually excluding. Both employ dialectical method to show how dominant values come to occupy the discursive centre (of the structure of language, the formation of psycho-sexual and/or socio-economic identities) in such a way as to effectively define all other values in negative relation to these norms. There is a common acknowledgement, also, that meanings are made *relationally*, in recognition of *difference*: which is to say, there is nothing *essential* in things themselves to discriminate their value from other things, apart, that is, from their relationships of difference and similarity with the signs that represent those *other* things. Marxist economic historian, Eric Hobsbawm, is no less anti-essentialist in his approach to identity politics than is Judith Butler:

> Collective identities are defined negatively; that is to say against others. 'We' recognize ourselves as 'us' because we are different from 'Them'. If there were no 'They' from whom we are different, we wouldn't have to ask ourselves who 'We' were. Without Outsiders there are no Insiders . . . Unionists and nationalists in Belfast, or Serb, Croat and Muslim Bosnians, who would otherwise be indistinguishable – they speak the same language, have the same life styles, look and behave the same – insist on the one thing that divides them, which happens to be religion.[5]

Other values

The concept of 'Otherness' has been central to the development of cultural theory, especially in studies of race, gender, ethnicity and, increasingly, of 'postcolonial' situations. Lacan explicitly linked negative identification with the discovery and symbolic articulation of subjectivity; made in reflection, by recognition of difference from self. Crucially, for cultural studies, identity formation is now understood to be the result of a communicative chain, structured 'like a language'. Jorge Larrain: 'The formation of cultural identities presupposes the notion of the "other"; the definition of the cultural self always involves a distinction from the values, characteristics and ways of life of others.'[6]

In contrast to much contemporary scholarship on related issues of race, culture and imperialism, Frantz Fanon's writings are precise with primary sources, suasively illustrated and to the point. He died in 1961, not long before the victory of Algerian nationalism and too soon to witness the revolutionary impact of French structuralism. *Black skin, white masks* (1952) and *The wretched of the earth* (1961) are remarkable books, not least for their early synthesis of Freudian and Marxist theory and technique. They connect individual and societal crises of identity. Their purview and period of production overlapped with the 'linguistic turn' of Althusser and Lacan's labours towards revised definitions of ideology and identity. I regret not having read Fanon until recently. A decade on from first reading Edward Said, I can now also appreciate the affiliation of Fanon's work with the formulation of *Orientalism* (minus Foucault), and, in retrospect, would undoubtedly have got more out of Foucault, Derrida and Lacan the first time round had I approached them with Fanon in mind. Concentrating on the key distinction between *relational* and *relativist* construals, it is instructive to compare Fanon:

> In a very concrete way Europe has stuffed herself inordinately with the gold and raw materials of the colonial countries: Latin America, China and Africa. From all these continents, under whose eyes Europe raises up her tower of opulence, there has flowed out for centuries towards that same Europe diamonds, oil, silk and cotton, wood and exotic products. Europe is literally the creation of the Third World.[7]

with Said:

> It is Europe that articulates the Orient; this articulation is the prerogative, not of a puppet master, but of a genuine creator, whose life-giving power represents, animates, constitutes the otherwise silent and dangerous spaces living beyond familiar boundaries.[8]

And:

> What we must reckon with is a long and slow process of appropriation by which Europe, or the European awareness of the Orient, transformed itself from being textual and contemplative into being administrative, economic and even military.[9]

I say minus Foucault because where Fanon insists on the material causes of uneven development, Said appears to accord primacy to orientalist texts; or, to put this in harsher terms, to privilege immaterial determination of the material world. In the afterword to the 1995 printing of *Orientalism*, while in the main reiterating the thesis, Said none the less took the opportunity to clarify the context of his earlier (1978) remarks:

> The construction of identity – for identity, whether of Orient or Occident, France or Britain, *while obviously a repository of distinct collective experiences*, is finally a construction – involves establishing opposites and 'others' whose actuality is always subject to the continuous interpretation and

> re-interpretation of their differences from 'us'. Each age and society re-creates its 'Others' . . . *We all need some foundation on which to stand* . . . My position is that in the case of an essential Islam or Orient, these images are no more than images, *and are upheld as such* both by the community of the Muslim faithful and (the correspondence is significant) by the community of Orientalists.[10]

Acute and eloquent as ever, the italicised phrases are Said's quiet reply to his detractors (notably Aijaz Ahmad),[11] showing a firm purpose of amendment on his part to correct any impression given of relativism or over-generalisation.

'Sealed into . . . crushing objecthood'[12] is how Fanon explained the generalised effects of reduction to a racial Other. Dialectically speaking, the 'feeling of inferiority of the colonised is the correlative to the European feeling of superiority. Let us have the courage to say it outright: it is the racist who creates his inferior.'[13] The experience of being objectified corresponds to and results from the reality of material imbalance. Relations of domination naturalise the cultural authority of hegemonic perspectives. These find a great variety of expressions, some of them, on the face of things, complimentary. Parallel to overtly racialist forms, to be fetishised as ethnic, primitive or authentic, in nostalgic praise of premodern societies; or as exotic, in awe and desire, is to limit the meanings of 'blackness' to exclusively 'native' characteristics. The deep structure of this discourse of discriminating judgements, recurrent in mainstream media, posits an anthropological contrast of civilisation and savagery. Achievements by black men in athletics or the arts, for example, are regarded as the gifts of nature; lawlessness, anomie and under-achievement, their inevitable corollary (surfeit of spontaneity and libidinousness; lack of cerebral capacity, social graces and self-control).

'The problem of race' is a persistent feature of the problem of racist society. For if Race is consistently represented as a problem, then 'race relations' may only be a problem. Furthermore, to couple the words woman and black, for instance, is to risk a double reduction, perhaps no less inferiorising for the ostensible good intentions (even when advocated and/or actively invited by some representative speakers). This compares with speaking of black writing and black art as if these were hyphenated terms, routinely restricting the limits of their artistry to blackness in a way that would be unimaginable if applied to white-writing or white-art. If the latter two are non-sequiturs, why not the former? Fanon's linguistic illustration reveals an answer:

> Nothing of the sort in the Antilles. The language spoken officially is French; teachers keep a close watch over the children to make sure they do not use Creole. Let us not mention the ostensible reasons. It would seem, then, that the problem is this: In the Antilles, as in Brittany, there is a dialect and there is the French language. But this is false, for the Bretons have not been civilized by the white man.[14]

The designations just cited are equivalent in the area of culture to the emergence of cessationalist strategies in the wider society. Intended to contest the systematic exclusions that result from the failure of the postwar universalist project, their objective is to carve out a civic space where oppressed communities of interest may seek to represent themselves; on their own terms and free of the routine prejudices of normative judgement and patronage. In doing so, it follows, cultural movements of this order consign themselves to ghettoised locations within a particularist public sphere, the critical value of which will be regarded (by authorities of normative judgement) as less than canonic. To some, the prospect of separate and distinct 'black' idioms and valuation is to be welcomed and worked for. To others, the reduction of their craft to ethnicist characteristics – 'neo-Tarzanism' is how Wole Soyinka terms the outlook of self-consciously Africanist critics of his writing[15] – represents a chauvinistic alternative barely preferable to colonialism. Racialism is a deep seated fact of life throughout the industrialised countries of Europe and north America. These material inequalities in turn contribute to the essentialising perception of polarity between 'white' and 'black' discourses and, therefore, unavoidably, tend also to rigidify the existence of these.

Cognisant of the absolute division between unionist–loyalist and nationalist–republican perspectives in NI and, arising from this, the absence of agreed or shared codes and cultural institutions, central government has acted to promote 'community relations' programmes. In education and cultural matters, as far as I can see, these come in two varieties. The main thrust of policy has been to sponsor schemes which will encourage 'integration' by 'bringing together' the 'two traditions' in order to demonstrate their equal value in the interests of tolerance and reconciliation. Good intentions apart, the prospects of secular, anti-sectarian identifications are not aided and have probably been hindered by official patronage of arts and education linked to cross-community criteria. For, as I've said elsewhere, two is not a plurality and in my view particularist 'cultural traditions' – in the NI context, this means triumphalism and irredentism – are not generally acceptable civic forms.[16] Integrationalism has the effect of affirming the dominance of religious definition of culture and community (in schooling, for example, children receive double helpings of religious instruction) and reinforces the duopoly of nationalist and unionist authority over civil society. (Other points of view, ways of organising and thinking don't get much of a look in.)

Not least in recognition of criticisms of this kind, latterly the statutory bodies have sanctioned 'single-identity work' to augment the consensualist agenda. This means that protestant, catholic *and other* community groups are able to apply for support on the basis of subjecting that identity to constructive self-reflection. Where *critical* representation of traditional culture is facilitated, this framework has produced interesting and valuable explorations. But the risk and likelihood is that the relativising discourse of 'parity of esteem' can be used to legitimise sectarianism. A spokeswoman for a loyalist community group, Ormeau Residents Demand Equal Rights, formed in reaction to RUC re-routing of Orange parades away from the catholic Lower Ormeau, characterised their aim as 'the beginning of a campaign to achieve civil rights for protestants'. Another appropriated Martin Luther King: 'I have a dream that my children and their children will live in a nation where they will not be judged on their religion but on their character.'[17]

Difference and truth

Discursive approaches have achieved the status of critical common sense in humanities and social science research in recent years. The realisation that all identities are 'constructed' has meant that 'representation' has come to be considered the critical issue.

It is a paradox of identity formation that while these are deeply felt – providing 'a sense of belonging', of integrity, at-oneness in commonweal – it is nevertheless true that cultures are made-up. Contrary to the perception of depth, modern identities develop in a way that more closely approximates a scattering or patchwork than a prehistoric rootedness to land, language and shared custom. Identities materialise on the surface of objects and activities – territorial emblems, institutional authorities, rituals, pastimes, agreed codes, and so on. Invariably derived from mixed and 'multivalent' origins, these are the skin-deep resources of identification from which unity and coherence are represented and the basis on which distinction from alternative identities is established. There is, indubitably, no core of essences to this, that or any other identity. Identities of all kinds are prone to instability and as such are subject also to what Said calls 'counterpuntal' strategies.

The breakthrough for anti-essentialist studies of culture has been to reveal the false universalism of dominant conceptions: of the Orient, of blackness, of sexuality, nationality, and so on. Thus the radical appeal of 'destabilizing theory'[18] – for 'third wave' feminist theorists and in cultural studies of race and the legacy of colonialism – lies in the pluralising promise to 'decentre' the exclusionary norms of dominant discourse, thereby 'empowering' oppressed interests to speak up from the peripheries. Modern, integrative narratives are said to be based on corrupting claims to universal, that is, totalising knowledge. In their stead, the proposition is to interpret the world according to 'logics of disintegration',[19] in which, by contrasting definition, there can be no singular explanatory horizon. Using relational method and linguistic metaphor to undermine 'logocentrisms' of all kinds, these 'deconstructive' techniques provide the means to disclose the inferiorising mentalities inscribed in culturally dominant codes (taken for granted even in reputedly transgressive texts) and permit critical recovery of Other ways of being, seeing and doing; in this way warranting revaluation of 'diasporic' arts and consciousness over the museum styles of modern culture and theory.

There are, then, at least two good reasons for choosing hybridity as an evaluative premise in studies of cultural formations. The first is to counter the authority of essentialism. Henry Louis Gates:

> I rebel at the notion that I can't be part of other groups, that I can't construct identities through elective affinities, that race must be the most important thing about me. Is that what I want on my gravestone: Here lies an African American? So I'm divided. I want to be black, to luxuriate in whatever I might be calling blackness at any particular time – but to do so in order to come out the other side, to experience a humanity that is neither colorless nor reducible to color. Bach and James Brown. Sushi and fried catfish.[20]

Advocating a dual subject as opposed to the inbred stupidity of purist mentalities, this model of non-reductive, extensive, civic identification founded on 'elective affinities' rather than primordial essences presents an egalitarian and politically enabling proposition: a knowing, open offer to know what Paul Gilroy refers to as 'double consciousness'[21] ('our mongrel selves' is Salman Rushdie's rallying slogan for diasporic self-representation).[22]

And second, as noted, anti-essentialist cultural studies calls for validation of hitherto marginalised 'local, specific and particular' perspectives.[23] Herein, however, abides a logical contradiction. This may be framed as two linked questions: (a) must local, specific and particular forms *always* merit critical support over and against universalist conceptions? (b) how is the 'micropolitical' to be categorically separated off from the undeconstructively chauvinist? This is more than pedantry. Orthodoxy, after all, does not have a monopoly on reactionary values, nor subaltern cultures a monopoly on virtue. The intellectual poverty and inferiorising effects of nativism, or of religious and/or indigene absolutisms are no less harmful and offensive in postcolonial or neo-colonial settings for being attributable to antecedent external rule. (A mark of the decency and courage of Said's 'secular' criticism has been his determination to indict sectarian values and behaviours on the anti-imperialist side of the great historic divide.)

Conventionalist critics insist, correctly, on the discursivity of identities in general, in order to subvert oppressive uniformities, and so, proffer intellectual and cultural liberation to colonised subjects. However, if we prefer non-reductive, plural conceptions, where the only real difference is semiotic difference, it follows that the foundations of each particular identity are bound to be as made-up and inauthentic as every and any other. On this logic, rational acts of discrimination – as between felicitous and harmful, just and unjust – become infeasible other than as 'a strictly irreducible conflict of interpretations'.[24] John Fiske, for example, contends:

> In 1985 . . . a New York based, Korean and Jewish owned company
> marketed a brand of sports shoe to inner-city Black and Latino men. The
> brand name was 'Troop'. Rapidly a rumor spread that it was owned by the
> Ku Klux Klan and that it was a strategy to use Black dollars to fund the
> Klan's operations . . . The substance of the rumor was 'untrue' in the
> objective sense, but the knowledge of an invasive economics was a true
> part of the Black experience . . . These two ways of knowing . . . may not
> be equivalent in their relationship to those empirical data which form the
> base of scientific rationalism, but they are equivalent in the social truth of
> contemporary racism.[25]

'True lies'. For Fiske there can be no truth, only competing claims to 'truth'.
Further, as for him universal values are incurably contaminated by association
with orthodox theories (liberalism, humanism, Marxism), the best strategic
option available is to serve and protect the interests of discursively subordinated
identities. Founded on historical knowledge and experience of injustice,
promoted on pragmatic grounds as a cure to the ills of wholesale discrimination, cultural chauvinism does have a rational, sectarian basis. Racial
particularism is advancing in the USA and elsewhere in the modern world, as
noted before, in step with the retreat from the 'inclusionary' policy platform of
the 'civil rights' period. Endeavouring to direct these resources of despair to
ultra-separatist agitation, Louis Farrakhan and his followers in the 'Nation of
Islam' advocate purely 'black' forms of economic, political and social organisation on principled racialist grounds.

On the postmodern premise that oppositional reading *per se* is progressive
because anti-universal, an effect of Fiske's fealty to Nietzschean anti-realism is
to legitimise the conceptual basis of reverse racialism and the slimy species of
'micropolitics' it cultures. On a similar sort of reasoning, loyalists have learned
to love the indiscriminate language of 'difference' as a way of sanctioning
'traditional' parades. Invoking the official credentials of 'mutual understanding',
unionist leaders now seek to dispel the material referent – invasive, triumphalist
marching – on to a discursive understanding of culture, as if an Orange march
were like a Lord Mayor's Parade and Orangeism a quaint folk culture akin to
Morris dancing. The aim is to justify a bellicose cultural practice by giving it
an *other* name. Reflecting on 'Drumcree 2' (to which I referred above), Assistant
Grand Master, Jeffrey Donaldson, asked: 'For the sake of fifteen minutes, and to
avoid all the problems of last year, can we not have a little bit of respect and
tolerance for a cultural tradition and identity?'[26] This, as Janet Wolff cautions, is
where irrationalist theories will lead, if 'in demonstrating the discursive nature
of the social', they are permitted to 'operate as a license to deny the social'.[27]

Cultural identities are hybrid things for sure. And yet, illogical though it
may appear, in opposing universalism root and branch, philosophical pluralism
often comes around to endorsing the diametric opposite of diversity: that is,

particularist identities. Fiskean idealism abandons material reality for the absurdist off-world of 'writerly' textualism. His writing is cited here as symptomatic of relativist double standards in that it fails or refuses to see resolute anti-foundationalism for what it truly is – a conceptual foundation no less totalising in its claims than other meta-narratives.

Identities are constructed, which is to say, determined in relation to a hierarchy of institutions of definitional authority. But construction depends upon the existence of foundations. These, in the case of the formation of cultural identities, are complex and multifactoral, not limited to any singular cause. Headed by state and economy, our relationships with bureaucracies and bosses, educators and guardians, kin, colleagues, enemies and friends – subject to the influence of common, objectifying conceptions about, for example, the lives, character traits and outlooks of others (cultures, societies, peoples) – are the measure against which social activity is structured, that is, in regard to which lives are lived.

Identities are thus the cultural expression of lived experience: positive and negative, enabling and constraining, in and from which personal and collective histories emerge. These dialectical relations between material and discursive authorities are finally reproduced by and circulated within the media of public communication. It is accurate, therefore, to say that power is articulated, given substance, made real in discourse. At the same time it must be stressed that the sources of 'systematic asymmetry' originate outside – though not (as Judith Butler properly insists) before – discursivity. In other words (and in the last instance), social meanings derive from the real world as opposed to the world of 'the real'. Perforce, women and men may 'make their own history, but they do not make it just as they please; they do not make it under circumstances chosen by themselves, but under circumstances directly encountered, given and transmitted from the past'.[28] The analytical importance of culture is as a site of (ideological) exchange between simultaneously occurring acts of making and encountering history. In this way both 'invented' and 'lived' amidst the material forces of culture, identities (of race, class, gender, to name only three) are, in Janet Wolff's words, 'real at the same time as being socially inscribed and discursively constituted'.[29]

I'd guess that Henry Louis Gates would not disagree that the opportunity to exercise autonomy over cultural preferences and occlusions in the formation of a diasporic consciousness will always be subject to the limitations of class, colour, gender and other impinging biographical details; such as talent, intellect, industry and, critically, the influence (to put it no stronger than that) of material circumstance. The unionists and nationalists in Belfast, or Serb, Croat and Muslim Bosnians, of whom Hobsbawm spoke, are doubtless mixed from common cultural material, unmonolithic, interrelated. Yet they are certain about 'the one thing that divides them, which happens to be religion'. It would be wrong to say these identities, made in difference, are unreal. Equally, it is true that these peoples do persist, amid the debris of postcoloniality, in living unhappily uniform and univalent cultural lives.

Metropolitan bias

It is a base element of modern thought and culture that because empire is outside, controlling but not immediately visible inside the imperialised zones, the piracies of colonial rule are not readily demonstrable in the forms of everyday discourse. As Jameson has remarked, the 'inner forms and structure' of metropolitan culture mediated and were a meditation upon the creative contradictions of modernity.[30] Social and political improvements hard-won by the organisations of working class representation in Britain and other leading empire economies depended integrally on the forcible subjugation and expropriation of the peoples and materials of more or less 'peripheral' lands. So much so that 'social imperialism' was a common foundation of centre, right and left party political agendas in the British state in the years 1895–1916.[31] The culture of jingoism that took hold in this period represented the material basis of a competition between metropolitan nation-states.

The perception of imperial foes differs materially from the otherness of colonised subjects. Writing in 1939, George Orwell in his study of boys' weeklies outlined the structure of inference in British culture as between protagonist and inferior Others (he dates its origins to 1910):

> As a rule it is assumed that foreigners of any one race are all alike and will confirm more or less exactly to the following patterns:
> > FRENCHMAN: Excitable. Wears beard, gesticulates wildly.
> > SPANIARD, MEXICAN etc.: Sinister, treacherous.
> > ARAB, AFGHAN etc.: Sinister, treacherous.
> > CHINESE: Sinister, treacherous, wears pigtails.
> > ITALIAN: Excitable. Grinds barrel-organ or carries stiletto.
> > SWEDE, DANE etc.: Kind-hearted, stupid.
> > NEGRO: Comic, very faithful.[32]

At the deepest level of social meaning-making, the inferiorising predispositions of imperialism have set down an intellectual infrastructure which, unseen, informs aesthetic and critical preferences in 'advanced' societies. Typically, the internalised presumptions of the culture of imperialism efface the empirical data of colonial relations (exploitation, underdevelopment), thereafter re-presenting these on to inverted forms of otherness (native indolence and indiscipline, childlike exuberance and promiscuity, comic naiveté, dependency theory and so on).[33] The revolutionary avant-gardes of the European early twentieth century were startling in their iconoclasm and formal determination to flatten established perspectives. Yet even these most celebratedly oppositional works appropriated and utilised African iconographies in an exoticising and reductive manner – for instance, in Picasso's *Les demoiselles d'Avignon* (1907).[34] None of this is to deny the progressive value of cubism or other modernist practices within the 'First World'. Rather, it focuses attention on an incongruities of the cultural logic of capitalist modernity.

Their emancipatory ethics notwithstanding, one intellectual legacy of the predominance of Eurocentric horizons has been to reinforce the weakness and marginality of 'Third World' perspectives. From this, two related lessons for the development of anti-imperialist cultural studies follow. First, fully justified scepticism of universal claims where the conceptual roots of these are discovered to be coextensive with western knowledge. Fairly representative of the theoretical strengths and limitations of the metropolitan Left, Orwell's essay 'Shooting an elephant' (1936) was both stirring in its indictment of colonial rule and patronisingly orientalist in attitude to the Burmese: 'In a job like that you see the dirty work of Empire at close quarters . . . We began questioning the people as to where the elephant had gone, and, as usual, failed to get any definite information. This is invariably the case in the East; a story always sounds clear enough at a distance, but the nearer you get to the scene of events the vaguer it becomes.'[35] The second imperative of postwar oppositional politics has been to recover and promote national definition as an insurgent means of liberating inferiorised minds and inspiring the defeat of occupying powers. 'Truth is the property of the national cause' was how Fanon put it.[36]

Circumstances change. British cultural studies came out of left-labourism (especially traditions of labour history and adult education) and the institutions of the Marxist left in mainland Europe. With distance gained from source, in north America and the Antipodes, the draw of culturalism and 'Western Marxism' diminishes.[37] Still, it is fair to say, I think, that the 'inner forms and structure' of the intellectual formations of metropolitan cultural studies have been overdetermined by the rhetoric of national identity, with the cognitively limiting consequence that other patterns of manifestly non-nationalist identification and analysis (notably, of race, sex and secular definition) were not inclined to be granted an appropriate measure of discursive prominence. The occlusions of culturalism were forcefully addressed by – and, arguably, have now undergone basic realignment in response to – writers such as Paul Gilroy:

> I have grown gradually more weary of having to deal with the effects of striving to analyse culture within neat, homogeneous national units reflecting the 'lived relations' involved; with the invisibility of 'race' within the field and, most importantly, with the forms of nationalism endorsed by a discipline which, in spite of itself, tends towards a morbid celebration of England and Englishness from which Blacks are systematically excluded.[38]

Night follows day: relations of systematic asymmetry give rise to cultural forms of otherness. Ulster protestants and unionists are not inferiorised others.

Nor are Ulster catholics and nationalists. Not now at any rate and not in the way that black immigrants in Britain have been. In past centuries Irish catholic lives and interests were inferiorised and reduced by racialist unionist domination. Material imbalances between catholic and protestant citizens remain. Measured in relation to the customary cleavages of capitalist class and patriarchy, furthermore, contemporary social conditions in NI are not comparable in scale (discursively or materially) with those of underdeveloped economies in the Third World. This is important because it makes the matter of left analysis and affiliation problematic. One of the arguments of my book *The trouble with reporting Northern Ireland* (1995) is that where studies of culture in NI rely on the dominant narrative of national belonging, these will limit the complexity of the conflict to incomplete equations. Worse, solutions formulated on the basis of the generic propositions of orthodox liberal consensus, constitutional nationalism, or the local form of anti-imperialism (the 'unfinished revolution' thesis) cannot, in my view, remedy or reduce the conflict and may contribute to its long lasting life.

Paradoxes endure. 'As a cultural ideal', Michael Ignatieff reports, 'nationalism is the claim that while men and women have many identities, it is the nation which provides them with their primary form of belonging'.[39] Not all nationalisms are retrograde. The chauvinism and essentialist swill of 'blood and belonging' are an offence against reason and deserve to be stood down. Alternatively, against essentialism and the scepticism of anti-foundationalist reason, the construction of civic, inclusionary models of enabling nation-state formations, mobilised on a protected foundation of 'materialised' rights and responsibilities of citizenship and a projected society and polity of 'regulated pluralism',[40] are to be aided and emulated. Evidently, in analysing culture, critical separation is required between national and nationalist forms. Fanon implied as much: 'if nationalism is not made . . . into humanism, it leads up a blind alley'.[41] Not all national expressions of Britishness (actual and feasible) are reactionary and imperialist: the anti-market design of the welfare state, for instance, is a principle of belonging surely worth defending.

Politics/theory/culture

The particularist conflict between nationalist and anti-nationalist definitions reflects a local history and the global conditions of 'late imperial' cultures. The hybridity of contemporary forms of identification is an empirical fact of capitalist modernity (the diasporic consciousness of dislocation, from periphery to core, is a universal motif of the current era).[42] In NI, as elsewhere, identities are discursive and real, inessential and essentialising. The intellectual preference for unitary definitions of subjectivity and belonging is an enduring sign of the intellectual hegemony of metropolitan values.

Debates known to students of cultural studies as 'the politics of identity' are integral to the 1998 Belfast agreement. The agreement proposes to install a balance of sectarian forces in the NI polity (brokered by the sovereign states) and requires 'parallel consent' between these in such a way as to ensure opposing aspirations – for internal as against north–south structures – stand or fall together. Whether or not it can solve the zero-sum at the core of the conflict, the historical significance of this document is that the British and Irish governments have reconceptualised national identity and belonging in NI in specifically dualist terms.[43] Item 1(vi), under *Constitutional Issues*, compels the signatories to

> recognise the birthright of all the people of Northern Ireland to identify themselves and be accepted as Irish or British, or both, as they may so choose, and accordingly confirm that their right to hold both British and Irish citizenship is accepted by both Governments and would not be affected by any future change in the status of Northern Ireland.

In addition, parsing Item 6 of Strand One arrangements, *Democratic Institutions in NI*, the document offers the prospect (at some utopian point in the future) 'to resignify the subject as a site of resignification':[44]

> At their first meeting, members of the Assembly will register a designation of identity – nationalist, unionist or other – for the purposes of measuring cross-community support in Assembly votes under the relevant provisions above.

Even more remarkable is the non-essentialist, diasporic disposition of the amended text of Article 2 of the Irish Constitution, drafted to replace the traditional irredentist claim to the national territory:

> It is the entitlement and birthright of every person born in the island of Ireland, which includes its islands and seas, to be part of the Irish nation. That is also the entitlement of all persons otherwise qualified in accordance with law to be citizens of Ireland. Furthermore, the Irish nation cherishes its affinity with people of Irish ancestry living abroad who share its cultural identity and heritage.

Cultural theory has practical, political value. That the radically relativist precepts of anti-foundationalism – where 'power is read as a text without the interference of materials of a different kind'[45] – are used as camouflage for cultural chauvinism is reason enough to be mistrustful of its subversive allure. With particular debt to Fanon and to Williams, in this chapter and in teaching media studies I prefer dialectical method, where cultural forms are understood to produce social meaning *in relation to* their historical and material contexts, and where minimally, the latter decisively 'set limits' on the former. The point is to analyse *representation* with a mind to uncovering the misperceptions produced by relations of domination: notably, in the NI context, to diagnose the errors that result from essentialism.

Notes

1   See Hall S, 'The emergence of cultural studies and the crisis in the humanities', *October*, 53, 1990.

2   Williams R, 'Drama in a dramatized society', *Writing in Society*, Verso, London, 1984, p. 18.

3   Butler J, *Gender trouble*, Routledge, London, 1990, p. 25.

4   'Gender as performance: interview with Judith Butler', *Radical Philosophy*, 67, 1994.

5   Hobsbawm E, 'Identity politics and the left', *New Left Review*, 217, 1996.

6   Larrain J, *Ideology and cultural identity*, Polity, Cambridge, 1994, p. 142.

7   Fanon F, *The wretched of the earth*, Penguin, Harmondsworth, 1967, p. 81.

8   Said E W, *Orientalism*, Routledge, New York, 1978, p. 57.

9   Said, p. 204.

10 Said E W, 'Afterword to the 1995 printing', *Orientalism*, Routledge, London, 1995, pp. 332–33.

11 Ahmad A, 'Orientalism and after: ambivalence and metropolitan location in the work of Edward Said', *In theory: classes, nations, literatures*, Verso, London, 1992.

12 Fanon F, *Black skin, white masks*, Grove Press, New York, 1967, p. 109.

13 Fanon, *Black skin, white masks*, p. 93.

14 Fanon, *Black skin, white masks*, p. 28.

15 Soyinka W, 'Neo-Tarzanism: the poetics of pseudo-tradition', *Transitions*, 48, 1975.

16 For fuller elaboration of this framework of analysis, see Chapter 3, 'Cultural identity and broadcasting in Northern Ireland', of my *The trouble with reporting Northern Ireland*, Avebury, Aldershot, 1995.

17 *Belfast News Letter*, 28 October 1996.

18 See Barrett M and Phillips A (eds), *Destabilizing theory: contemporary feminist debates*, Polity, Cambridge, 1993.

19 See Dews P, *Logics of disintegration: logics of post-structuralist thought and the claims of critical theory*, Verso, London, 1987.

20 Gates H L Jr, *Colored people*, Viking, London, 1995, p. xv.

21 Gilroy P, *The Black Atlantic: modernity and double consciousness*, Verso, London, 1993.

22 Taken by Stuart Hall as title of an article for *New Statesman and Society*, 5, 207, 1992.

23 Barrett M and Phillips A, 'Introduction', Barrett and Phillips (eds), *Destabilizing theory*, p. 1.

24 Norris C, 'Old themes for new times: postmodern theory and cultural politics', *New Formations*, 18, 1992.

25 Fiske J, *Power plays, power works*, Viking, London, 1993, pp. 245f.

26 *Irish Times*, Dublin, 1 February 1997.

27 Wolff J, 'Interdisciplinarity in the study of art', in Grossberg L, Nelson C and Treichler P (eds), *Cultural studies*, Routledge, London and New York, 1992, p. 791.

28 Marx K, 'The eighteenth Brumaire of Louis Bonaparte', in *Marx and Engels: selected works in one volume*, Progress Publishers, London, 1968, p. 97.

29 Wolff J, *Feminine sentences*, Polity Press, Cambridge, 1990, p. 138.

30 Jameson F, 'Nationalism, colonialism and literature: modernism and imperialism', *Field Day Pamphlet*, 14, Derry, 1988, p. 6.

31 See Semmel B, *Imperialism and social reform*, Allen and Unwin, London, 1960.

32 Orwell G, 'Boys' weeklies', *The Penguin essays of George Orwell*, Penguin, Harmondsworth, 1984, p. 94.

33 See Said E W, *Culture and imperialism*, Chatto and Windus, London, 1993.

34 See, for example, Jordan G and Weedon C, 'Primitives, politics and the avant garde: modern art and its others', *Cultural politics: class, gender, race and the postmodern world*, Blackwell, Oxford, 1995, pp. 315–94.

35 'Shooting an elephant', *The Penguin Essays of George Orwell*, pp. 25f.

36 Fanon, *The Wretched of the Earth*, p. 39.

37 See Anderson P, *Considerations on Western Marxism*, NLB, London, 1976.

38 Gilroy P, *There ain't no black in the Union Jack*, Hutchinson, London, 1987, p. 12.

39 Ignatieff M, *Blood and belonging: journeys into the new nationalism*, BBC Books, London, 1994, p. 3.

40 John B. Thompson's term, used in relation to broadcasting in *Ideology and modern culture*, Polity, Cambridge, 1990, pp. 260–64.

41 Fanon, *The Wretched of the Earth*, p. 165.

42 See Hall S, 'Cultural identity and diaspora', in Rutherford J (ed.), *Identity: community, culture, difference*, Lawrence and Wishart, London, 1990; 'The formation of a diasporic intellectual: an interview with Stuart Hall by Kuan Hsing Chen', in Morley D and Kuan Hsing Chen (eds), *Stuart Hall: critical dialogues in cultural studies*, Routledge, London, 1996, pp. 484–503.

43 My quotations are from the full text of the agreement reproduced in the *Irish Times*, 11 April 1998.

44 The phrase is Judith Butler's: see 'Contingent foundations: feminism and the question of postmodernism', in Butler J and Scott J W (eds), *Feminists theorize the political*, Routledge, London and New York, 1992, p. 14.

45 Jameson F, *Postmodernism*, Verso, London, 1991, p. 186.

12   Education for what? The politics of pedagogy in cultural studies

Alan O'Shea

In the turbulent years of the late 1960s and early 1970s, students occupied their campuses (in Britain, continental Europe and, especially, the USA) in protest against an education which they saw as transmitting received knowledge without reference to what they felt they needed to know in order to live more fulfilled lives and to understand and modify their world: the key demand was student participation in developing curricula relevant to their needs. This was substantially a revolt of the privileged – a rejection of the repressive conformism required by the 'affluent society' from the point of view of often utopian countercultures whose goal was to remove hierarchies and maximise individual freedom. These ideas spread throughout the educational system: there was a movement to 'deschool society' and the establishment of independent 'free schools'. The sense that knowledge/power relations could somehow be dispersed, rather than simply reconfigured, now looks naively idealist. Nevertheless the question of what education is *for*, and who decides that, was apt – and explosive.

In 1968, at the height of these struggles, Raymond Williams connected the student demands for control over their own curricula to a longer history of working class demands for education:

> In these uneasy months, I remember the history of men without rights and without property demanding the means to understand their world; the complicated interaction between their own self-organising institutions and not only those who could control or buy them but also those who know, from direct experience, how hard, disturbing and endlessly flexible any real learning is.[1]

He was articulating the countercultural moment to a different tradition of radical pedagogy: to the conception of 'really useful knowledge', as the nineteenth-century working-class self-educators called it, which had carried through into the Adult Education classes of the postwar period, taught by, among others, Williams and Richard Hoggart, and exemplified by the 'history from below' of E P Thompson's *The Making of the English Working Class* (1963) and by the establishment of Ruskin College, Oxford to provide an academic education for trades unionists.

It was during this heady moment that the working practices of the small postgraduate Centre for Contemporary Cultural Studies at Birmingham University were being established. Here both these agendas were in play: disciplinary knowledges were subjected to critique, and there was also a concern to challenge the exclusion of subordinate groups from the process of knowledge production and validation. At the Centre there was an emphasis on collaborative work, on student participation in planning seminar programmes, and on interventionist projects. This was no golden moment: in the negotiations over topics, theories and pedagogic modes, the process of claiming and conceding inclusion was often difficult and painful on all sides. Nevertheless the processes of teaching and learning were consciously on the agenda, particularly the awareness that knowledge-production always has a political dimension – for containment or change. The intention was that students would use their studies to develop those understandings which would enable them to intervene in their social worlds as political subjects.

Between that point and the present day the field of cultural studies has expanded massively: it represents a vibrant, international field of research and debate, one which has influenced many cognate disciplines. The huge expansion of higher education has included the development of many courses in, or strongly informed by, cultural studies. Despite fierce debates and differences within this field, there remains a consensus that claiming to work in 'cultural studies' is synonymous with aspirations to be interventionist. One object of transformation has been academia itself – developing interdisciplinarity, breaking down traditional compartmentalisations of knowledge and exposing academic discourses for their complicity with social inequality and exclusion. But usually there has also been an aspiration to intervene in the social formation more directly, by opening up for scrutiny the often subtle ways in which existing forms of oppression and marginality are sustained through cultural processes. Direct public intervention has not been easy, except for the few 'stars': most of the critical writing has not reached a readership beyond the circle of those already 'inside' this kind of sociocultural critique. What is rarely acknowledged is that for most academics their *teaching* offers the most scope for significant intervention.

I have suggested elsewhere why cultural studies academics in Britain have given little attention to pedagogy over the past twenty years: first, their concern to establish their academic credentials and institutional positions – a preoccupation required for any newly emerging field, but particularly for one which questions the foundations of more established disciplines; second, funding mechanisms which privilege research over teaching and hence tie promotion to research output; third, the absence of a wider, radical debate about education over this period; fourth, the inexorable reduction of resources, forcing workloads to expand; and, finally, ever more burdensome forms of accountability, such that the sheer grind of teaching and administration militates against innovative thinking about pedagogy.[2]

Against all these pressures, it is crucial that cultural studies academics give priority to a renewed attention to pedagogy. At a time when formal politics is increasingly being turned into a marketing exercise, when citizenship is represented as just another form of consumer choice, when the idea that individuals can become agents of change is seen as utopian, indeed when existing social arrangements are increasingly naturalised as how life has to be – at such a time it is all the more urgent to encourage critical distance from, and scrutiny of, such arrangements in a way which stimulates a vigorous engagement with them.

This chapter will consider what might be the goals and methods of a 'critical pedagogy', examine exactly how both 'experience' and 'identity' might be brought into this pedagogic process, and consider how these politico–academic concerns connect to the investments of present-day students.

A critical pedagogy?

I have mentioned the lack of public debate on such a pedagogy in Britain. But there has been a recent and welcome resumption of the question of education for social change by Henry Giroux and colleagues in the USA.[3] Giroux has argued for a 'critical pedagogy' which is directed towards the creation of a new public sphere – educating people 'to be active and critical citizens capable of fighting for and reconstructing democratic public life'. The main task is seen as enabling marginal cultures to find a voice, such that 'radical educators can bring the concepts of culture, voice and difference together to create a borderland where multiple subjectivities and identities exist as part of a pedagogical practice that provides the potential to expand the politics of democratic community and solidarity'.[4] Giroux's rhetoric is radical: his talk of cultural studies as providing an 'oppositional rhetoric' and supporting an 'insurgent practice' sounds hopelessly vanguardist in the context of the conservatism of the wider US political culture. His practical proposals are more modest and reformist: his account of his own classroom practice reveals achiev-able, if not exactly 'oppositional', goals and an interesting prefiguring of 'active citizenship' – students negotiate both course content and modes of assess-ment.[5] But is 'critical citizenship' a useful formulation of a goal for cultural studies?

Tony Bennett makes the (understated!) point that 'reconstructing democratic public life' is 'asking a lot of teachers and of the school'.[6] There is of course no existing political force which is about to rapidly transform the public sphere. Stuart Hall has made the point that the political agenda developed in debates in cultural theory has no emerging historical movement to attach itself to.[7] The (post-liberal) public sphere proposed by Giroux is an imagined space. But, as Gramsci has pointed out, the strategy in times of retrenchment should not be to withdraw from activism until a revolutionary moment presents itself: rather, we should engage in a 'war of position', building alliances slowly and securing small transformations until these accrue into more significant shifts in the balance of forces. Whatever our particular political emphases are, there are spaces for intervention at this level. Across our societies there is dissent and grievance, which can be articulated in struggles against injustice, inequality and oppression. These are all potential points of pressure for change. Bennett suggests that Giroux's vision of 'voice and difference', far from encouraging 'insurgency', is merely offering what the state has always required of public education: the shaping of citizens 'in a highly governmental organisation of voices in order that some voices be supported and others be corrected and revised . . . with the teacher as technician of the soul'.[8] But this Foucauldian reading is a monolithic and non-contradictory model of the social formation. Citizenship is seen as inevitably a category of containment rather than as a site of struggle, the terrain where any 'war of position' is played out. Of course this site is bounded: we are talking about capitalist democracies. But the discourses of democracy offer plenty of space for radical struggles: we have only to note the number of radical movements which have in recent years deployed discourses of rights, equality and justice. This is not to underestimate the forces ranged against a more egalitarian and collectivist society, simply to assert that it is possible to contest them on this terrain, and that small changes matter. It then becomes significant *which* voices (or rather, what kinds of discursive space) are supported in educational institutions and which are not.

The fact that mainstream politics also deploys the term 'active citizenship' is a useful rather than a negative feature. The term is polysemic – open enough to be inflected in very different political directions. It means that radicals can fight a more subtle battle with it; they can articulate their demands 'from within' by pointing up the mismatch between the principles the dominant culture asserts and its practices of unfreedom and exclusion. While a term like 'socialism' can be represented as Other, 'equality' cannot be so easily shrugged off. In sum, a plural and self-reflexive discursive space which is based on those principles constitutes a political arena in which a radical politics can operate. On this model, any, however temporary, prefiguring of a community which is critical but inclusive, which recognises diversity but reaches across difference, is worth attempting.

But how do we construct a curriculum which encourages our students to become 'critical citizens'? We must consider thematic content and pedagogy. In terms of themes and issues, despite the fierce contestation over the past decade over what counts as 'cultural studies', some elements of common ground are discernible. I have mentioned two: the interventionist aspiration and the push towards an interdisciplinary, multidimensional approach. There is also the relation between culture and power, the examination of how cultural practices, representations and processes are caught up in sustaining or challenging power relations. This is achieved by revealing not only the partiality of any representation, but also the historicity and contingency of what appears to be natural, given, fixed. An associated objective is to explore both the distinctiveness of, and the interconnections between, different kinds of power relations – especially those of gender, sexuality, race, ethnicity, nation and class. The difficulties of talking across such 'differences' are acknowledged and there is, in fact, plenty of sectarianism and conflict among cultural studies practitioners. Nevertheless, in recent years, a consensus-in-principle has been acknowledged around the necessity both to take seriously, and to reach across, difference: towards self-reflexiveness concerning one's own partiality, and towards recognising 'the other in oneself'. These aspirations offer a discernible content for a cultural studies syllabus.

However, a critical syllabus does not guarantee a critical pedagogy. The rapid institutionalisation of cultural studies programmes is a splendid achievement, but also produces a concomitant concern: that a once dynamic and interventionist discipline may be hardening into an orthodoxy which can be passively learned and parroted back in examinations like any other subject. There may not be a consensus on a standard textbook, but there are various firm tendencies, and secondary texts to validate these, such that any particular course can present itself as a received orthodoxy for uncritical consumption by students. If we claim to be producing *critical* knowledge, but pay no attention to pedagogy, how do we know whether we are making it possible for students to appropriate it as such – as practical knowledge which they can use for their own social projects, but also subject to interrogation, rather than simply as a radical discourse to be reproduced in essays and exams but without this impinging upon how they engage with their social world?

The distinction between these two forms of learning was pivotal to the radical critiques of education in the 1960s and the demand for a student-centred pedagogy. These demands were underpinned by the cognitive psychologies of Jerome Bruner and Jean Piaget, whose theories were deployed in arguments for a 'child-centred' curriculum, particularly in primary schools. They proposed that knowledge was structured as a system for interpreting the world: acquiring new knowledge involves restructuring the system. We make sense of events by trying to squeeze them to fit our interpretative categories ('assimilation' in Piaget). But often new experiences cannot be grasped within existing categories and may even bring them into question; in such situations we modify our existing categories to explain events more adequately and to make new connections ('accommodation' in Piaget, 'recoding' in Bruner).[9] Learning is a process of connecting new knowledge to existing knowledge in a way which transforms it. It was argued by educationalists that it was possible to 'learn' at a superficial level ('recognition knowledge' or 'school knowledge'), so that you could repeat this back in exams, or 'know' something when it is pointed out to you; but that, unless the process of assimilation and accommodation took place, this knowledge would not become internalised as a tool with which to think ('action knowledge'). This was more likely to take place if the pupil/student was encouraged to talk through this new knowledge with the tutor or with other students, and to deploy it in tackling problems.[10] These arguments ignore other, more sociological and cultural aspects of the classroom situation, but as psychological models of individual learning they still hold up.

How can we maximise the chance of students assimilating the knowledges offered by cultural studies as tools to think with? On the above argument it would have to be by engaging with existing experience and understandings; but I will propose that we must move beyond questions of cognition to addressing students' desires and aspirations, and also take account of some of the costs to students if they engage in critiques of the everyday world they inhabit. This involves discussing, first, 'identity work' and, second, some of the concrete investments students bring into the classroom.

Identity work and its pitfalls

It is not surprising that in a period when the most vigorous forms of politics have been struggles around identity – particularly those of gender, race, ethnicity and sexuality – attempts to keep cultural studies politicised and at the same time to connect to students' experience have taken the form of working on social identity. I will suggest this is not a *sufficient* basis for a cultural studies curriculum, but still a very important one. The issue is how, rather than whether, such work should be carried out, so as best to help students understand the insights of cultural studies and deploy them in thinking about their own lives.

Again, the work of Giroux and colleagues provides a very useful starting point for this discussion. I want to take issue with one important tendency in some of their arguments, which could impede their intention of opening up the political possibilities summarised above. At one point Giroux cites approvingly a class on multicultural education in which students are asked to talk about their ethnic and cultural backgrounds: the African-American students talk easily, but the white students are at a loss – 'I don't know much about my background. In fact I don't even have a culture'. The teacher remedies the situation by helping them recover their working class, Irish histories.[11] Giroux offers this instance in the context of a concern to problematise whiteness, to make white students 'understand how their own identities are beyond neither ethnicity, history, privilege nor struggle'. This is a commendable aim: of articulating difference in order to open up the positionality and the partiality of all discourses, particularly those which appear universal. But to encourage the voicing of difference is a tricky strategy. Racism and fascism are also vocalisations of 'difference': is the goal really a plurality of voices, or is it rather to combat marginalisation and inequality? If so, Bennett is partly right: we have a regulation of voices rather than an unfettered opening up. And if the project is actually about inclusion and egalitarianism, why the enthusiasm to attach identities to individuals, and particularly ethnic ones? First, it is not clear how the opening up of (working-class) Irishness will produce insights on *dominant* whiteness. Second, the autobiographical, confessional route into the discussion of ethnicity can encourage a celebration of ethnicity which hardens it – possibly a step on the slippery slope towards essentialism, in which ethnicity becomes the *primary* marker of cultural difference, the 'real' identity. Of course there are moments when such a hardening is an important political strategy, a 'strategic essentialism' which provides a basis for a collective unity and energy focused on a political project. Such identity assertions have opened up ways of seeing not easily available before, and have allowed subordinate groups to reinterpret what had been experienced as personal inadequacy as political oppression, and thus to become subjects of history. In particular they have been a mechanism for demanding rights without having to accept sameness. But narratives of difference slip easily into assertions of superiority or of a noble victimhood (or both at the same time). Chandra Mohanty speaks of a 'more-authentic than thou' syndrome.[12] This positioning allows the claim to a privileged relation to the truth, and the imposition of a guilty silence on others. Also (and this is particularly significant for the classroom situation) it appears that only subordinate identities are encouraged in this autobiographical approach: the middle-class, male WASP is still excluded from participation.

Moreover we may ask: does the production of (white, liberal) guilt have a productive political effect? This was the strategy of some 'racism awareness' projects of the 1980s, and also of recent demands that contemporary political leaders apologise for atrocities committed by earlier regimes. There is no evidence that such production of guilt (frequently accompanied by resentment) encourages thought and dialogue leading to understanding about the partiality and potential oppressiveness of all narratives. Giroux looks for 'a pedagogy of "whiteness" which enables white students to move beyond positions of guilt and resentment', but still wants to offer whiteness 'as a racial identity that can play a crucial role in refashioning an anti-racist politics'.[13] But is the only strategy to 'provide identities'?

This is not to argue against the retrieval of repressed histories, which contribute to the analysis of knowledge/power relations in the present as well as to a more complex understanding of the past. But there are alternative ways of handling them in the classroom which enable *all* the students to connect these histories to their own experience and their own sense of self. One of the central insights of cultural studies is that identities, however deep-rooted, are contingent and historically produced – including those based on 'race' or ethnicity. Rather than encouraging students to attach a recovered ethnic (or gendered) history to the validation of an identity and an authenticity claim, why not shift the agenda towards an examination of the *historicity* of such identity narratives? To argue that an ethnic or other identity is a historically contingent cultural construction is not to deny its concrete reality in constituting subjects. Some postmodernist versions of anti-essentialism appear to equate 'contingency' with both fleetingness and agency: because an identity can be historicised it can be taken up or discarded at will. This is why Paul

Gilroy has insisted on an 'anti-anti-essentialism', 'a model whereby identity can be understood neither as a fixed essence nor as a vague and utterly contingent construction to be reinvented by the whim and will of aesthetes, symbolists and language-gamers'.[14] He argues that there may be many cultural differences among the black populations of the Americas and Europe, but that there are also some common elements which have been slow to develop and also remain relatively resistant to change; these common cultural elements (which he calls the Black Atlantic) do not derive from belonging to the same race, but from a shared history of transportation, slavery, emancipation, the difficulty of entering white-dominated societies and migration.

The term 'historically contingent', then, should not be taken to imply that identities change easily through a ready agency, but to posit, one the one hand, powerful historical determinants, and, on the other, the possibility of continued transformation. 'Contingency' keeps alive the notion that things could have been, and might still be, otherwise: it allows us to think 'counter-factually', to imagine different forms of social relations. To teach this requires a careful balancing act: to acknowledge the rootedness of identities (and their deep internalisation by all of us) while opening up their historical determinacy, and hence their openness to historical change. This allows at least an *analytic* separation of identities (as discourses) from the students to which they are contingently attached, so that they can be considered as *social* phenomena 'out there' in the discursive formation. This allows, in principle, all students to examine all identifications as cultural phenomena.

The particular engagement with identity that I am proposing keeps students' own experience and investments as a key component of discussion, but avoids making 'confession' compulsory: pride, anger and guilt are thus less of an obstruction to a sharpened understanding of how identity and difference operate. Students still engage in autobiographical work but in an analytic mode; they 'recover' identities but to situate them as determinate cultural phenomena, and then to explore their own formation in relation to them. Thus, if the distinctness between the individual and identification is opened up, when we turn to whiteness, all students can contribute to an investigation of how it operates as an invisible norm and frames, differentially, each of their identities. This approach treats 'difference' as 'real' and deep-rooted, while also bringing out a more abstract commonality across the group: by beginning to grasp the formation of their own subjectivity, they can empathise with that process in others.

Furthermore, subjectivity comprises *multiple* identities. People set apart by one difference (eg ethnicity) may be connected by another (eg a common gender). We live in networks of connectedness as well as difference. To grasp these processes, it is necessary to talk about the specificities of each dimension of power/identity separately but also to reconnect them. To speak 'as a black person' or 'from a woman's perspective' assumes a homogeneity of experience which will not stand up to empirical scrutiny. As Angela McRobbie points out:

> When feminists talk about women, this too is a representation. It does not automatically and unproblematically refer to and reflect a pre-existing material reality. Instead it constructs and gives an identity to a social group who might previously have been known as ladies, girls, housewives or mothers . . .[15]

The feminist conception of 'women' is constitutive of identity: 'women', and other positionalities such as 'global sisterhood,' are political mobilisations around an asserted commonality of interest, and important as such. But this assertion of commonality effaces important differences. McRobbie points out that postcolonial and poststructuralist feminists quickly asserted that 'this global category of "women" is one which is based on a Eurocentric confidence which claims to know what all women need to achieve equality'. One can make precisely the same arguments about the category 'black women': all such categories inescapably assume a homogeneity rather like any form of stereotyping. McRobbie points to Spivak's neat way of responding to students who assert such identity-claims in her seminar.[16] She asks the student how the community, which the student claims to embody, benefits from this act of representation in the classroom. This could be experienced as a sharp putdown in the wrong context. But posed gently, in the context of a group that has already aired some of the above debates, it can produce several important reminders: that all assertions of positionality are made in historically concrete contexts to particular addressees; that such assertions are constitutive, not (simply) descriptive – that is, designed (however unconsciously) to have political effects; and that speakers should reflect on the discourses which have produced them as this subject who can speak on behalf of specific others.

Identity statements are always oversimplifications. Avtar Brah argues for opening up the diverse experiences and cultures which terms such as 'black' can subsume, and also proposes that thinking multiple identities together can reduce the likelihood that a challenge to one form of oppression leads to the reinforcement of another: 'It may be over-ambitious, but it is imperative that we do not compartmentalise oppressions, but instead formulate strategies for challenging all oppressions on the basis of an understanding of how they interconnect and articulate.'[17]

This is why self-identity and the exploration of experience, while important elements, are not *sufficient* starting points for a cultural studies pedagogy. Some broader mapping is necessary to achieve the above objective: mappings of, one the one hand, the theoretical/political perspectives which address such compartmentalisations and articulations and, on the other, the specific sociocultural formations which embody them, so that students can situate those aspects of a conjuncture with which they wish to engage within the broader 'relations of force' to identify which are the points of leverage and which the points of fixity.[18] In other words, 'active citizens' also need a body of knowledge which allows them to locate their immediate concerns in the bigger picture.

These knowledges are not necessarily 'identity-knowledges': they can be knowledges of particular historical forms or structures, or more general conceptions of power, history or representation. Not all 'really useful knowledge' is of the learner's own immediate situation. And while I have argued that to become 'action knowledge' new knowledge has to be assimilated into, or accommodated by, existing knowledge, this does not mean that students have to work *from* experience to acquire new knowledge. Students do not need to reinvent wheels: just like academic researchers they can learn a lot through secondary sources, including the accounts offered in lectures by their tutors. The fact of lecturing does not locate us back in a 'transmission' model of pedagogy. Students do not assimilate messages (eg the lecture) undigested: they read them through their existing cultural codes – they *negotiate* the 'text'. The important thing is to encourage such negotiation.

Thus the politics of the pedagogy resides largely in the how rather than the what – in the overall social relations of the course or the specific classroom situation.

Student investments

The above discussion is, unashamedly, an argument at the level of theory, but one which informs the cultural politics of the classroom. But to maximise the possibility of serious engagement, tutors have to be aware of the specific investments students bring with them into the classroom, and to address or at least allow for these in their pedagogic practice. At this level of concreteness the experience in each institution will be different. The following account is derived from my own experience in a 'new university' in the metropolis where the student cohort is multiethnic and multiclassed, and with a higher proportion of mature students than school-leavers. Readers will be able to refer to their own experience, and modify this sketch for their own purposes.

Students bring very diverse investments with them. A minority of them already have a politicised social awareness and want to explore culture/power relations. Some (often younger students) are there because they like the (city) location and they believe that their subcultural needs will be met; they have chosen this course because it claims to connect to the students' own cultural interests, and perhaps because it includes media production. Others (usually mature students) will be there because this is their local university, the only one they can attend because of their domestic responsibilities; many of these choose cultural studies because of the range of its disciplinary reach, because they like the idea of working on literature and film and taking a historical approach (the parts of secondary schooling they remember enjoying most). Others are there because their friends or relatives have enjoyed the course, and they expect to find caring and dependable teachers. Whatever else they want, they will want to achieve a good degree classification which will give them access to good jobs. Many will also be concerned to acquire the skills required of the modern workplace: skills in communication (written, spoken and IT based, and maybe also in the audio-visual media), in working in groups, in problem-solving, and so on.

They will bring different attitudes to the course, ranging from deep engagement from the very beginning to a cynical, instrumentalist desire for a qualification with the minimum of investment. Some (mainly mature) students will have deep anxieties about study at HE level, about what is expected in an essay and about their ability to engage with the 'elaborated codes' and abstract arguments of academia; others are already confident readers and communicators. Others struggle to commit sufficient time to study, because of the extensive paid work they have to keep up in order to pay the bills, and/or because of heavy domestic commitments. For most students, their course will be a three or four year commitment on their way to something else.

But, for all the distractions from serious study, most students enter higher education at a moment of transition in their lives, at a moment when they are repositioning themselves in their social relations: a moment of openness. This may be a moment of 'growing up' (away from parents); or (for working-class and female mature students in particular) it could represent a transition from being a manual worker or a housewife/mother to becoming a knowledge worker. A degree programme could support these processes or inhibit them. If the students work through the course dutifully and are then assessed simply for their understanding of the material we provide, we are in effect teaching obedience: it is a pedagogy of containment.

We must also recognise that the engagement I am proposing, if this really includes scrutiny of one's own identifications, can have a cost. If students take a distance from their everyday culture and open up for examination the implicit assumptions of texts and practices with which they are already familiar, this can involve something of a crisis, a period of self-reflection and reorientation. Our own students have frequently talked about this: it could simply be the new impossibility of watching TV or reading fiction without 'reading' it for strategies of representation or for closure. Or, more significantly, students speak of a perceptual gap opening up between themselves and their friends or family (which can take the form of an uncomfortable and reluctant form of élitism). In short, 'taking cultural studies seriously' can unsettle both relationships and inner security. For students for whom higher education is being used as a moment of transition, this revaluation can be exhilarating and liberating, at least along some dimensions. But even in this group crises can be provoked: many young men find an analysis of masculinities challenging, and may resist it strongly.[19] Other students, whose lives are relatively settled, in terms of a domestic, local culture, may not want to put their gendered identity, their ethnicity or their religion up for scrutiny.

In areas of such sensitivity, attempts to force a self-scrutiny will be counterproductive: they will have a distancing effect. In any case our role is not that of 'thought control', but to open up the possibility of learning those things which will help them succeed in their future projects. We can put questions of culture, identification and power on the agenda, and offer tools of analysis, but in the end the students will decide which of those identifications that inform their sense of self they are going to explore openly and seriously. And for this they will need a context of trust and support. One strategy is to introduce this approach in relation to identities which are clearly of important social significance but may not be a part of most students' most intimate selves. In contemporary Britain *national* identity may be an appropriate choice: it is deeply contested and offers multiple positionings, but is rarely a sensitive element of students' subjectivities. There are also plenty of contemporary textual materials for analysis, as well as historical studies. The theme lends itself to autobiographical narrative, but without demanding the deeply personal confession that a focus on sexuality or even gender might demand. The class would research and map out narratives of nation, including those drawn from their own autobiographies; they would discuss their differential inscription in these discourses, and the processes through which institutional practices sought to construct and interpellate individuals as national subjects. After this students may have developed sufficiently in confidence and trust to approach other identities in the same way, especially in their individual essays, or in group project work where the group and topic have been self-selected.

An effective pedagogy has, then, to be sensitive to the social relations of the course – the relations between students as well as between tutor and students. Moreover, regardless of specific conditions, certain kinds of pedagogic practice are on the side of 'action knowledge' – those where students talk through their relationship to the material of the course: in seminars (subdivided if necessary, so that all can include themselves in the discussion); in dialogue with other students (this can be where they learn most, if the situation is purposive and oriented to specific issues and/or to making joint reports); in group projects; in written assignments which encourage them to apply concepts to issues and materials with which they have some engagement; and especially where the students have had a hand in devising the project, in formulating the questions, and even in deciding in what form to present their arguments. Even with large groups of students there are ways of enabling these kinds of student involvement. Perhaps the most defining element of any course, in terms of its politics of pedagogy, is the kind of assignments it sets, and how it assesses them: how much credit students are given for attempting to *use* the knowledge they have encountered.

Tony Bennett, in his critique of Giroux and his colleagues, worries that an unremitting focus on the exploration of identity/sociocultural positioning will detract attention from other competencies that our active and critical citizen (and employee) will need, from the skills and knowledges which do not derive from this focus. But if we adopt the above kinds of pedagogy, we will be simultaneously providing training in 'transferable skills'. Just as 'active citizenship' is both a widely legitimised goal for education and a space for social and cultural critique, so the skills demanded in recent years by state and industry sound remarkably compatible with those we might suppose are needed by a radical intellectual. Over the past ten years employers' organisations have been asking not for graduates who are efficient, docile and unquestioning, but for 'enterprising' individuals who are able to evaluate information critically, to innovate, to think strategically, to solve problems and make complex judgements, to work well in teams and alone, and to communicate effectively in writing and orally. Whether employers would be entirely happy if they actually obtained a workforce of this kind is another matter. But the skills enumerated here are precisely those which enable students to develop critiques of existing sociocultural relations and also to make effective interventions in such relations – including those of the course itself.

To encourage this kind of work is against all the odds in present-day higher education: the pressure on academics is to routinise their teaching and it is not easy to break down the resistance of some students to letting go a cynical instrumentalism. In the end we cannot force them to. But we can *encourage* a different kind of engagement, and we can support all those who, for their various reasons, want to move beyond this kind of alienated relation. My experience is that once they have begun to make the connections with their own social selves, most students find it sometimes disturbing but mainly deeply satisfying. And for academic staff, engaged students make all the difference in terms of job satisfaction. Most cultural studies academics are already familiar with these arguments – but they slip away in the face of continual and worsening pressures. But if we let go the goal of this kind of engaged learning, what is left of the famous 'political edge'?

Notes

1 Williams R, 'The teaching relationship: both sides of the wall', in Rubenstein D and Stoneman C (eds), *Education for democracy*, Penguin, Harmondsworth, 1970, p. 208.

2 See O'Shea A, 'A special relationship? Cultural studies, academia and pedagogy', *Cultural Studies*, Vol 12 No 4, 1998, pp. 513–27.

3 See Giroux H, *Border crossings*, New York, 1992; 'Resisting difference: Cultural studies and the discourse of critical pedagogy', in Grossberg L, Nelson C and Treichler P (eds), *Cultural studies*, Routledge, London and New York, 1992; *Disturbing pleasures*, Routledge, London and New York, 1994; 'White squall: resistance and the pedagogy of whiteness' *Cultural Studies*, Vol 11 No 3, 1997; and

Giroux H and McLaren P (eds), *Between borders*, Routledge, New York and London, 1994.

4 Giroux, *Border crossings*, pp. 199, 206.

5 See Giroux, *Disturbing pleasures*, pp. 133ff.

6 See Bennett T, 'Out in the open: reflections on the history and practice of cultural studies', *Cultural Studies*, Vol 10 No 1, p. 151.

7 Hall S, 'Cultural studies and its theoretical legacies', in Grossberg L *et al.* (eds), *Cultural studies*, p. 281.

8 Bennett, 'Out in the open', p. 151.

9 See Piaget J, *Genetic epistemology*, Columbia University Press, New York, 1960; Bruner J, *Towards a theory of instruction*, Belknap Press, Harvard, 1966.

10 Barnes D, *From communication to curriculum*, Penguin, Harmondsworth, 1976.

11 See Giroux and McLaren, p. 51.

12 See Mohanty C, 'On race and voice: challenges for liberal education in the 1990s', *Cultural Critique*, in Giroux and McLaren, p. 153.

13 See Giroux, 1997, p. 384.

14 See Gilroy P, *The Black Atlantic*, Verso, London, 1993, p. 102.

15 McRobbie A, 'The Es and the anti-Es: new questions for feminism and cultural studies', in Ferguson M and Golding P (eds), *Cultural studies in question*, Sage, London, 1997, p. 176.

16 McRobbie, p. 178; cf. Spivak G, *Outside in the teaching machine*, Routledge, New York, 1993, pp. 18f.

17 Brah A, 'Difference, diversity and differentiation' in Donald J and Rattansi A, *'Race', culture and difference*, Sage, London, 1992, p. 144.

18 Cf. Gramsci A, trans. Nowell Smith G and Hoare Q, *Selections from the prison notebooks*, Lawrence and Wishart, London, 1972, pp. 180ff.

19 See Williamson J, 'How does girl number 20 learn about ideology?', *Screen Education*, 40, 1981.

Notes on contributors

Nannette Aldred is a lecturer in the Centre for Continuing Education at the University of Sussex. She has been Arts Officer for East Sussex County Council and now lectures in Visual Culture while maintaining links with the regional cultural industries. She has written about cultural institutions and policy including a contribution to a forthcoming collection of essays about culture in postwar Britain for Routledge. She has also published work on 'A Canterbury Tale: Powell and Pressburger's Film Fantasies of Britain' in the catalogue for *A Paradise Lost: Neo-Romantic Art in Britain 1935–55* (1987). More recently she has contributed a number of entries for the *Twentieth Century Britain* encyclopaedia published by Garland, and written on 'Figure paintings and double portraits' in *David Hockney* for Manchester University Press.

David Butler is Principal Lecturer in Media Studies at the University of East London. He studied at the University of Ulster and taught there as a Lecturer in Media Studies (1991–99). He is the author of *The Trouble with Reporting Northern Ireland* (Avebury, 1995).

Eddie Chambers was born in Wolverhampton in 1960. He completed a Foundation Course at Coventry Lanchester Polytechnic in 1980 and went on to do a Fine Art degree course at Sunderland Polytechnic. From 1980 onwards he has been involved in organising and curating a number of artists' exhibitions in the United Kingdom. In December 1996 he completed a fifteen-month residency as Curator in Residence in the History of Art Department at the University of Sussex and in March 1998 he was awarded his Ph D in History of Art from Goldsmiths' College, University of London. He took as his subject 'Black Visual Arts Activity in England Between 1981 and 1986: Press and Public Responses'.

Jane Elliott is a Lecturer in Women's Studies and has been the co-ordinator of the programme for Women's Studies in the Department of Adult Continuing Education, University of Wales Swansea since 1992. She has developed courses at non-award bearing, undergraduate and postgraduate levels. Her work is informed by her long-term interest in all aspects of equal opportunities and she has delivered training in this area for voluntary groups and local government employees. Her interest in women's education and in encouraging mature women to return to education is reflected in her research interests. She has written articles and chapters in the field of the teaching of Women's Studies and recently co-edited, with Roseanne Benn and Pat Whaley, *Educating Rita and Her Sisters: Women and Continuing Education* (NIACE, 1998).

Heiko Henkel studied history and pedagogy at the University of Hamburg and anthropology at the University of Sussex. He is currently writing a PhD thesis at Princeton University on Religion and Secularism in contemporary Turkey, the Turkish diaspora, and Western Europe.

Richard Johnson is Professor of Cultural Studies at Nottingham Trent University. He has published widely on adult education and cultural politics. His most recent book is *Schooling Sexualities* (with D. Epstein: Open University Press, 1997).

Christina Lupton grew up in Australia, where she studied Literature and Politics. She has studied and taught Postcolonial Theory at the University of Sussex, and is currently at Rutgers University writing her PhD thesis on issues of authority and property in settler colonialism.

Andy Medhurst teaches Media Studies at the University of Sussex. He is the co-editor of *Lesbian and Gay Studies: A Critical Introduction* (Cassell, 1997), the author of many articles on questions of cultural politics and identity, and is currently completing a book on comedy and Englishness called *A National Joke* (for Routledge). Outside, or adjacent to, his academic work, he is a critic, journalist and broadcaster for numerous magazines, newspapers, radio and television programmes.

Jim McGuigan is Senior Lecturer in Sociology at Loughborough University and sometime Reader in Cultural Studies at Coventry University. He is the author of *Cultural Populism* (1992) and *Culture and the Public Sphere* (1996), editor of *Cultural Methodologies* (1997) and co-editor of *Studying Culture* (second edition, 1997). His forthcoming publications include *Technocities* (Sage) and *Modernity and Postmodern Culture* (Open University Press). He serves on the editorial boards of the *International Journal of Cultural Policy* and *Keywords – A Journal of Cultural Materialism* and is a member of the management committee of the Raymond Williams Society and of the executive committee of the Association for Media, Communication and Cultural Studies.

Alan O'Shea is Professor and Head of Cultural Studies at the University of East London. He is editor, with Mica Nava, of *Modern Times: Reflections on a Century of English Modernity*, Routledge, 1996.

Martin Ryle is a Lecturer in the Centre for Continuing Education at the University of Sussex, where he teaches literature and cultural studies. He has published articles on cultural theory and literary criticism and has contributed to collective volumes on policy and pedagogy in adult education. His major current research interests are in landscape, travel and their literary and cultural representations, and his recent book *Journeys in Ireland: Literary Travellers, Rural Landscapes, Cultural Relations* is published by Ashgate Publishing.

Kate Soper is Professor of Philosophy at the University of North London. Her books include *Troubled Pleasures* (Verso, 1990) and *What is Nature? Culture, politics and the non-human* (Blackwell, 1996). She has contributed regularly to *Radical Philosophy* and *New Left Review* and is a columnist for *Capitalism, Nature,*

Socialism: CNS Journal. She is currently working on myth, philosophy and ecology, and is also involved in a collective research project on women and the Enlightenment.

Angeliki Spiropoulou has worked as a Lecturer in the Communication Studies Department at Mediterranean College, Athens in collaboration with Coventry University, UK. Her publications include articles in the Greek national daily, *Eleftherotypia*; 'Fashion and PostModern Identities' in Kalogeras G and Pastourmatzi D (eds), *Nationalism and Sexuality: Crises of Identity* (Thessaloniki, 1996); and 'Structuralism and Literature' and 'Oedipus Tyrannus: How many Readings' in the Greek journal *Diavazo*. Recent articles on Virginia Woolf and Greece and on gym culture and the female body are due to be published. She edited and introduced *Representations of Femininity: Feminist Approaches* (Athens: Centre for Research and Documentation, 1994), and her translations into Greek include Gillian Dyer's book *Advertising as Communication* (Athens, 1993). Her current research interests are literature, popular women's culture, feminism and cultural theory with an emphasis on consumer culture, sexuality and the body.

Tom Steele is Senior Lecturer in Adult Education at the University of Glasgow. He moved to Glasgow in 1996 from Leeds, where he had worked as an Organising Tutor for the WEA and subsequently as a Lecturer in the Department of Adult Education at the University of Leeds. His books include *Alfred Orage and the Leeds Arts Club* (Scolar, 1990), *Learning Independence – A political outline of Indian Adult Education* (with Richard Taylor, NIACE, 1995) and *The Emergence of Cultural Studies: Adult Education, Cultural Politics and the English Question* (Lawrence and Wishart, 1997). He is currently working on a study of popular knowledges, academic disciplines and the educational role of social movements in Europe from 1850 to 1950.